A Metaphysics for the Mob

The Philosophy of George Berkeley

JOHN RUSSELL ROBERTS

OXFORD

UNIVERSITY PRESS

2007

OXFORD
UNIVERSITY PRESS

Oxford University Press, Inc., publishes works that further
Oxford University's objective of excellence
in research, scholarship, and education.

Oxford   New York
Auckland   Cape Town   Dar es Salaam   Hong Kong   Karachi
Kuala Lumpur   Madrid   Melbourne   Mexico City   Nairobi
New Delhi   Shanghai   Taipei   Toronto

With offices in
Argentina   Austria   Brazil   Chile   Czech Republic   France   Greece
Guatemala   Hungary   Italy   Japan   Poland   Portugal   Singapore
South Korea   Switzerland   Thailand   Turkey   Ukraine   Vietnam

Published by Oxford University Press, Inc.
198 Madison Avenue, New York, New York 10016

www.oup.com

Oxford is a registered trademark of Oxford University Press

Library of Congress Cataloging-in-Publication Data
Roberts, John Russell.
A metaphysics for the mob : the philosophy of George Berkeley /
John Russell Roberts.
p. cm.
Includes bibliographical references and index.
ISBN 978-0-19-531393-2
1. Berkeley, George, 1685–1753.   2. Metaphysics.   I. Title.
B1349.M47R87 2007
192—dc22   2006048303

1 3 5 7 9 8 6 4 2

Printed in the United States of America
on acid-free paper

To my wife,
Alicia K. Smith,
and her built-in bullshit detector

Phaedrus: It is somewhere here at which Boreas is said to have carried off Orithyia from the banks of the Ilissus.... I wonder Socrates, do you believe this tale?

Socrates: I should be quite in the fashion if I disbelieved it, as the men of science do. I might proceed to give a scientific account of how the maiden, while at play with Pharmacia, was blown by a gust of Boreas down from the rocks hard by, and having thus met her death was said to have been seized by Boreas. For my part, Phaedrus, I regard such theories as no doubt attractive, but as the invention of clever, industrious people who are not exactly to be envied, for the simple reason that they must then go on and tell us the real truth about the appearance of centaurs and the Chimera, not to mention a whole host of such creatures, Gorgons and Pegasuses and countless other remarkable monsters of legend flocking in on them. If our skeptic, with his somewhat crude science, means to reduce every one of them to the standard of probability, he'll need a deal of time for it. Now I have no leisure for such inquiries; shall I tell you why? I must first know myself, as the Delphian inscription says; so long [as] I am still in ignorance of my own self, it seems to me ridiculous to inquire into extraneous matters. And therefore I bid farewell to all this; the common opinion is enough for me. For, as I was saying, I want to know not about this, but about myself: am I a monster more complex and swollen with pride than Typho, or a being whom heaven has blessed with a simple and quiet nature?

—Plato, *Phaedrus*

Acknowledgments

I am deeply indebted to Simon Blackburn, Don Garrett, Jay Rosenberg, and Daniel Dennett. I suspect that anyone familiar with their work will, upon reading this one, recognize that debt. Less obvious to readers, but no less real, will be the debt owed to Stephen White and William Lycan. Dan Dennett deserves additional thanks for his ceaseless moral support. I would also like to thank Karen Bailey for skillfully and, above all, patiently playing the role of midwife to many of the formative ideas of this work. Some of them were rather ugly babies when they first emerged. Thanks for not flinching. Thanks are also owed to Katya Hoskings for a pivotal slap upside the head (or two) at just the right time. Adrienne Martin's wonderful brain provided excellent questions and her friendship provided sustenance. Two anonymous readers for Oxford University Press supplied very helpful comments; thank you to you both, whoever you are. Thanks also go to Thomas Flint, Alvin Plantinga, and Notre Dame's Center for Philosophy of Religion. Their generous support provided much needed and much appreciated time to do research as well as providing me with easy access to the library of that greatest of all Berkeley scholars, the late A. A. Luce. Similarly, I would like to thank Florida State University and the Department of Philosophy for their support. Mike Woodring and Alicia Smith both deserve praise for helping me to make the manuscript look less like it was prepared by a distracted chimp. Thanks also to Lara Zoble, Peter Ohlin, Merryl Sloane, and Stacey Hamilton at Oxford University Press. Finally, to Alicia, I am grateful for far more than can be expressed in a mere book, however long. I am forgetting many people who helped along the way. I thank them for their help and for their forgiveness, in advance.

Contents

Abbreviations

All references to Berkeley's writings are from A. A. Luce and T. E. Jessop, eds., *The Works of George Berkeley: Bishop of Cloyne*, 9 volumes (Nelson, 1948–1957). This is referred to in the notes as simply *Works*.

In referring to Berkeley's individual works, I use the following abbreviations:

A   *Alciphron or the Minute Philosopher*
DM   *De Motu or the Principle and Nature of Motion and the Cause of the Communication of Motions*
NTV   *An Essay toward a New Theory of Vision*
PC   *Philosophical Commentaries*
P   *A Treatise Concerning the Principles of Human Knowledge*
S   *Siris: A Chain of Philosophical Reflexions and Enquiries*
TD   *Three Dialogues between Hylas and Philonous*

Other abbreviations used:

PWD   Rene Descartes, *The Philosophical Writings of Descartes*, ed. John Cottingham, Robert Stoothoff, and Dugald Murdoch, vols. I–III (Cambridge University Press, 1985–1991)
Enquiry David Hume, *An Enquiry concerning Human Understanding*, 3d ed., ed. L. A. Shelby-Bigge and P. H. Nidditch (Oxford University Press, 1975)
Essay   John Locke, *An Essay concerning Human Understanding*, ed. P. H. Nidditch (Oxford University Press, 1975)
THN   David Hume, *A Treatise of Human Nature*, 2d ed., ed. L. A. Shelby-Bigge and P. H. Nidditch (Oxford University Press, 1978)

Introduction

Hume's Legacy

I side in all things with the Mob.
—Berkeley[1]

Some 130 years ago, the single most influential voice in English-language philosophy of the age, John Stuart Mill, thought that the time was ripe for a reappraisal of Berkeley's work. In part buoyed by the publication of the first complete edition of Berkeley's writings,[2] Mill wrote, "[W]e think it will be recognized that [of] all who, from the earliest times, have applied the powers of their minds to metaphysical inquiries, he is the one of greatest philosophic genius."[3] But, after all these years, little has changed. While Berkeley's works continue to be taught in English-speaking universities everywhere, they are presented, at best, as a challenge piece and, at worst, as a cautionary tale. To this day, our own philosophical identity remains both bound up with and strangely alienated from the Bishop's philosophical legacy. We recognize Locke, Berkeley, and Hume as our founding fathers and their work as the original tilling that provided us with much of our common philosophical soil but, at the same time, we are unsure of Berkeley's proper place and our connection to him. In what sense and to what extent are we the Bishop's heirs? We remain partly grateful, while still partly wary. As one commentator memorably put it, "Berkeley's metaphysics rises in the garden of British thought like some fantastic plant—beautiful and extravagant."[4] If that final 'and' were replaced with a 'but,' it would capture our sentiments toward Berkeley's work perfectly.

The ultimate aim of this work is to make plain that the roots of Berkeley's metaphysics are ancient and that the ground from which it grows is common to us all. But there are serious difficulties waiting for anyone who undertakes such a task. Standing in the way are two fundamental and interrelated problems of interpretation. Both were brought out by Hume's work and continue to be associated with him. The first is succinctly captured in a well-known footnote in his *An Enquiry concerning Human Understanding*.

[Dr. Berkeley] professes ... in his title-page (and undoubtedly with great truth) to have composed his book against the sceptics as well as against the atheists and free-thinkers. But that all his arguments, though otherwise intended, are, in reality, merely sceptical, appears from this, *that they admit of no answer and produce no conviction.*[5]

Few would go as far as to say that Berkeley's arguments "admit of no answer," but the spirit of Hume's positive assessment is still felt. One reason Berkeley's works continue to be taught is because his attack on material substance provides us with an excellent model of the analytic hatchet job. When it comes to the craft of philosophical criticism, Berkeley is our mentor. As for the negative part of Hume's assessment, it seems that little qualification is called for. We don't teach Berkeley's works with the expectation that they will produce converts to immaterialism. On the contrary, we teach his works with the expectation that his conclusions will clash with the standing convictions of our students, thereby spurring them to engage in some philosophical criticism of their own.

Russell, somewhat puckishly, once suggested that "the point of philosophy is to start with something so simple as not to seem worth stating, and to end with something so paradoxical that no one will believe it,"[6] and by this measure, Hume and history have judged Berkeley's efforts to be an unqualified success. However, Berkeley would not have been able to take Russell's quip lightly. As he saw it, too many of the intellectuals of his time were seriously in the grip of just such an opinion, and the effects of this were not, in his estimation, merely academic. To Berkeley, philosophy was very serious business with important consequences for humanity. He often took time to impress this point upon his readers. For instance, in the *Three Dialogues between Hylas and Philonous*, we find the following:

> Hylas: I was considering the odd fate of those men who have in all ages, through an affectation of being distinguished from the vulgar, or some unaccountable turn of thought, pretended either to believe nothing at all, or to believe the most extravagant things in the world. This however might be borne, if their paradoxes and scepticism did not draw after them some consequences of general disadvantage to mankind. But the mischief lieth here; that when men of less leisure see them who are supposed to have spent their whole time in the pursuits of knowledge, professing an entire ignorance of all things, or advancing such notions as are repugnant to plain and commonly received principles, they will be tempted to entertain suspicions concerning the most important truths, which they had hitherto held sacred and unquestionable.[7]

Berkeley designed his philosophical works to provide a counter to such affectations and their deleterious consequences.

> If the principles, which I here endeavour to propagate, are admitted for true; the consequences which, I think, evidently flow from thence, are, that atheism and scepticism will be utterly destroyed, many intricate points made plain, great difficulties solved, several useless parts of science retrenched, speculation referred to practice, and men reduced from paradoxes to common sense.[8]

Clearly, far from seeing his views as literally incredible, he saw his work as directed toward important practical aims that drew at least part of their value from the fact that they support *common sense*. As he once famously remarked, "I side in all things with the Mob."[9] Therein lies our first problem: what is the reader to make of Berkeley's repeated insistence that his philosophy is not only consonant with but even a defense of common sense?

As I see it, the fundamental link between Berkeley's philosophy and common sense ultimately runs through his account of *spirits*. Here's why: however you spell it out, the concept *material substance* is, when all is said and done, a philosophical creation. Common sense and a rejection of material substance are not intrinsically at odds. However, even those, such as Hume, who find no fault with Berkeley's arguments against material substance are not moved to embrace his metaphysics, and that is because when Berkeley is done one feels that he has left one with nothing to embrace. What Berkeley gives us is what we might call a "negative metaphysics." The great bulk of his effort is directed toward a negative point, i.e., establishing that reality in no way consists of material substances. Even should one find his arguments against material substance compelling, their influence will be limited so long as one is not given an alternative positive account of that which reality *does* consist.

Now, of course, Berkeley does have a positive metaphysics. He is what A. C. Fraser aptly labeled a "spiritual realist."[10] According to Berkeley, the basic entities of the world are "spirits," what Berkeley interchangeably refers to as "minds." Reality, at the most fundamental level, consists not of material substances, but rather of *spiritual substances*. Unfortunately, whereas Berkeley's attack on material substance is developed in great detail in two separate works, *A Treatise concerning the Principles of Human Knowledge* and *Three Dialogues between Hylas and Philonous*, he did not leave behind anything comparable in the way of an account of spirits. Instead, his remarks on the nature of spirits are scattered throughout his writings and are, for the most part, brief. Consequently, having left only half of a metaphysics, at best the effect can only be to convince by half. Even should one think his arguments "admit of no answer," still those arguments will only fail to produce conviction, for having been convinced of what one should *not* believe in, one is left with little idea of what one *should* believe in.

The upshot is that there is little hope of establishing a coherent connection between Berkeley's metaphysics and common sense so long as we lack an account of Berkelian spirits. This, in turn, would seem to point the way toward a solution to our first interpretive problem. We must comb Berkeley's works and do our best to piece together his account of spirits from what Berkeley did leave us. Once this is done, we will hopefully have a much clearer idea of just what we are to make of the relationship between his philosophy and common sense.

Prima facie, this sounds like a nice, straightforward project. Unfortunately, it brings us right up against the second basic interpretive problem. It is widely believed that there is no coherent account of spirits to be found in Berkeley's works. To most, what little Berkeley did say about the nature of spirits is extremely unsatisfactory or, worse, flat-out inconsistent. The complaints against Berkeley's view of substance take many forms, but the basic objection is associated with Hume and is now a commonplace. One of Berkeley's central arguments against material substance proceeds from the premise that what we perceive immediately is only our own ideas, to the conclusion that the objects of perception are no more than collections of ideas. Hume, so this line of criticism would have it, simply follows through and proceeds to do much the same with respect to spiritual substances.[11] As Hume famously put it,

I may venture to affirm of the rest of mankind, that they are nothing but a bundle or collection of different perceptions, which succeed each other with an inconceivable rapidity, and are in a perpetual flux and movement.[12]

In Hume's work, we seem to find an explanation for why Berkeley left us no developed account of spirits. Roughly, the conjecture is that some time after presenting his attack on material substance, Berkeley came to recognize that a consistent application of his own principles undermines the ontology of his positive metaphysics of spiritual substances.

This view of the situation gets support from the fact that Berkeley had originally planned to go into more detail about the positive side of his metaphysics. The first edition of the *Principles* is labeled "Part I," and the preface to the first edition of the *Three Dialogues* makes mention of a forthcoming "second part" of the *Principles*. In addition, extant is a pair of notebooks, commonly known as the *Philosophical Commentaries*, which Berkeley kept in the course of the development of "Part I" of the *Principles* and of his first major work, *An Essay toward a New Theory of Vision*. From these notebooks, we learn that Berkeley originally projected at least four parts to the *Principles*. What we have of the *Principles* is, in a sense, only a fragment. It was the second part that was to focus more fully on the subject of spirits, both the finite ones (us) and the infinite one (God), and therefore, it would have dealt with the heart of his positive metaphysics. The third part was to take up the subject of natural science, and the fourth was to deal with mathematics. We can assume that Berkeley's essay *De Motu* gives us at least some of what we might have expected from the former, and another essay, *The Analyst*, some of the latter. But the second part of the *Principles* never saw publication, and he did not leave us anything like a *De Motu* or *The Analyst* with regard to the topic of spirits.

Why? The only explanation we have from Berkeley himself is in a letter to his American friend Samuel Johnson.[13] In prior correspondence, Johnson had expressed interest in the promised second part of the *Principles*. In his reply Berkeley writes,

> As to the second part of my treatise concerning the principles of human knowledge, the fact is that I had made a considerable progress in it, but the manuscript was lost about fourteen years ago during my travels in Italy; and I never had leisure since to do so disagreeable a thing as writing twice on the same subject.[14]

In the years that followed the writing of this letter, it seems Berkeley never did find the requisite leisure.

Despite what he tells us in this letter, an alternate explanation of why Berkeley failed to bring Part II to press has been far more popular. According to it, the reason we do not have the second part of the *Principles* is because Berkeley gradually came to realize just what the consistent application of his principles meant for spiritual substances and, in turn, the foundation of his positive metaphysics.[15] Now, if this Humean take on the facts is correct, then there is no great interpretive problem after all. It simply bears out what one is already inclined to believe: there is little sense to be made of the connection between Berkeley's philosophy and common sense because that connection ultimately ran through his account of spirits and since, as even Berkeley came to realize, he has no coherent account of spirits, no meaningful connection exists. Our interpretive problems are at an end.

But things are not so simple. The fact that this Humean perspective supports what we are already inclined to believe about the relationship between common sense and Berkeley's work has probably helped us to ignore the fact that there are some very serious problems facing this interpretation. First, the application of his own invention, the bundle account of objects, to minds was not a possibility that Berkeley somehow managed to overlook. From the *Philosophical Commentaries*, we know that he had already hit on the bundle account of the mind very early in his philosophical inquiries. He considered its strengths and weaknesses, and by the time his first philosophical work appeared, the *Principles*, he had rejected the account in favor of the simple substance view of the self.[16] This fact should be viewed against the backdrop of another. In the appendix to the *Treatise*, Hume tells us that, on reflection, he has found that he cannot render the bundle account of the self coherent. When his next major work, *An Enquiry concerning Human Understanding*, is published, the bundle account of the self is omitted and nothing has replaced it. Nor is the topic ever revisited in any subsequent work. Hume's second thoughts in the appendix proved to be his last published ones on this particular subject.

These considerations suggest that the received interpretation gets things exactly backward. It suggests that, perhaps, it was Berkeley who understood Hume's troubles, not the other way around. It suggests that there may be an alternative dialectic, one that Berkeley understood but one that history has overlooked, according to which consideration of both the bundle theory's attractions and shortcomings serves merely as something of a stepping-stone on the path that is the development of Berkeley's understanding of the self as a simple substance. This alternative interpretation gets further support from the fact that more than twenty-five years before the publication of Hume's *Treatise*, Berkeley explicitly addressed the bundle view in print and attacked a key part of the reasoning that Hume would later use in the body of the *Treatise* for rejecting the simple substance view.[17] To this, we can add the fact that Hume's argument for the bundle theory in the body of the *Treatise*, as well as his second thoughts in the appendix, fail to address Berkeley's published attack on the bundle theory and his reasons for rejecting the argument against simple substances.

We now have the two fundamental problems of interpretation before us. We want to know what to make of Berkeley's claim that his philosophy is of a piece with common sense. But the answer to that question depends upon our having a clear understanding of Berkeley's positive metaphysics. This, in turn, relies upon the viability of his view of spirits. But it is no more obvious what we are to make of the viability of his view of spirits than it is what we are to make of the claimed connection between his philosophy and common sense.

In the pages that follow, I defend Berkeley's claim that his philosophy is consonant with common sense, and that, in fact, it does serve to defend it. This should not be confused with the aim of trying to get the reader to regard Berkeley's philosophy *as* common sense. The common use of 'common sense' is, after all, as an evaluative expression, and this is primarily an interpretive work rather than an exercise in immaterialist apologetics. But with that said, my contention is that there is a meaningful, sensible connection between Berkeley's metaphysics and common sense. My central aim is to make this connection clear. This, of course, requires that I provide a coherent account of Berkelian spirits. However, an account of spirits is not possible without an account of two other items that are central to Berkeley's philosophy: the active/passive distinction and the so-called divine language thesis.

As for the active/passive distinction, it is the fundamental distinction of Berkeley's metaphysics and, as such, underlies the basic division of his ontology. Reality is twofold. There are spirits, and there are ideas. To a first approximation, spirits are active; ideas are passive. No account of his ontology, and therefore no account of spirits, can be complete without an interpretation of the active/passive distinction.

As for the divine language thesis, it is quintessential Berkeley. Against the prevailing mechanistic model of nature, Berkeley presented this striking alternative. He proposed that we view the entirety of the natural world as being organized— not mechanically, but rather *linguistically*. The heart of this approach is the view that "[i]deas which are observed to be connected together are vulgarly considered under the relation of cause and effect, whereas, in strict and philosophic truth, they are only related as the sign to the thing signified."[18] For Berkeley, denying that ideas stand in causal relations is equivalent to denying that ideas possess any *causal powers*. This is important because, on Berkeley's view, *causal power* is to be understood in terms of *activity*. Consequently, causal power belongs only to spirits. Ideas are utterly inert—in a word, *passive*. Still, ideas make up the whole of the natural world and, in doing so, mediate the relations between different spirits. The divine language thesis is, then, Berkeley's way of explaining why this mediation is not tantamount to a kind of Leibnizian monadic isolation. It is the linguistic ordering of nature that allows for the intelligible interaction of the individual active finite spirits. The divine language thesis is the conceptual tool that Berkeley uses to close the otherwise problematic gap separating his two fundamental ontological categories and is an essential part of the solution to his own unique version of the interaction problem.

Of these four topics—common sense, spirits, the active/passive distinction, and the divine language thesis—only the first two have drawn much scholarly attention. The active/passive distinction has been largely ignored, and the divine language thesis has mostly been treated as being intriguing but peripheral. However, given the preceding and the fact that the link between Berkeley's metaphysics and common sense runs through his account of spirits, the topics of the active/passive distinction and the divine language thesis form central themes of this work.

Since no analysis of activity is possible in a metaphysics in which activity is treated as basic, an account of activity must take another form. I begin this task in chapter I by exploring Berkeley's understanding of related concepts lying close to that foundation. I provide an elucidation of Berkeley's view of the nature and meaning of existence and its relationship to his understanding of the concepts of simplicity, identity, unity, and substance. In addition to moving us closer to an understanding of the nature of activity, one of the more valuable products of this discussion is an explanation of the fundamental error that lies behind any attempt to interpret Berkeley as having some sort of bundle view of the mind. Somewhat ironically, bundle accounts of Berkelian spirits have been very popular, especially of late. While there are many problems facing bundle interpretations of spirits in general, this chapter lays bare what I regard as the fatal problem for bundle interpretations of spirits. As we will see, Berkeley's understanding of the nature of existence rules out any form of a bundle account of Berkelian spirits.

In chapter II, I turn to Berkeley's philosophy of language. The topic is of central importance to our understanding of the divine language thesis because our understanding of the divine language thesis is constrained by our understanding of Berkeley's philosophy of language. The key claim of this chapter is that we have misread Berkeley's famous "Introduction" to the *Principles* in an important way. A reexamination of the "Introduction" reveals that Berkeley identified the ideational theory of meaning and understanding as the root cause of some of the worst of man's intellectual errors, not "abstract ideas." Abstract ideas are, rather, the most debilitating symptom of this underlying ailment. Furthermore, I defend the position that, in place of the ideational theory, Berkeley offered the rudiments of what we would now call a "use theory." The latter half of this thesis was first suggested by Anthony Flew. However, Flew took it to be a late development of Berkeley's and one that threatened other essential aspects of his work. I argue that neither of those claims is true. Quite to the contrary, Berkeley regarded materialism and the ideational theory as two sides of the same coin.

Chapter III begins my account of spirits by approaching them from the issue of our knowledge of other minds. Here, I start to explore the important ramifications that the attribution to Berkeley of a use theory of meaning has for the interpretation of his divine language thesis, and, in turn, how this impacts the way we should understand the relationship between individual spirits as well as the nature of spirits themselves. In this chapter more than the others, I make anachronistic use of several familiar contemporary philosophical devices to render Berkeley's admittedly unusual approach more familiar. I compare and contrast Berkeley's views with Daniel Dennett's familiar views about the "intentional stance" to develop an analogy with noncognitivism in ethics that is designed to elucidate the way in which Berkeley regards our relations with other spirits as being mediated by irreducibly normative relations. The considerations of this chapter help to clarify just what the fundamental nature of spirits will have to be if they are going to fulfill their all-important role in Berkeley's metaphysics.

The task of providing an account of spirits is not directly addressed until chapter IV. In this chapter, I begin with the obvious, but too often overlooked, point that, prima facie, Berkeley's descriptions of spirits as simple, immaterial substances suggest that spirits are close kin to Cartesian minds. However, while there would certainly seem to be good reason to connect the two, there is also a serious problem about how spirits can be *simple* substances (Cartesian or otherwise) so long as they must be both active and passive in nature. Solving this problem requires three things: a clear interpretation of the active/passive distinction, an account of how the linguistic ordering of nature serves to render the sensory world intelligible, and an understanding of the relationship between Berkelian spirits and Lockean persons. The position I develop and defend in this chapter is that Berkeley's spirits must be understood to be a kind of hybrid of Lockean persons and Cartesian simple substances.

Chapter V is somewhat different from all the other chapters in that it is primarily an application of the various interpretive tools so far developed. Here, I turn to one of the thorniest problems facing Berkeley's philosophy: the specter of occasionalism. Although Berkeley claimed his philosophy was fundamentally different from that of Malebranche, he has long been dogged by comparisons. The most troublesome of these comparisons claims that Berkeley's own views on human and divine agency imply a commitment to some form of occasionalism. The aim of this chapter is to apply the interpretation of Berkeley's metaphysics developed over the previous chapters so as to reveal just how deeply incompatible Berkeley's views and occasionalism are and to show how difficult it is within Berkeley's metaphysics to raise the sort of problems that motivate occasionalism in the first place.

Finally, in chapter VI, I return to our primary interpretive problem: the question of just what to make of Berkeley's repeated claims that his philosophy is not only of a piece with but even a defense of common sense. But there is little point in providing anything by way of a preface for this chapter now. That is the job of the first five chapters.

A Metaphysics for the Mob

I

The Berkelian Basics

Why *Esse* Is Not *Percipi*

'[T]is on the Discovering of the nature & meaning & import of Existence that I chiefly insist.... This I think wholly new. I am sure 'tis new to me.

—Berkeley[1]

1. A Philosopher of Substance

Being and substance emerged hand in hand from the primordial philosophical ooze. They are as ancient as they are inseparable, and they are so inseparable as to be nearly synonymous. That is to say, a substance is a being. The synonymy, however, is not perfect, and, in fact, the point of invoking the language of substance is to mark off a contrast in the ways of being. Substances exist; everything else merely subsists.

Those who have worried over first philosophy have found that, inevitably, they must employ some such distinction. Where the disagreement lies is in how it is to be understood. One of the surest ways into the pantheon of great philosophers is to make a fundamental contribution to this debate. All who were raised in the Western philosophical tradition stand either in the shadow or on the shoulders (depending on one's attitude) of the dialectic between Platonic and Aristotelian conceptions of the contrast and order of beings. The characteristic Platonic view gives the "forms" priority over the familiar beings of the world. The latter have what reality they do by way of the lowly act of "imitating" those eternal, immutable forms. In contrast, the defining Aristotelian impulse is to locate priority with the more mundane items of workaday life. From the perspective of the Aristotelian program, the being of the *abstracta* must be understood as, in some sense, dependent upon the *contreta*.

The dialectic between Platonic and Aristotelian conceptions of the priority of beings is developed, sometimes with inscrutable sophistication, right up to the early modern period (and, to be sure, into the present). At that point, Descartes intervened and revitalized first philosophy. He accomplished this, in part, by introducing a dualism of types of finite beings, the material and the mental, while at the same time denying any priority ordering between them. Material and mental entities exist side by side, neither *dependent* upon the other. This characteristic Cartesian move brings the "independence criterion" to the forefront in accounts of what distinguishes something as a substance, replacing the more traditional focus on substances qua subject of predication. But even given all his originality, ontological priority orderings still play an ineliminable role in Descartes' work. Any reader of the *Meditations* will remember that his philosophical desiderata are unreachable without recourse to the notorious distinction between "formal being" and "objective being." And of course, *finite* mental and material substances, though not dependent upon one another, are dependent upon the *infinite* mental being, God. In fact, according to Descartes, God alone is substance in the strict sense because only God's independence is absolute.

The renaissance in metaphysics that followed is largely the result of the impetus that Descartes imparted. Most who followed were working through, modifying, or attempting to exorcise his innovations. Malebranche, Spinoza, Leibniz, and Locke all make fundamental and original contributions. Throughout, however, we find that the need to mark, not only a contrast, but also a priority in the order of beings persists. There is no more telling testimony to this than the fact that even in Hume's works, those great antidotes to metaphysics, we find his cardinal distinction between *impressions* and *ideas*—the former standing as the original beings with respect to the latter.

As the quotation that begins this chapter indicates, Berkeley understood himself to be contributing to the heart of this debate. As he saw it, his great discovery concerns the nature, meaning, and import of existence. I believe Berkeley was right; he did make a discovery of fundamental importance about existence. I further believe that the only way to understand the very basics of Berkeley's metaphysics is to get a handle on the nature of this discovery. That is the task of this chapter and, in a sense, of this entire work. However, before we can even begin, we must first remove an obstacle. Standing in our way is our own deep-seated and surprisingly resilient tendency to start off with our perspective of Berkeley's views about existence turned almost perfectly upside down. A convincing demonstration of this is all too easily had.

2. *Esse* Is Not *Percipi*

Merely consider the fact that very few philosophers enjoy the honor of having their intellectual legacy communicated to posterity by a catchphrase. But Berkeley does. No sooner does one hear his name than the words "*esse* is *percipi*" spring to mind. As a result, what everyone starts out knowing about Berkeley is that he argued for an extraordinary view about the nature of existence. Unfortunately, as a result of the attention given to the catchphrase, it is all too common to be told that what Berkeley's view about existence amounts to is that "to be real is to be perceived" or that "to exist is to be perceived."[2] This in turn leads to Berkeley being labeled a "subjective idealist"—an advocate for a uniquely bizarre form of solipsism, a sort of group solipsism, wherein reality consists of what *I* do or may perceive, plus what *you* do or may perceive, plus what *he, she,* or *it* does/did/may perceive. And, of course, sometimes it will be added, it includes what God perceives as well.

All who know Berkeley will recognize this caricature, whether they participate in its upkeep or not. Consequently, students coming to Berkeley for the first time should have the following basic axiom drilled into their heads as often and as vociferously as is necessary: Berkeley did not say "*esse* is *percipi*." He did not say "*esse* is *percipi*" any more than Commander Prescott said "Fire until you see the whites of their eyes!" In the former, as in the latter, what's deleted makes all the difference. The infamous *percipi* catchphrase is lifted from Berkeley's *A Treatise concerning the Principles of Human Knowledge* where, in §3 of Part I, he writes,

> [A]s to what is said of the absolute existence of unthinking things without any relation to their being perceived, that seems perfectly unintelligible. Their *esse* is *percipi*, nor is it possible they should have any existence, out of the minds or thinking things which perceive them.[3]

Berkeley tells us, "[t]heir *esse* is *percipi*." Clearly, the 'their' is anaphoric on 'unthinking things,' what Berkeley also sometimes refers to as "sensible things" and sometimes as "ideas." What Berkeley taught is that the being of *sensible things* consists in their being perceived. But with that said, two all-important points have to be insisted upon immediately.

First, the same is not true of *minds*, what Berkeley more frequently calls "spirits" but also refers to (equivalently) as "souls," "wills," and "agents." The being of spirits does not depend on their being perceived. In fact, spirits *cannot* be perceived.

> [T]he words *will, soul, spirit*, do not stand for different ideas, or in truth, for any idea at all, but for something which is very different from ideas, and which being an agent cannot be like unto, or represented by, any idea whatsoever.[4]

The *esse* of spirits is *not percipi*.

The second point is even more important: Berkeley is a *monist*. His is a monism of *minds*.

> Nothing seems of more importance, towards erecting a firm system of sound and real knowledge, which may be proof against the assaults of *scepticism*, than to lay the beginning in a distinct explication of what is meant by *thing, reality, existence*: for in vain shall we dispute concerning the real existence of things, or pretend to any knowledge thereof, so long as we have not fixed the meaning of those words. *Thing* or *being* is the most general name of all, it comprehends under it two kinds entirely distinct and heterogeneous, and which have nothing common but the name, to wit, *spirits* and *ideas*. The former are *active, indivisible substances*: the latter are *inert, fleeting, dependent beings*, which subsist not by themselves, but are supported by, or exist in minds or spiritual substances.[5]

The fundamental items of Berkeley's ontology are spirits. Spirits alone are substances. In one sense, of course, it is a simple point, but it is also of the first importance. Prejudices early acquired tend to persevere. We are all students of the caricature first; only later, if at all, do we come to recognize the error. The danger is that the hacked and hackneyed *esse* is *percipi* shibboleth will continue to have the effect of focusing our attention on the *dependent* things of Berkeley's ontology and away from both the contrasting and proper priority ordering of beings.[6]

3. Bundled Selves and the Berkelian Basics

One should not think that this confusion infects only the philosophical novice. Even the seasoned are not entirely immune. I suspect that the caricature has influenced contemporary interpretations of Berkeley's view of spirits. It must be admitted, however, that here it does not work alone. Instead, it finds aid and comfort in the form of an old ally, Hume's well-known attack on spiritual substances from his landmark *A Treatise of Human Knowledge*.[7] Hume does not mention Berkeley by name in that attack, but others soon cemented the connection. In an influential passage, Thomas Reid wrote,

> [Hume] proceeds upon the same principles [as Berkeley], but carries them to their full length; and, as the Bishop undid the whole material world, this author, upon the same grounds, undoes the world of spirits.[8]

The idea here is simple. One of Berkeley's central arguments against material substance proceeds from the premise that what we immediately perceive is only our own ideas, to the conclusion that the objects of perception are no more than collections of ideas. Hume, so this line of criticism would have it, is simply being more consistent than Berkeley. He argues that the same follows for the objects of "inner perception."

> If any impression gives rise to the idea of self, that impression must continue invariably the same, through the whole course of our lives; since self is supposed to exist after that manner. But there is no impression constant and invariable. Pain and pleasure, grief and joy, passions and sensations succeed each other, and never all exist at the same time. It cannot therefore be from any of these impressions, or from any other, that the idea of self is derived; and consequently there is no such idea.... [Selves] are nothing but a bundle or collection of different perceptions, which succeed each other with an inconceivable rapidity, and are in a perpetual flux and movement.[9]

There are no two ways about it; Hume's criticism has made a lasting impression on philosophy. But it's had a very unusual—one might even say ironic—impact on Berkeley scholarship in particular. It has helped a number of contemporary commentators to the conclusion that, all things considered, it is preferable that we not take Berkeley's description of spirits as "simple substances" too seriously. Instead, they recommend that we read him as holding some sort of bundle account of spirits. Clearly, this move will be especially attractive to anyone in the grip of the *esse* is *percipi* caricature because now, since spirits consist of perceptions, the *esse* of spirits is *percipi*.

My aim in this chapter is to present an interpretation of the very basics of Berkeley's metaphysics and to do it in such as way as to flush the hidden influence of the caricature out into the open. To this end, I will treat the bundle approach to spirits as something of a stalking horse. Currently, there are three different strategies for attributing one version or another of the bundle account of spirits to Berkeley. One, due to Robert Muehlmann, reads Berkeley as holding a fairly straightforward Humean view of spirits, except that Berkeley's bundles include not only ideas but individual volitions as well.[10] Another, due to Stephen Daniel, sees in Berkeley's work some

Suarezian influences that lead to an account of minds as bundles of "particular and determinate apprehensions" of ideas.[11] The third is due to Ian Tipton and sees Berkeley as identifying spirits with Lockean *persons* and as thereby treating minds as collections in something like the way a herd is a collection.[12]

Now, my main interest is making plain the systemic problem that undoes all three of these attempts and indeed any attempt to provide a bundle account of spirits. However, before beginning that task, we should note that two of these interpretations suffer from a distinct problem that lies much closer to the surface. Both Muehlmann's and Daniel's interpretations rely heavily on a series of entries from the *Philosophical Commentaries* in which Berkeley appears to be endorsing a bundle or what he might have called a "congeries" approach to spirits.

+ The very existence of Ideas constitutes the soul.

+ Consult, ransack y^r Understanding w^t find you there besides several perceptions or thoughts. W^t mean you by the word mind you must mean something that you perceive or y^t you do not perceive. a thing not perceived is a contradiction. to mean (also) a thing you do not perceive is a contradiction. We are in all this matter strangely abused by words.

+ Mind is a congeries of Perceptions. Take away Perceptions & you take away the Mind put the Perceptions & you put the mind.

+ Say you the Mind is not the Perceptions. but that thing wch perceives. I answer you are abus'd by the words that & thing these are vague empty words wthout a meaning.[13]

These early notebook entries were all marked by Berkeley with the + sign. While the exact interpretation of the sign's meaning is disputed, the standard reading takes it to mark, if not outright rejection of the view expressed, then at least some level of dissatisfaction. Sometimes, the dissatisfaction is only with part of the content of the entry. Other times, it seems to be simply a matter of an infelicitous wording. Still other times, it simply is not clear why the entry is marked. But with that said, the central problem facing anyone who would use these entries to support the attribution of any sort of bundle account of spirits to Berkeley is that we certainly appear to have conclusive evidence that so far as these particular entries are concerned, the + sign indicates a rejection of the view expressed. In his published works, Berkeley consistently refers to spirits as *simple substances*. With this in mind, I propose the following interpretive constraint:

Constraint 1: When there is a conflict, one should reject early views that the author chose not to publish in favor of later views that the author chose to publish repeatedly.

Since both Daniel's and Muehlmann's interpretations rely heavily upon the use of such notebook entries, I take it that their interpretations prima facie violate this constraint.

Daniel does not directly address the problem created by the conflict between these notebook entries and Berkeley's repeatedly endorsed description of spirits as simple substances, so I will set his interpretation aside.[14] Muehlmann, however, does address it. He claims that Berkeley never really rejected the congeries view, but instead chose to *conceal* it in his published works. According to Muehlmann, Berkeley is a master of the "arts of misdirection and camouflage."[15] Naturally, one immediately wonders why Berkeley would do such a thing. Muehlmann's answer is disappointing. We are told it is because he has ambitions in the Church and fears that a bundle view of spirits will offend "Church-men" because "it cannot be easily squared with theological dogma."[16]

So far as I can see, the "dogma" being referred to is the belief that the soul is naturally immortal. Since bundles are collections, they are also divisible (i.e., mere natural processes can destroy them). Simple substances, by contrast, are indivisible and, therefore, are naturally immortal. A belief in the natural immortality of soul is certainly a "dogma" which Berkeley believed. To be plain, this is an extraordinary claim to make against anyone, but laying the charge at the feet of a deeply religious man who is well known for the integrity of his character only increases the burden of proof. Muehlmann admits that the evidence for attributing such systematic and lifelong deceit to Berkeley is "thin," but I don't think he recognizes just how thin.[17] His key piece of evidence is entry 715 of the *Commentaries*. It reads,

> N.B. To use utmost Caution not to give the least Handle of offence to the Church or Church-men.[18]

From this entry, we learn that Berkeley does not want to give anyone in "the Church" reason to attack his work on the grounds of it being offensive. I am unable to see in this grounds for attributing to Berkeley an intention to engage in an elaborate, sustained deceit about the fundamentals of his philosophy. But even if we set that aside, it is still very hard to connect this entry with Berkeley's ambitions in the Church because in the very next entry, 716, Berkeley comments on that previous entry, 715, by adding,

> Even to speak somewhat favourably of the Schoolmen & shew that they who blame them for Jargon are not free from it themselves.[19]

The reference to the "Schoolmen" in connection with "the Church" rather strongly suggests that Berkeley is here concerned with not giving "handle of offence" to the Roman Catholic church. But certainly, Berkeley had no ambitions in *that* church.

The most intriguing and best motivated of the bundle account interpretation is due to Ian Tipton. Tipton's interpretation is not motivated (at least not primarily) by the aforementioned notebook entries. Instead, in connecting Berkelian spirits with Lockean persons, his interpretation is built upon the sensible assumption that Locke's famous discussion of the distinction between spiritual substances and persons would have been closely studied by Berkeley. I think there is a valuable insight at the heart of Tipton's proposal once it is separated from the bundle interpretation. I will discuss this aspect of his view in chapter IV.

Of more immediate concern is to get about the business of undoing the damage done by the *esse* is *percipi* caricature so that we can have a good, clean start with Berkeley's positive metaphysics. From here, I will trace a historical path, elucidating Berkeley's views on existence by locating them with respect to two traditions of the early modern period that inform and compete with his, those of Descartes and Locke. This will occupy the rest of this chapter. When the argument of this chapter is complete, the fundamental error behind the attribution of *any* sort of bundle account of spirits will be made plain, and by exposing the error we will have a much clearer view of the Berkelian basics.

4. Two Traditions about Existence: Descartes and Locke

As is often the case, it's best to begin with that great French grandfather of us all, Descartes. We tend to see Descartes' dualism as ontologically profligate. We like bare, Quinean, desert ontologies. We like the sharp, clean edge of Occam's razor. This ontological aesthetic is firmly fixed and helps to support a long-standing antagonism toward Descartes' metaphysics. But what we flatly fail to appreciate is that Descartes wielded Occam's razor like a scythe.

To get off on the right foot with Descartes, you must see him first and foremost as a radical ontological reductionist. His philosophy took the ascendancy over an elaborately developed and well-established Aristotelianism. His scholastic predecessors and contemporaries had recourse to a vast menagerie of kinds of substances. Descartes' project was to show that we could make do with only two kinds of substances: *extended things* and *thinking things*. His bold claim was that not only could we meet the explanatory needs of both science and self with recourse to a mere two kinds of substances, but that by doing so we could actually make better sense of the world and our place in it. Descartes' sleek, stripped-down ontology gave birth to a new generation of philosophers who felt as if a great weight had been lifted from them. 'Scholasticism' became a term of abuse. Philosophy, it seemed, had been given a fresh start.

5. The Cartesian Bifurcation of Being

But there was a cost. Descartes' radically minimalist metaphysics required an even more radical reconceiving of the very concept of *division* in the ways of being. Because we were all raised downstream from this conceptual shift, it's hard for us to fully appreciate just how challenging it was.

Here's one way to gain perspective: for the Aristotelian, it makes sense to say that the nature of a domestic cat is really quite different from the nature of a snail. And it makes sense to say that a cat's nature is even more distant from the nature of a piece of coal. By comparison, the nature of a cat is not so very different from that of a lion. The point is that the plurality of kinds of Aristotelian substances is such as to admit of degrees of difference in the ways of being. However, in the Cartesian metaphysics, the notion that the difference in kinds of substances is a difference of degrees has absolutely no place. From the Cartesian perspective, the being of matter and the being of mind are utterly distinct, completely incommensurable. The nature of matter is to be *extended*. The nature of mind is to *think*. And never the twain shall commune. Forget apples and oranges. Bodies are material. Minds are *immaterial*. As Descartes suggests in the "Synopsis" to the *Meditations*, "The natures of mind and body are not only different, but in some way opposite."[20] The Cartesian distinction between matter and mind is as absolute a distinction as that between *being* and *nothingness*, yet at the same time it is to be conceived as a distinction *of beings*. Would-be Aristotelian converts to Cartesianism are asked to make one giant conceptual leap and can be forgiven if they balk after sizing up the chasm.

To further illustrate the point, it's helpful to note that it is precisely Descartes' reconceiving of division in being that makes the infamous "interaction problem" so stark. As others have pointed out, Descartes is not alone in having an interaction problem. In the early modern period, causal interaction was largely thought of as an interaction that leads to one substance transferring something to a second, distinct substance. But transferring *what* and *how*? Perhaps we have the interaction of billiard balls in mind and are imagining that what is transferred is simply the cue ball's direction of motion to the eight ball. But that motion is a property of the first substance, the cue ball. How can it be transferred to the eight ball, a distinct substance? As a property, it depends upon, "inheres in," its substance. How can one substance's dependent become another substance's dependent? Must papers be signed? The Aristotelians have no better answer to this problem than do the Cartesians. However, the Aristotelian does have the advantage in that she is only conceiving of the transfer of the kinds of properties that both substances can support, e.g., *motion* in one particular substance bringing about *motion* in a distinct, but not incommensurable, substance. She doesn't have to explain how the property of *thought* in an *im*material substance can bring about the completely distinct, incommensurable property of *motion* in a material substance, or vice versa. The problem is only further highlighted by that other distinctive feature of Descartes' dualism, i.e., its lack of priority ordering with respect to the two kinds of finite substances. Since neither enjoys any kind of metaphysical priority over the other, the possibility that perhaps the greater can somehow control its dependent is patently unavailable.[21] Descartes' radical bifurcation of being had the effect, not of creating the interaction problem, but of making it manifest.

6. The Cartesian Bifurcation of Epistemology

The ontological independence of mind and body are matched by their conceptual independence. It is only through our grasp of their peculiar conceptual independence that we come to recognize that body and mind are *substances*.

> Whatever exists can either be conceived by itself (*seul*) or it cannot. There is no middle ground, for the two propositions are contradictory. Now whatever can be conceived by itself and without thinking of another thing—whatever, I say, can be conceived by itself as existing independently of some other thing, or can be conceived without the idea we have of it representing some other thing—that is certainly a being or a substance.[22]

The quotation here is from Descartes' most talented and famous disciple, Nicolas Malebranche. Malebranche was particularly keen to emphasize the importance of this point. He regarded the distinctively Cartesian conception of mind and body as "the foundation of the principal tenets of philosophy," and he believed that if we paid due attention to it, we could rightly draw "an infinite number of conclusions."[23]

Both the concepts of *extension* and *mind* enjoy independence from one another. Malebranche begins with extension.

> Now, enter into yourself, and do you not find that you can think of what is extended without thinking of some other thing? Do you not find that you can perceive what is extended by itself alone? Hence, extension is a substance and in no way a state or manner of being. Hence, extension and matter are but one and the same substance.[24]

The conceptual independence of extension helps to reveal its ontological independence because the Cartesian approach to the concept of substance *identifies* a substance with its essence. So, in grasping the essence of the substance, we grasp all there is to know about the substance. Descartes' own references to extension as matter's "principle attribute" are potentially misleading.[25] Extension is not a property of matter; it is all there is to matter. It is the very being of the substance itself. Again, Malebranche is clearer on this point.

> Extension is not a state of being: it is itself a being. As the modification of a substance is simply the substance itself in some particular state.[26]

Malebranche's greater clarity about this point provides him with one of his more effective rhetorical devices for explaining the conceptual independence of mind and matter.

> Modifications of extension consist entirely in relations of distance. Now, it is evident that my pleasure, my desire, and all my thoughts are not relations of distance. For relations of distance can be compared, measured, exactly determined by principles of geometry; and we can neither compare nor measure in this way our perceptions and our sensations. Hence, my soul is not material. It is not the modification of my body. It is a substance which thinks and which has no resemblance to the extended substance of which my body is composed.[27]

Spatial measurement has no nonmetaphorical application to the modalities of thought. They are conceptually unrelated—independent.[28]

6.1. The Pure Intellect

Coordinating with this conceptual dualism is an epistemic dualism. Descartes posits two different sources for acquiring the two different concepts of being. For the concept *material being* (i.e., *body* or *material substance*), we must turn to the "pure intellect." For the concept *mental being* (i.e., *mind* or *mental substance*), we must turn to "reflection." I begin with the pure intellect.

A substance, in the strict sense, is above all a genuine individual. It is not composed of parts in any sense of either 'composition' or 'parts.' It is simple. This in mind, there is a difficulty about just how we acquire the idea of any given substance. To see why this is so, let's, following Descartes, "take, for example, this piece of wax."

> It has just been taken from the honeycomb; it has not yet quite lost the taste of the honey; it retains some of the scent of the flowers from which it was gathered; its

colour, shape and size are plain to see; it is hard, cold and can be handled without difficulty; if you rap it with your knuckle it makes a sound. In short, it has everything which appears necessary to enable a body to be known as distinctly as possible. But even as I speak, I put the wax by the fire, and look: the residual taste is eliminated, the smell goes away, the colour changes, the shape is lost, the size increases; it becomes liquid and hot; you can hardly touch it, and if you strike it, it no longer makes a sound. But does the same wax remain? It must be admitted that it does; no one denies it, no one thinks otherwise. So what was it in the wax that I understood with such distinctness? Evidently none of the features which I arrived at by means of the senses; *for whatever came under taste, smell, sight, touch or hearing has now altered—yet the wax remains.*[29]

Descartes can be read as making a classical point. Our senses present us with a *flux*. We say we see, smell, feel one and the same thing—an individual, in this case a piece of wax. But what our senses present us with is a multimodal plurality of sensations both at an instant and over the period of time in question. Among this plurality there is no one individual thing present at an instant or throughout.

It will be worthwhile to lay the problem out explicitly. Paraphrasing Descartes' example a bit, we can explain the problem in the following way: the perceiver starts out at time t_1 with an olfactory sensation of a scent of flowers, which we shall name α; a visual sensation of a yellow honeycomb shape (β); a cold, hard tactile feeling (γ); and the sound of a sharp, clear knock (δ). By the end of the discussion, time t_2, there is either no longer a sensation of the scent of flowers or, at most, a much fainter one (ε); the yellow honeycomb shape is absent and instead he now has a visual idea of a blanched, somewhat larger, irregular shape (ζ); there is now a soft, warm tactile sensation (η); and the sharp knock is replaced by a dull, quiet thud (ν).

There is both a synchronic and a diachronic problem for the claim that we perceive the wax with the senses. The synchronic problem is that at t_1 we are supposed to have *an* idea of the wax. But as far as our senses are concerned, we do not have before the mind any one single idea but rather several ideas: $\{\alpha, \beta, \gamma, \delta\}$. Which of these is the idea of the wax itself? And of course, we can't say it is the collection because what we are said to have is an idea of the wax *as a substance*, a genuine individual. The collection is just that, a *collection of ideas*, not the *idea of a collection*. The latter requires that we conceive of the collection as a unit, but currently we have no idea what it is that unites these ideas into a collection.[30]

The diachronic problem is then even easier to see. At t_1 we have ideas $\{\alpha, \beta, \gamma, \delta\}$. At t_2 we have ideas $\{\varepsilon, \zeta, \eta, \nu\}$. Not a single one of the ideas present at t_1 is present at t_2. What then grounds the assertion that anything at all, let alone something we have reason to call "the wax," *remains* from t_1 through to t_2? In short, what warrants our claim that we perceive *one thing*? The sensory ground is too unstable, constantly shifting. The senses simply lack the authority to issue such a warrant.

Happily, however, we are not just sensory creatures. Our cognitive resources run deeper. We have in addition to sensation a faculty of *imagination*. The imagination can form copies of our sensory ideas in the form of images. It can repeat them, store them, and recall them at a later time, thus providing us with memory. The imagination can also dissect its copied images, combine and rearrange them into novel patterns that have not (yet) been met within our sensory perceptions. Its powers are certainly remarkable, and so Descartes considers the possibility that it is this faculty that allows us to be acquainted with something we can dub "this piece of wax."

> Perhaps the answer lies in the thought which now comes to my mind; namely, the wax was not after all the sweetness of the honey, or the fragrance of the flowers, or the whiteness, or the shape, or the sound, but was rather a body which presented itself to me in these various forms a little while ago, but which now exhibits different ones. But what exactly is it that I am now imagining? Let us concentrate, take away everything which does not belong to the wax, and see what is left: merely something extended, flexible and changeable. But what is meant here by 'flexible' and 'changeable'? Is it what I picture in my imagination: that this piece of wax is capable of changing from a round shape to a square shape, or from a square shape to a triangular shape? Not at all; for I can grasp that the wax is capable of countless changes of this kind, yet I am unable to run through this immeasurable number of changes in my imagination, from which it follows that it is not the faculty of imagination that gives me my grasp of the wax as flexible and changeable.[31]

The question is, how are we to account for our grasp of the wax as containing an immeasurable number of unactualized and thus unperceived possibilities? The faculty of imagination is marvelous but still finite. My grasp of the wax as a thing capable of innumerable changes exceeds the reach of my imagination. Now, that certainly does indicate some sort of problem, but what is the problem exactly? We can think of it this way: Descartes has, at that very moment, a conception (an idea, a representation, a grasp) of the wax. It is the concept of something capable of *countless* changes of shape. The imagination's representational powers reach no further than the production of individual images. But no matter how much time one gives the imagination, it cannot provide representations of each of the possible shapes the wax can take, and so it cannot supply a complete representation of the wax itself. Simply put, the imagination is finite; the possibilities are infinite. But to push more deeply into the heart of the problem, we must appreciate what I take to be Descartes' key question in the passage: "what is meant here by 'flexible' and 'changeable'? Is it what I picture in my imagination?" Central to Descartes' concept of the wax *as a substance* is his grasp of it as something *capable* of taking on different shapes. The point that must be drawn out is that the concept *substance* is intimately tied to the concept *power*. The wax is able to do things. Importantly, however, material substances possess only what both Descartes and Malebranche would call "passive power." This concept of power is not equivalent to the concept of efficient cause. It is not the concept of something that is able to *bring about* changes. It is rather the concept of something that can be modified. It can receive changes, but not cause them.

The upshot is that if the imagination is to be the source of our idea of the wax itself, the wax qua substance, it must provide us with a representation of the wax's power. The problem then is that this means it cannot be the imagination which accounts for Descartes' grasp of the wax because the imagination cannot supply him with a representation of this power. Here is another approach to the problem: even if we allowed that, somehow, the imagination does manage to produce an infinite number of representations at an instant, we still would not have a grasp of the wax *itself*. The imagination would only be providing us with representations of the various *states* the wax could take. What it is about the wax that makes it capable of taking on all these various states and thus, what it is that gives us reason to unite all these representations and regard them as *states of one thing*, i.e., of a substance, is not thereby represented. From imagination, we can get no conception of the power that ties this vast number of representations together into a bundle.

So it seems that it is neither from sense nor imagination that we acquire the concept "material being."[32] Still, we continue to talk as if we do have a grasp of just such a thing. We say things like "This piece of wax was cool, but it is now hot." And "This wax was stiff, but it is now flexible." Is this talk illegitimate? Descartes' answer is no. His contention is that we have not yet exhausted all our perceptual faculties.

> [H]ere is the point, the perception I have of [the wax] is a case not of vision or touch or imagination—nor has it ever been, despite previous appearances—but of purely mental scrutiny.[33]

"Purely mental scrutiny" is something only a special faculty, distinct from sense and imagination, can achieve. If we were restricted to receiving sensory representations or forming only imagistic representations, as are the senses and imagination, respectively, we would be acquainted with nothing more than actual and possible *states* of an extended thing. Enter the "pure intellect." From the fact that we do grasp that the wax remains—as Descartes puts it, "It must be admitted that it does; no one denies it, no one thinks otherwise"—Descartes concludes that we do have an ability to represent more than just states of a body. What makes the pure intellect's representational capacities unique is its ability to produce *non-imagistic* representations. "Pure mental scrutiny" is a mode of perception, but it is not a mode of sensory perception. Its representations have no sensorial/imagistic content. It is this faculty that allows us to grasp the wax by way of its *essence*, extension. And extension is the essence of the substance which is the wax; it is not merely a state or property of that substance. In grasping it, I grasp the wax qua substance.

Now, this is not to say that we could have the idea of this individual piece of wax without sense and imagination. Their participation is integral. The activity of the pure intellect requires input from the senses and imagination on which to work. Without them, we might have the idea of extension, but not the idea that there is a particular extended being (e.g., a piece of wax) in my hand right now. However, once the pure intellect forms its representation of that particular extended being, that representation is non-imagistic. What we then become acquainted with is the extended thing itself: a body stripped of its sensory guise. Descartes' Platonic point here is that if we are to find what is lasting, what is real, we must rise above the blooming, buzzing confusion of sense and imagination and turn toward a higher faculty. Deepening the Platonic nature of his orientation here is the fact that Descartes identifies the activity of the pure intellect as *judgment.* But, for our purposes, the important point is that the unique perceptual-representational powers of the pure intellect serve as a sort of unity detector, if you will, allowing us to perceive the essence of material being.

Thus, this gives us the first half of Descartes' bifurcated epistemology.

6.2. Reflection

Since the pure intellect provides us with the concept of one kind of substance, matter, the obvious question is, how do we acquire our concept of the other kind of substance, mind? Descartes' answer: through the faculty of *reflection.* Reflection, like the pure intellect, is a faculty for perceiving unity. And such a faculty has its work cut out for it. Like the outer, the inner realm confronts us with a flux as well, only it is a flux of thoughts, intentions, volitions, emotions, pains, pleasures, etc. It is precisely at this point that Hume's critique of spiritual substance enters the dialectic, because when Hume looks inward, he finds no more than a flux.

> For my part, when I enter most intimately into what I call myself, I always stumble on some particular perception or other, of heat or cold, light or shade, love or hatred, pain or pleasure. I never can catch myself at any time without a perception, and never can observe any thing but the perception.[34]

Famously, from this he draws the conclusion that there is no genuine individual answering to the terms 'self,' 'soul,' or 'mind.' Instead, we are just a bundle of these perceptions. But Hume does offer a concession.

> If any one, upon serious and unprejudiced reflection, thinks he has a different notion of himself, I must confess I can reason no longer with him. All I can allow him is, that he may be in the right as well as I, and that we are essentially different in this particular. He may, perhaps, perceive something simple and continued, which he calls himself; though I am certain there is no such principle in me.[35]

Descartes is such a person. As he sees it, in reflection we do not encounter merely a flux of thoughts. Although he would allow that we do not encounter a simple sensory continuant in reflection that we identify as our self, we do, however, encounter our thoughts, feelings, pains, etc., *as ours* and in doing so we encounter ourselves *as a unity.* Moreover, according to Descartes, his grasp of that fact is unusually sound. It is every bit as indubitable as is the belief that he exists. In the "Second Meditation," Descartes writes,

> Is it not one and the same 'I' who is now doubting almost everything, who nonetheless understands some things, who affirms that this one thing is true, denies everything else, desires to know more, is unwilling to be deceived, imagines many things even involuntarily, and is aware of many things which apparently come from the senses? *Are not all these things just as true as the fact that I exist,* even if I am asleep all the time, and even if he who created me is doing all he can to deceive me?...The fact that it is I who am doubting and understanding and willing is so evident that I see no way of making it any clearer.[36]

According to Descartes, the unity of a self is self-evident to reflection.

This is not the time to adjudicate the debate between Descartes and Hume on reflection.[37] At present, the more important point is that we have before us now the basics of Descartes' dualistic ontology and his matching dualistic epistemology of that ontology. There are two substances. Equivalently, the universe admits of two fundamental kinds of unity: material and mental. The nature of the unity of a material thing is completely different from that of a mental thing, a self. The former are unities in virtue of the fact that they have *extension* as their essence and the fact that their being coincides with their essence, i.e., they are *extended* things. The latter are unities in virtue of the fact that they have *thought* as their essence and the fact that their being also coincides with their essence, i.e., they are *thinking* things. We are able to grasp the unity of things existing in the mode of extension by way of the perceptions of the pure intellect. We are able to grasp the principle of the unity of things existing in the mode of thought by way of reflection.[38]

7. Locke and the Empiricist Strategy

Characteristic of what has become known as early modern "empiricism" is an antagonism toward the pure intellect.[39] The paradigm empiricist attempts to show that we can account for all our knowledge via the acquisitive capacities of sense perception. There are two intertwined components to this approach. The first is a requirement that one make do without recourse to *innate* ideas. There is an emphasis on the need for ideas to be *acquired*.[40] The empiricist regards the appeal to innate ideas as explanatorily bankrupt. It is a dodge, a deus ex machina designed to silence debate, not deepen it.[41] The empiricist embraces the old scholastic dictum *Nihil est in intellectu quod non prius fuit in sensu*, but she does so with an unprecedented vigor. This, in turn, provides the second key aspect of the empiricist approach. The empiricist is hostile to the possibility of *non-imagistic mental representations*. Since nothing can be in the intellect that was not first in sensation, ideas must maintain their sensorial character. Just what will count as sensorial enough may vary from thinker to thinker, but one thing is agreed upon: the radically non-imagistic representations of the pure intellect are excluded. When it comes to ideas, being non-imagistic is as bad as being innate.

The obvious question then is, how will the empiricist be able to account for all our knowledge, most important, our knowledge of things like this piece of wax? After all, the entire point of introducing the pure intellect was to take advantage of its uniquely *non-sensory, non-imagistic* representational powers so that we could account for this sort of knowledge. How will we find the unity that is the wax among the ever-changing wash of sensation without the pure intellect?

Locke put together a powerful strategy for dealing with this problem. The first part of his strategy involves a reevaluation of the faculties of sense and imagination with the aim of seeing if one cannot squeeze more fodder for concept formation out of them than was previously thought possible. He coordinates this with an effort to curb our pretension toward certain kinds of knowledge.[42] The goal is to show that we neither have nor need a faculty like the pure intellect. That is to say, we neither have nor need knowledge of the sort that the pure intellect and its non-imagistic representations are supposed to provide. The combined strategy is fairly simple: the less we are seen to need in the way of conceptual prowess, the more likely it is that mere sense and imagination can meet those needs.

8. Reevaluating the Understanding

Locke, much like his predecessors, divides the understanding by way of its different representational faculties. And, also in the spirit of his predecessors, he identifies its two main faculties as *sensation* and *reflection*. However, instead of the pure intellect, he adds to this a capacity to form ideas by a process called "abstraction." Sensation and reflection are representational cum perceptual faculties; abstraction is not or, at least, not exactly. I review each in turn, beginning with sense.

Locke reserves 'sense' for the familiar five perceptual modalities: sight, scent, touch, taste, and hearing. Sensation is distinguished from reflection by the "location" of the source of their ideas. They provide us with ideas of "things without." The sensory ideas, or sensations, we receive are distinct both intermodally and intramodally:

> Though the qualities that affect our senses are, in the things themselves, so united and blended, that there is no separation, no distance between them; yet it is plain, the ideas they produce in the mind enter by the senses simple and unmixed. For though the sight and touch often take in from the same object, at the same time, different ideas; as a man sees at once motion and colour; the hand feels softness and warmth in the same piece of wax; yet the simple ideas, thus united in the same subject, are as perfectly distinct as those that come in by different senses: The coldness and hardness which a man feels in a piece of ice being as distinct ideas in the mind, as the smell and whiteness of a lily; or as the taste of sugar, and smell of a rose. And there is nothing can be plainer to a man, than the clear and distinct perception he has of those simple ideas; which, being each in itself uncompounded, contains in it nothing but one uniform appearance, or conception in the mind, and is not distinguishable into different ideas.[43]

The now-familiar distinction between "simple" and "complex" ideas is important because it provides Locke with a basic anatomy of the perceptual realm and then a taxonomy by which to define the scope and limit of the powers of both the various sensory faculties and the faculty of imagination. The imagination has the power to copy and carve the sensory world at the joints. It can recall, arrange, and rearrange simple ideas into complex ideas. However, it cannot create any new simple ideas. It can only work with what it is given by sensation and reflection.

Limited as we are to sensation and imagination, we have no capacity for "purely mental scrutiny." Our sensory ideas are ideas of the properties of "outer" objects. We have no additional faculty for peering through those presentations and grasping the inner principle of the unity of objects.

8.1. Reflection

As for the faculty of reflection, Locke is keen to emphasize its affinity to the other perceptual modalities.

> The other fountain from which experience furnisheth the understanding with ideas, is the perception of the operations of our own mind within us, as it is employed about the ideas it has got; which operations, when the soul comes to reflect on and consider, do furnish the understanding with another set of ideas, which could not be had from things without. And such are Perception, Thinking, Doubting, Believing, Reasoning, Knowing, Willing, and all the different actings of our own minds; which we being conscious of and observing in ourselves, do from these receive into our understandings as distinct ideas, as we do from bodies affecting our senses. This source of ideas every man has wholly in himself; and though it be not sense, as having nothing to do with external objects, yet it is very like it, and might properly enough be called internal sense. But as I call the other sensation, so I call this REFLECTION.[44]

Reflection is "inner sense." Locke wants to make it plain that he regards reflection as just another sensory modality. His point here is that the ideas with which reflection provides us do not differ in kind from those provided by outer senses. According to Locke, we quite literally have a "sixth sense." Consequently, since reflection is no more than inner sense, reflection is not capable of "purely mental scrutiny" either. It doesn't possess a special power for grasping the inner principle of unity of these "internal" items. It was Locke's conception of reflection that Hume would embrace and drive to its logical conclusion.

8.2. Abstraction

The only other idea-forming faculty we have is the power of abstraction.

> The use of words then being to stand as outward marks of our internal ideas, and those ideas being taken from particular things, if every particular idea that we take in should have a distinct name, names must be endless. To prevent this, the mind makes the particular ideas received from particular objects, to become general; which is done by considering them as they are in the mind, such appearances, separate from all other existences, and the circumstances of real existence, as time, place, or any other concomitant ideas. This is called abstraction, whereby ideas, taken from particular beings, become general representatives of all of the same kind, and their names general names, applicable to whatever exists conformable to such abstract ideas.[45]

Since we encounter only *particulars* and not general beings in perception, we cannot be acquiring our "general ideas" from sense or imagination. Abstraction allows us to *acquire* general ideas by *making* them. Unfortunately, Locke's discussion of this power has left more than one reader wondering if abstraction perhaps provides us with a power to form something akin to non-imagistic representations. And if this question is not clearly answered, then one could be excused for wondering if Locke is unwittingly allowing the pure intellect, or at least something much like it, in through the back door.

Ultimately, however, there's little reason to see Locke's abstract ideas as radically non-imagistic in the way the ideas of the pure intellect are. According to Locke, we do not have access to anything like an object's inner essence, and that's nothing to be too terribly upset about because individual objects simply do not have essences.

> There is nothing I have that is essential to me. An accident, or disease, may very much alter my colour, or shape; a fever or fall, may take away my reason or memory, or both, and an apoplexy leave neither sense nor understanding, nor life. Other creatures of my shape may be made with more and better, or fewer and worse faculties than I have; and others may have reason and sense in a shape and body very different from mine.[46]

Locke rejects the identification of substance and essence, and so at *Essay* II.i.10, contra the Cartesians, Locke famously argues that minds need not always think. And as he tells as *Essay* III.vi.4, the concept *essence* only has application when it comes to sorting individuals into *kinds*.

> That essence, in the ordinary use of the word, relates to sorts; and that it is considered in particular beings no farther than as they are ranked into sorts; appears from hence: That take but away the abstract ideas, by which we sort individuals, and rank them under common names, and then the thought of any thing essential to any of them instantly vanishes; we have no notion of the one without the other; which plainly shows their relation.

Abstraction is the process whereby we come to have sortal ideas, and thus abstraction is concerned with forming concepts of the essences of things only insofar as they are categorized into kinds. This is a less powerful representational faculty than the pure intellect, but then, since objects don't have essences, we have little cause to complain.

Further insulating abstraction from the pure intellect is Locke's distinction between "nominal" and "real" essences.

> When general names have any connexion with particular beings, these abstract ideas are the medium that unites them: So that the essences of species, as distinguished and denominated by us, neither are nor can be any thing but these precise abstract ideas we have in our minds. And therefore the supposed real essences of substances, if different from our abstract ideas, cannot be the essences of the species we rank things into.[47]

Abstraction lacks the power to carve the world by way of the "real" essences of objects; the best it can provide us with is the "nominal" essences of objects.

> It is true, there is ordinarily supposed a real constitution of the sorts of things; and it is past doubt, there must be some real constitution, on which any collection of simple ideas co-existing must depend. But it being evident, that things are ranked under names into sorts or species, only as they agree to certain abstract ideas, to which we have annexed those names: The essence of each genus, or sort, comes to be nothing but that abstract idea, which the general, or sortal (if I may have leave so to call it from sort, as I do general from genus) name stands for. And this we shall find to be that which the word essence imports in its most familiar use. These two sorts of essences, I suppose, may not unfitly be termed, the one the real, the other nominal essence.[48]

Since, outside of sense, reflection, and imagination, the only other representational faculty we have concerns itself solely with nominal essences, it seems
Locke has a very different view, not only of the nature of objects themselves, but
also of the nature of our grasp of those objects. As Locke sees it, our ideas of the
various substances of the world (e.g., you, me, the Washington Monument, a piece
of iron, a diamond, etc.) are *complex* ideas. Our grasp of any of these things consists
almost entirely in our grasp of the various *qualities* of these objects.

> It is the ordinary qualities observable in iron, or a diamond, put together, that make
> the true complex idea of those substances, which a smith or a jeweller commonly
> knows better than a philosopher; who, whatever substantial forms he may talk of, has
> no other idea of those substances, than what is framed by a collection of those simple
> ideas which are to be found in them.[49]

My grasp of this piece of iron in front of me is not a matter of my pure intellect
grasping something other than the qualities of iron. As Locke sees it, even if there
were something more for such a faculty to grasp, knowledge of it wouldn't be of
much value to us. My knowledge of this bit of iron consists almost entirely in knowledge of the nominal essence *iron* (i.e., the complex idea of the qualities of iron).
However, although a grasp of the qualities of a substance makes up the greater part
of our concept of it, there is still something more to them. We group some collection of simple ideas together into a complex one under a name like 'iron' or
'diamond' because in our experience, as Locke puts it, "these simple ideas go
constantly together," and the reason for this, we presume, is because they "belong to
one thing."[50] Therefore,

> our complex ideas of substances, besides all those simple ideas they are made up of,
> have always the confused idea of some thing to which they belong, and in which they
> subsist. And therefore, when we speak of any sort of substance, we say it is a thing
> having such or such qualities: As body is a thing that is extended, figured, and capable
> of motion; spirit, a thing capable of thinking; and so hardness, friability, and power to
> draw iron, we say, are qualities to be found in a lodestone. These, and the like fashions
> of speaking, intimate, that the substance is supposed always some thing besides the
> extension, figure, solidity, motion, thinking, or other observable ideas, though we
> know not what it is.[51]

Something is responsible for uniting these ideas in our experience, but as Locke
makes clear here, he sees nothing in our concept of either extension or thought that
accounts for the unity of an object's qualities. Extension and thought seem as much
in need of substantial support as anything else. They seem to be merely qualities of
substances, not substances themselves. As for the nature of substantial support, we
have only the vaguest of ideas.

> [Substance] being nothing but the supposed, but unknown support of those qualities
> we find existing, which we imagine cannot subsist, "sine re substante," without some
> thing to support them, we call that support substantia; which, according to the true
> import of the word, is in plain English, standing under or upholding.[52]

But here is the point: as Locke sees it, our thin, sad grasp of that which supplies
the qualities of an object with their substantial unity is nothing to be concerned

about. Even if we had it, it wouldn't help us much. Our working knowledge of objects is overwhelmingly concerned with nominal essences, and those nominal essences are complex ideas consisting almost entirely of ideas of the qualities of objects. Our faculties may be limited, but just the same, they are well suited to our needs.

8.3. *Lockean Simple Ideas and the Concept of Unity*

In many respects, it seems that Locke's view of the understanding does not involve a radical reconception of the powers of sense and imagination from that of the Cartesians. Ultimately, like the Cartesians, Locke regards the deliverances of the senses as ideas. And as in the Cartesian tradition, ideas are understood to be representational intermediaries standing between the perceiving subject and the world as it is in-itself. Moreover, although the Cartesians didn't make much of the distinction between "simple" and "complex" ideas, their conception of the basic powers of the senses and imagination seems similar enough. The important differences seem to be the limitations that Locke sets for himself: our perceptual capacities do not include the powers of the pure intellect. Ideas must be sensations or sensation-like images. No appeal to radically unpicturable ideas is allowed. And so, our problem remains, *how do we account for our grasp of the wax?* Granted, Locke has dissuaded us from a pretension toward knowledge of the real essences of things as well as of the nature of substance. But still, we do have a grasp of the wax *as an individual*, i.e., as a unitary being, a "unity." The mere claim that we are ignorant of the nature of substance or the real essence of an individual requires that we have the concept *individual*. In Locke's case, he tells us that we find that certain ideas "go constantly together," and we presume this is because they proceed from a unitary source, as Locke puts it, they "belong to one thing." Out of the murky waters of the ever-altering river of sensation, we somehow manage to spot an individual. Whatever else there might be to say about it after we get it up on shore, towel it off, and give it a good looking over, it seems we already know this much: it is at the very least an individual "thing." And to do even this much cognizing, we must have somehow, somewhere, somewhen acquired the concepts *unity* and *being*—exactly the concepts that you need in order to have the concept *individual thing*. This, however, is precisely what Descartes argued our faculties of sense and imagination alone did not supply. So how do we acquire such ideas?

Locke's surprising answer is that the ideas *unity* and *existence* are not at all hard to come by. In fact, we can't avoid having them; they are met with in every perception, whether of sense or reflection.

> Existence and unity are two other ideas that are suggested to the understanding by every object without, and every idea within.[53]

What's going on here? How is that Locke comes by so easily what others struggled to account for? Consider *unity*; what he tells us is that

> [w]hatever we can consider as one thing, whether a real being or idea, suggests to the understanding the idea of unity.[54]

But this is clearly a nonstarter. What Locke tells us is that we acquire the concept *unity* by "consider[ing] as one thing" a real being or idea. The concept *one thing* is not distinct from the concept *unity*. The account presupposes what it is designed to explain. It amounts to the unhelpful claim that we *acquire* the concept *unity* by *applying* the concept *unity*.

Providing an account of how we get the concept *unity* is clearly central to the success or failure of Locke's brave new epistemology. So how do we explain such a lapse? The best one can do is to engage in some speculation, but I think the following is plausible. When it comes to the concept *unity*, Locke's taxonomy itself is already doing all the heavy lifting. In Book II of the *Essay*, almost immediately, Locke introduces the distinction between "simple" and "complex" ideas. He presents it as "plain" that we have simple ideas. Little to no argument is offered. Rather, Locke presents himself as making explicit a distinction we all implicitly recognize. The problem is that 'simplicity' is just one of the many aliases of 'unity.'[55] If something is "simple," it is a true unity. It lacks parts and is thus *one single individual* thing. Since both sensation and reflection provide us with simple ideas, we get the concept *unity* with every sensation, whether it be from "inner" or "outer" sense. If true, then the concept *unity* is just part and parcel of perceiving. If this is your view, then you won't be able to say anything very helpful about how we acquire the concept *unity* through perception. Any attempt to do so would likely produce the kind of idle account Locke provides.[56]

This line of speculation gets further support from Locke's well-known corpuscularian sympathies. The corpuscularian view of substance is, of course, a variety of atomism. The fundamental entities of the world are indivisible corpuscles. They possess only size, shape, and motion. These are the basic beings of the world. All other beings are dependent upon them by way of being complex compounds of these simple elements. The basic principles of geometry and the laws of motion combined with the sizes, shapes, and original motions of these atoms determine what combinations of complex beings the simple ones can form. These simple corpuscles provide the unchanging foundation of reality. In such an ontology, the primary/secondary division of being cuts along the simple/complex line.

Locke, it seems, presents an atomistic epistemology. Consider again how Locke introduces the notion of simple ideas.

> Though the qualities that affect our senses are, in the things themselves, so united and blended, that there is *no separation, no distance* between them; yet it is plain, the ideas they produce in the mind enter by the senses *simple* and *unmixed*.[57]

Notice that being *simple* is contrasted with a lack of "separation" and "distance" between ideas. Focusing on such features is the hallmark of an atomistic conception of substance. Atoms are substances because they can exist *spatially distanced* from other atoms without suffering any change in-themselves. When appeals to simplicity by way of separation and distance are brought to bear in the sensory context, simplicity suggests a "perceptual atomism." In the realm of the understanding, there are two kinds of beings: simple ideas and complex ideas.

Following this path, we have uncovered one, if not the central, explanation for Locke's attitude toward the concept of substantial support. Having banished inner essences, what remains forever vague or even empty in our concept of substance is our grasp of the nature of its substantial *support*. Locke cannot find any adequate account for that which gives a collection its unity. At *Essay* II.xxiii.23, he goes to the trouble of making plain for us the problem that faces the corpuscularian account of the unity of bodies.

> For though the pressure of the particles of air may account for the cohesion of several parts of matter, that are grosser than the particles of air, and have pores less than the corpuscles of air; yet the weight, or pressure of the air, will not explain, nor can be a cause of the coherence of the particles of air themselves. And if the pressure of the aether, or any subtler matter than the air, may unite, and hold fast together the parts of a particle of air, as well as other bodies; yet it cannot make bonds for itself, and hold together the parts that make up every the least corpuscle of that materia subtilis. So that hypothesis, how ingeniously soever explained, by shewing, that the parts of sensible bodies are held together by the pressure of other external insensible bodies, reaches not the parts of the aether it self; and by how much the more evident it proves, that the parts of other bodies are held together by the external pressure of the aether, and can have no other conceivable cause of their cohesion and union, by so much the more it leaves us in the dark concerning the cohesion of the parts of the corpuscles of the aether itself.[58]

In light of this, we should not be surprised to find Locke denying that we lack anything like a clear concept of substantial support. That is inevitable, given that he draws his concept of unity from the unity of perceptual corpuscles.

9. Berkelian Individuals

> [M]ind, soul, or spirit truly and really exists.... bodies exist in only a secondary and dependent sense.[59]

With the basic features of both the Cartesian and the Lockean accounts of substance and existence as background, I turn now to the task of elucidating the basics of Berkeley's view of these issues.

We should already be (almost painfully) aware that Berkeley is a monist; the only substances his ontology admits are spirits. And we are equally aware that this means that Berkeley draws a contrast and marks a priority ordering among beings. As he surveys metaphysics' past, he remarks,

> There are two sorts of philosophers. The one placed Body first in the order of beings, and made the faculty of thinking depend thereupon, supposing that the principles of all things are corporeal; that Body most really or principally exists, and all other things in a secondary sense, and by virtue of that. Others, making all corporeal things to be dependent upon Soul or Mind, think this to exist in the first place and primary sense, and the being of bodies to be altogether derived from and presuppose that of the Mind.[60]

Here, Berkeley is recalling a remark made by Proclus, but his point in doing so is that the perspective is one he shares. The quotation is from Berkeley's last major work, *Siris*. One of that work's central aims is to show that Berkeley's metaphysics has its roots in an ancient and venerable tradition that shares his fundamental metaphysical thesis: *it places minds first in the order of beings*.[61] Although he is often remembered for his originality, Berkeley saw himself as the most recent contributor to a tradition that stretches back beyond Plato.

Central among his contributions to the tradition is a more perspicuous account of its view of both the contrast and priority of beings. He connects the themes of the ancient tradition with the modern philosophy by taking up the modern focus on the conceptual connection between substance and independence that Descartes fostered.

Berkeley's most familiar and well-developed presentation of his central metaphysical thesis is in the negative form of "immaterialism." It is the claim that "unthinking things"—whatever is not a spirit, a mind—do not have an "absolute existence" without any relation to minds whatsoever.[62] He spells this out in terms of a denial of independence to unthinking things.

Berkeley's understanding of the nature of dependence is richly developed, often subtle, and easily misinterpreted. This last aspect is due in no small part to the fact that *dependence* and *independence* are not the fundamental categories of Berkeley's metaphysics. *Activity* and *passivity* are the fundamental categories of Berkeley's metaphysics. The use of the (then) familiar language of 'dependence' and 'independence' is to some extent an expository device. In many ways, it's a very successful device, but not so surprisingly, it has a cost. No doubt, this cost has been exaggerated by the fact that we never got to see Part II of the *Principles*. Without that work and its promised discussion of the nature of spirits, the relationship between independence/dependence and activity/passivity is harder to sort out than it probably would have been.

One of the central interpretive aims of the entirety of the present work is to provide an account of Berkeley's active/passive distinction. The first step toward this is to provide an account of his use of the independence/dependence distinction.

10. Dependence One: 'In'

The way to elucidate Berkeley's use of the dependence/independence distinction is to begin by focusing on 'dependence.' The obvious reason for looking to dependence is that Berkeley's account of the nature of the dependence of matter, his immaterialism, is the subject of so much of his extant work.

Berkeley's account of dependence has two main threads to it. The two are carefully interwoven, presenting a single line of thought. However, for expository purposes, we must pull them apart. I will mark the distinction by referring to two different "senses" of 'dependence.' This is not perfectly satisfactory, but it is expedient.

Complicating matters further is the fact that, as a writer, Berkeley was decidedly strategy oriented. So, for instance, with respect to the *Principles*, he tells his friend Percival:

> I omitted all mention of the non-existence of matter in the title-page, dedication, preface, and introduction, that so the notion might steal unawares on the reader.[63]

With respect to the dependent nature of bodies, his strategy in Part I of the *Principles* is first to introduce the two key senses of dependence gently, right at the outset, then, a bit later, to state them more flatly and forcefully. He first gives them a chance to steal unawares on the reader.

So, in *Principles* 1, we get our first glimpse of both senses of 'dependence.' The first half presents the first sense of dependence and the second half presents the second. Both then find more explicit expression later in the text. With that in mind, let's begin with the first sense of dependence and, thus, the first half of *Principles* 1. It reads,

> It is evident to any one who takes a survey of the objects of human knowledge, that they are either ideas actually imprinted on the senses, or else such as are perceived by attending to the passions and operations of the mind, or lastly ideas formed by help of memory and imagination, either compounding, dividing, or barely representing those originally perceived in the aforesaid ways. By sight I have the ideas of light and colours with their several degrees and variations. By touch I perceive, for example, hard and soft, heat and cold, motion and resistance, and of all these more and less either as to quantity or degree. Smelling furnishes me with odours; the palate with tastes, and hearing conveys sounds to the mind in all their variety of tone and composition.[64]

This half of *Principles* 1 prepares us for the most familiar sense of dependence, the one that has become synonymous with the *esse* is *percipi* catchphrase. It is made more explicit at *Principles* 3.

> That neither our thoughts, nor passions, nor ideas formed by the imagination, exist without the mind, is what every body will allow. And it seems no less evident that the various sensations or ideas imprinted on the sense, however blended or combined together (that is, whatever objects they compose) cannot exist otherwise than in a mind perceiving them. I think an intuitive knowledge may be obtained of this, by any one that shall attend to what is meant by the term exist when applied to sensible things.... For as to what is said of the absolute existence of unthinking things without any relation to their being perceived, that seems perfectly unintelligible. Their *esse* is *percipi*, nor is it possible they should have any existence, out of the minds or thinking things which perceive them.[65]

Then, the first line of *Principles* 4 delivers the short, sharp shock.

> It is indeed an opinion strangely prevailing amongst men, that houses, mountains, rivers, and in a word all sensible objects have an existence natural or real, distinct from their being perceived by the understanding.[66]

Berkeley often expresses the first sense of dependence by saying that ideas exist "in" minds. What does he mean by this? Simply this: ideas of sense are *sensations* and so are "in minds," that is, they depend upon minds in exactly the same way that sensations depend upon their sentient subjects. Ideas of imagination are *images* and so are "in minds," that is, they depend upon minds in exactly the way that our imaginings do. We have here one of the ways in which Berkeley seeks to be "eternally banishing metaphysics and recalling men to common sense."[67] Even the vulgarest of the vulgar have first-person acquaintance with both sensation and imagination. And so, as we saw at *Principles* 3, when it comes to establishing the dependence of ideas on minds, Berkeley insists that "an intuitive knowledge may be obtained of this, by any one that shall attend to what is meant by the term 'exist' when applied to sensible things."[68]

Just the same, it must be acknowledged that Berkeley's use of 'in' has caused no end of interpretive consternation. The key to keeping clear of confusion begins with the dependence of ideas of sense. Despite the fact that minds are substances and these ideas exist "in" them, they do not exist in minds in the way that properties or "attributes" were traditionally conceived to exist in their substances, i.e., by "inhering in" them. Neither do ideas of sense exist in minds by being *modes* of their subject. When it comes to an idea of sense, it is not in the mind in the sense of being "predicated of the subject in which it exists."[69] Rather, ideas of sense

> are in the mind only as they are perceived by it, that is, not by way of *mode* or *attribute*, but only by way of *idea*; and it no more follows, that the soul or mind is extended because extension exists in it alone, than it does that it is red or blue, because those colours are on all hands acknowledged to exist in it, and no where else. As to what philosophers say of subject and mode, that seems very groundless and unintelligible.[70]

Berkeley is here taking advantage of philosophical common ground. The manner of dependence of ideas of sense is "by way of idea." This sense of dependence is recognized "on all hands." Berkeley's point is that no more is needed. When it comes to "all the choir of heaven and furniture of the earth, in a word all those bodies which compose the mighty frame of the world,"[71] we need only this already familiar sense of dependence to understand the manner of their subsistence. The familiar dependence of ideas upon minds eliminates any need to appeal to more extravagant, opaque metaphysical notions like inherence.

11. Active and Passive

Having separated 'in' from its traditional metaphysical interpretation, we can begin our elucidation of Berkeley's understanding of the basic categories of his metaphysics, *activity* and *passivity*. As I said above, 'in' denotes dependence, and the nature of that dependence is familiar. Ideas of sense are sensations and so depend upon minds in exactly the same way that sensations depend upon their sentient subjects. Ideas of imagination are images and so depend upon minds in exactly the way that our imaginings do. But what I carefully passed over is that we are here familiar with two distinct manners of dependence. In the preceding section, I focused on ideas of sense, but ideas of sense do not depend upon us in the same way that ideas of imagination do. Ideas of sense depend on us in a *passive* manner. Ideas of imagination depend on us in an *active* manner. This requires some spelling out.

It is tempting to simply line up Berkeley's active/passive distinction right alongside his familiar ontological distinction between minds and ideas: minds are *active* things; ideas are *passive* things. This is not wrong so much as it is potentially misleading.[72] *Finite minds*, i.e., all of us who are not God, are not *absolutely* active. When it comes to perception, we are passive. We passively receive our ideas of sense. Thus, the ideas of sense are dependent upon our minds in a wholly passive way, qua *recipient* of the ideas. Their primary dependence is on God's activity. Whereas they *passively* depend upon us as their *recipient*, they *actively* depend upon God as their *source*.

> Things by me perceived . . . exist independently of my mind, since I know myself not to be their author, it being out of my power to determine at pleasure, what particular ideas I shall be affected with upon opening my eyes or ears. They must therefore exist in some other mind, whose will it is they should be exhibited to me. The things, I say, immediately perceived, are ideas or sensations, call them which you will.[73]

According to Berkeley, activity is *volition*. I experience these ideas of sense because God *wills* it. As a finitely active being, I am in no position to resist God's will. It is "out of my power to determine at pleasure, what particular ideas I shall be affected with." Minds are active things. But finite minds are only finitely active and as such are subject to perception. Perception, strictly speaking, is only the having of ideas of sense, and so, ideas of sense are "in the mind" passively. Their dependence on our mind is *passive dependence*.

The same is not true with respect to ideas of imagination. With respect to ideas of imagination, we are *active*. As Berkeley puts it at *Principles* 28:

> I find I can excite ideas in my mind at pleasure, and vary and shift the scene as oft as I think fit. It is no more than willing, and straightaway this or that idea arises in my fancy: and by the same power it is obliterated, and makes way for another. This making and unmaking of ideas doth very properly denominate the mind active.[74]

Ideas of imagination are not "in the mind" passively. They actively depend upon us and so are "in the mind" actively.

> The ideas formed by the imagination are faint and indistinct; they have besides an entire dependence on the will. But the ideas perceived by sense, that is, real things, are more vivid and clear, and being imprinted on the mind by a spirit distinct from us, have not a like dependence on our will.[75]

Although here Berkeley describes the dependence of ideas of imagination on our own will as "entire," he, at the same time, recognizes limits to our activity in this respect. These ideas involve memory, and through memory we produce no new ideas but rather merely copies of the ideas of sense.[76] Moreover, compared with their originals, these copies are inferior, being less vivid, distinct, and regular. Their dependence upon us, and thus our activity with respect to them, is, in one sense, limited. Their dependence on us is "entire" in the sense that if we stop willing to have them, they cease to exist.

But there is still more to the dependence of ideas of imagination. Through the activity of imagination, we can take those ideas stored in memory and "compound" and "divide" them into new complex ideas. From my recollection of seeing a dog, I divide away the head and then, making two copies of that head, I then compound them with the body. In this way, I form an image of the guardian of Hades, Cerberus. The point is that the being of ideas of imagination also depends upon the

contribution of our imaginative activity in the sense that it supplies ideas of imagination with their manner of *organization*. But in order to fully appreciate the
importance of this last point, we must move on to the second thread of Berkeley's
account of dependence.

12. Dependence Two: The Unity of Sensible Things

The second thread of Berkeley's account of dependence begins with the second half
of *Principles* 1:

> [A]s several of these [ideas] are observed to accompany each other, they come to be
> marked by one name, and so to be reputed as one thing. Thus, for example, a certain
> colour, taste, smell, figure and consistence having been observed to go together, are
> accounted one distinct thing, signified by the name apple. Other collections of ideas
> constitute a stone, a tree, a book, and the like sensible things.[77]

With this, Berkeley introduces into philosophy the now-familiar bundle account of objects. Two paragraphs later, he introduces its complement, *conditional
analysis*.

> The table I write on, I say, exists, that is, I see and feel it; and if I were out of my study
> I should say it existed, meaning thereby that if I was in my study I might perceive it,
> or that some other spirit actually does perceive it. There was an odour, that is, it was
> smelled; there was a sound, that is to say, it was heard; a colour or figure, and it was
> perceived by sight or touch.[78]

Although immaterialism has not proven popular, Berkeley's pioneering use of
reductive analysis has proven extremely influential. Its pervasive influence only
makes more puzzling the fact that we have managed to overlook that Berkeley's use
of this analytical tool is driven primarily by a distinct, second sense of 'dependence.' No doubt, this has something to do with the fact that, unlike the first sense
of dependence, this second sense is not made explicit until *Principles* 12. Consequently, we have not properly connected the content of *Principles* 12 with the
bundle theory. *Principles* 12 reads,

> That number is entirely the creature of the mind, even though the other qualities be
> allowed to exist without, will be evident to whoever considers, that the same thing
> bears a different denomination of number, as the mind views it with different respects.
> Thus, the same extension is one or three or thirty six, according as the mind considers
> it with reference to a yard, a foot, or an inch. Number is so visibly relative, and
> dependent on men's understanding, that it is strange to think how any one should
> give it an absolute existence without the mind. We say one book, one page, one line;
> all these are equally units, though some contain several of the others. And in each
> instance it is plain, the unit relates to some particular combination of ideas arbitrarily
> put together by the mind.[79]

What special attention *Principles* 12 has received has been due to Frege. Frege
reads Berkeley as having anticipated a key point he wishes to make about the
conceptual relativity inherent to the practice of numbering.[80] The more tradi-

tional reading of *Principles* 12 sees it as simply making plain the fact that Berkeley's hostility to abstractions extends to "abstract particulars," i.e., numbers.[81] However, among other things, that would make its placement particularly odd since it is not until much later in the *Principles*, beginning with §118, that Berkeley takes up the topic of arithmetic and the status of numbers. I contend that, here at *Principles* 12, Berkeley's aim is decidedly more ambitious and his point far more fundamental than either the Fregean or the traditional interpretation recognizes.[82]

Berkeley works in sympathy with that aspect of the Platonic tradition that identifies *ens* with *unum*.[83] Keeping this in mind, we can see that *Principles* 12— and, as we shall see, its companion, *Principles* 13—is designed to help elucidate the sense of dependence according to which the very *being* of natural objects (i.e., "sensible things") requires minds in order to provide them with some kind of unity. What Berkeley says here is not that *numbers are a* creature of the mind, but rather that *number is the* creature of the mind. Berkeley's more radical thesis is that our concept *unit*, of strict "numerical identity," cannot be derived from the natural, sensible world because sensible things have no genuine unity in-themselves. Berkeley rejects not only abstract individuals but, more sweepingly, he rejects any nonspiritual individuals, in the strict sense of the term 'individual.' As he sees it,

> [S]ensible things are rather *considered as one than truly so*, they being in a perpetual flux or succession, ever differing and various.[84]

According to Berkeley, minds are the only true unities. They are simple, active substances. Nothing else is. And so, according to Berkeley, the concept *number* is not to be derived from the sensible world despite the fact that

> the contrary opinion of supposing *number* to be an original primary quality in things, independent of the mind, may obtain among the moderns.[85]

At this point, it will be helpful to recall the wax discussion. Berkeley does not deny what Descartes asserts; he does not deny that the wax remains. But where Descartes took this as grounds for positing the presence of a non-imagistic idea of the wax, Berkeley does not. Instead, Berkeley takes the bold step of identifying the wax with the collection of transient ideas that Descartes regarded as the mere sensory guise of the wax.

Now, this will seem to present a problem. It was not an option for Descartes to account for his grasp of the wax by way of an appeal to the collection of sensory and imagistic ideas he had of the wax. There were two interrelated problems. First, a *collection of ideas* is not the *idea of a collection*. He has to account for his regarding these ideas as composing a unit of some sort, as being representations of *one thing*. Second, how are we to account for our grasp of the wax as containing an immeasurable number of unactualized and, thus, unperceived possibilities? As we saw, an appeal to the imagination would not help; it can only give us more of the same. The imagination can produce representations of merely *possible* states of the wax, but in doing so, it cannot represent for us all the possible states of the wax and so cannot be responsible for supplying us with our complete concept of the wax as something changeable. What's more, even if it somehow could supply us with representations of all the possible states of the wax, this would not do anything to explain why we regard all these possible states as representations of states of *one thing*. In other words, appeal to the imagination does nothing to solve our first problem.

In Descartes' case, it was the so-called passive power of the wax that gave these actualities and possibilities unity and thereby made possible our conceiving of them as states of the wax. Thus, a complete concept of the wax had to include a representation of the passive power of the wax. Descartes solved this problem by appeal to the unique, non-imagistic, representational powers of the pure intellect.

Now, Berkeley does not face quite the same problem. He does not take his various ideas to be *representations*, and so they are not representations of states of something. As Berkeley writes in the *Commentaries*, entry 660, "The referring Ideas to things which are not Ideas; using the Term, 'Idea of' is one great cause of mistake."[86] Berkelian ideas are not *ideas of* things; they are not *representations of* something else. Ideas are the objects themselves.

The other key point about sensible things is that they, being no more than ideas, are completely lacking in any kind of power; they are perfectly passive.

> All our ideas, sensations, or the things which we perceive, by whatsoever names they may be distinguished, are visibly inactive, there is nothing of power or agency included in them. So that one idea or object of thought cannot produce, or make any alteration in another. To be satisfied of the truth of this, there is nothing else requisite but a bare observation of our ideas. For since they and every part of them exist only in the mind, it follows that there is nothing in them but what is perceived. But whoever shall attend to his ideas, whether of sense or reflexion, will not perceive in them any power or activity; there is therefore no such thing contained in them.[87]

As far as Berkeley can see, passivity is the *opposite* of power; it is not a form of power (i.e., "passive power" is an oxymoron).[88] There is only one concept of power and that is acquired by reflection on ourselves as things which *act*. Power is *activity*. And as we know, activity is *volition*. Power is, thus, volition. And so the concept of power is only applicable to spirits. At the heart of the second sense of 'dependence' is Berkeley's revolutionary move of eliminating from nonspiritual objects these suspect powers, whatever their aliases, e.g., substrata, real essences, substantial forms. Sensible things are *"inert, fleeting, dependent beings."*[89] In place of substantial powers, he offers a reductive analysis of their supposed inner sources of unity. In effect, the bundle/conditional account of sensible objects is designed to provide a strategy for analyzing the substancehood out of the would-be material substances. Its purpose is to supply something akin to an error theory—that is to say, it provides justification for our talk of nonspiritual individuals without inflating our commitments to them so as to include "absolute existence," i.e., an existence independent of minds.

Since objects lack any inherent unity, Berkeley has no need to appeal to the pure intellect and its unique, representational powers. "Pure intellect I understand not," he writes at *Commentaries* 810.[90] Now, of course, Locke would agree in rejecting the pure intellect and its mysterious representational powers. But his gambit of giving us access only to the nominal but not the real essences of substances just introduces room for skepticism. As Berkeley puts it,

One great inducement to our pronouncing our selves ignorant of the nature of things, is the current opinion that every thing includes within it self the cause of its properties: or that there is in each object an inward essence, which is the source whence its discernible qualities flow, and whereon they depend.[91]

Such a doctrine will only lead us to believe that

we are under an invincible blindness as to the true and real nature of things. This [the skeptics] exaggerate, and love to enlarge on. We are miserably bantered, say they, by our senses, and amused only with the outside and shew of things. The real essence, the internal qualities, and constitution of every the meanest object, is hid from our view; something there is in every drop of water, every grain of sand, which it is beyond the power of human understanding to fathom or comprehend.[92]

This problem isn't solved merely by the introduction of the *esse* is *percipi* thesis. The deeper problem is the attribution of an "internal" unity to natural objects, i.e., a unity independent of all minds whatsoever, or again, an "absolute existence independent of all minds." 'Real essence' is simply Locke's name for these supposed nonmental sources of internal unity.[93]

So objects are nothing but collections of ideas. But a collection of ideas is, once again, just that: a collection. To talk about apples and oranges, we need the ability to talk about the ideas *as a collection*. In other words, the ideas must be *united* into bundles one way or another. If the string that ties these bundles of ideas together is not supplied by the objects' substrata, or by real essences, etc., then what does supply it? Berkeley's answer: we do.

In things sensible and imaginable, as such, there seems to be no *unity*, nothing that can be called *one*, prior to all *act of the mind*; since they, being in themselves aggregates, consisting of parts or compounded of elements, are in effect many.[94]

Berkeley derives the unity of sensible things from the activity of the simple substances of his ontology, i.e., the activity of *minds*.

[A] cherry, I say, is nothing but a congeries of sensible impressions, or ideas perceived by various senses: *which ideas are united into one thing . . . by the mind*.[95]

Our treating them as one is an act of the mind. Fittingly, we find in *Siris* that Berkeley cites approvingly Aristotle's commentator Themistius when he writes, "the mind, by virtue of her simplicity, conferreth simplicity upon compounded beings."[96] We "collect up" ideas and then *act* toward them as if they were one thing, a genuine individual, when in fact, they are not.

It helps to take notice of the way in which this aspect of dependence compares with the manner of dependence found in our ideas of imagination. Beyond depending on us to copy and call up these images, their dependence upon our activity lies in supplying them with their manner *of organization*. We divide up the ideas of sense and rearrange them into new complex ideas of imagination. These complex ideas of imagination acquire their newfound unity from the organization that our imaginative activity—the activity of a spirit—imposes on them.

Importantly, however, sensible things (ideas of sense, "real things") are not likewise dependent upon us. Their unity is ultimately provided by *God's* activity.

The ideas of sense have ... a steadiness, order, and coherence, and are not excited at random, as those which are the effects of human wills often are, but in a regular train or series, the admirable connexion whereof sufficiently testifies the wisdom and benevolence of its Author. Now the set rules or established methods, wherein the mind we depend on excites in us the ideas of sense, are called the Laws of Nature: and these we learn by experience, which teaches us that such and such ideas are attended with such and such other ideas, in the ordinary course of things.[97]

God wills that we be affected with such and such perceptions, and so the being of the ideas of sense depend upon his activity. But they also depend upon God's activity in that it is his will that certain ideas of sense are regularly "observed to go together." It is God who presents these ideas of sense to us, and it is God who makes the conditionals true. God's activity makes it true that right now I do not see my desk, but that if I were now in my study I would now be seeing it, and that if I should soon enter my study, I will see it.

We discover these regularities in the course of experience and keep track of them (in part) by way of the introduction of *names*. The activities that make up our linguistic practices help us to act toward these collections *as if* they were genuine individuals. It is in this sense that sensible things can be said to depend upon us (us humans) for their unity. For it is by way of our activity of applying a name to them that they are "*accounted one distinct thing.*"[98] In light of this, consider again Berkeley's remark regarding the unity of a cherry, this time with the deleted parenthetical statement restored:

[A] cherry, I say, is nothing but a congeries of sensible impressions, or ideas perceived by various senses: which ideas are united into one thing (*or have one name given them*) by the mind.[99]

It is through the activity of naming that we organize our experience into pragmatically useful unities.

13. Sense and Simplicity

I will have more to say about naming, object unity, and ontological pragmatism in chapter II. At this point, it is more important that we distinguish Berkeley's conception of the sensory from Locke's. As we reviewed earlier, Locke has an atomistic conception of the sensory. There are simple ideas that can be combined into complex ones. Now, given that Berkeley talks of "complex ideas" at *Principles* 1, given that he will sometimes tell us, as he has above, that things sensible and imaginable are in themselves "aggregates," consisting of "parts" or "compounded elements," and given the undeniable influence of Locke's simple/complex taxonomy of the sensory on many other thinkers of the time, it is certainly tempting to infer that Berkeley accepts *simple ideas*. If that's the case, then he is wrong to say "In things sensible and imaginable, as such, there seems to be no unity." It would seem that there is at least the unity of simplicity that sensory elements enjoy, i.e., the unity of Lockean simple ideas. Thus, Daniel Flage writes,

Minds and ideas are Berkeley's ontological primitives (fundamental entities). Objects of both kinds are *inherently individuals*. Physical objects are composed of ideas (*Principles* 1), and, as such, they are ontologically secondary, that is, they are collections of ideas.[100]

The inference is tempting and even sensible, but it is a mistake just the same. Berkeley's talk of "complex ideas" does not indicate a commitment to simple ideas. According to Berkeley, simple ideas are, in fact, a species of that most dangerous of all philosophical Frankensteins, "abstract ideas." Luce was the first to emphasize that Berkeley regarded simple ideas as abstract ideas and that Berkeley's references to "complex ideas" had made it seem that Berkeley just took over the Lockean taxonomy of ideas as others would do.[101] More recently, Kenneth Winkler has taken certain aspects of Luce's point to heart and written searchingly on this topic.[102] I will assume that it now enjoys general acceptance, and, instead, I want to draw our attention to the fact that his rejection of simple ideas means that the concept *unity* cannot be drawn from perception via the (supposed) simplicity of ideas, as Locke would have it. In fact, right after Berkeley explains that "number [i.e., *unit*] is entirely a creature of the mind" in *Principles* 12, he then goes on in *Principles* 13 to tell us:

> Unity I know some will have to be a simple or uncompounded idea, accompanying all other ideas into the mind. That I have any such idea answering the word unity, I do not find; and if I had, methinks I could not miss finding it; on the contrary it should be the most familiar to my understanding, since it is said to accompany all other ideas, and to be perceived by all the ways of sensation and reflexion. To say no more, it is an abstract idea.[103]

There are no simple sensory ideas, and so no genuine unities are to be found in the natural world.[104] Consider a more familiar idea about the nature of qualia. Let's use Sellars' favorite example, our experience of a pink ice cube. Physical theory tells us that a pink ice cube is made up of mostly empty space populated by lots of individual imperceptible particles. However, to take the case of vision,

> the ice cube presents itself to us as something which is pink through and through, as a pink continuum, all the regions of which, however small, are pink. It presents itself to us as ultimately homogenous.[105]

Our experience of that pink is "grainless," as Sellars elsewhere puts it.[106] Berkeley agrees and would proceed to point out that the same is true of the *whole* of our visual field, or any of our sensory fields. The fact that there is variation within any given field does not add grain to it. The visual field as a whole presents itself as *colored* through and through. We must be careful to distinguish between *sensory simples* and *minima sensibila*, the latter of which Berkeley does accept. A 'minimal sensible' merely refers to the smallest color expanse of which one's visual field admits. One can arrive at it by putting a spot of red ink on the wall and retreating from it until it disappears. At the last moment before it vanishes, it is a *minima visibilia*.[107] But this process does not isolate and thereby acquaint us with a simple idea in the required sense. That small red point is only experienced as a color variation in what presents itself as the fully colored continuum that is one's present visual field. The fact that we might well refer to a *minimal sensibile* as a visual "point" should not be allowed to mislead us. That "point" is seamlessly embedded in our visual field. That field as a whole is no more "grainy," no less "homogeneous" than is one's experience of the pink of a pink ice cube. It too is colored through and through. A visual point is not a sensory *atom*.

The upshot is that, as far as Berkeley is concerned, in experience we meet with no genuine individuals. Experience acquaints us merely with what we might describe as a "sensory plenum" or, perhaps, an atomless phenomenal gunk.[108]

14. Atomism and "Outness"

Before moving on, I want to take advantage of our present perspective to point out that Berkeley's hostility toward atomism, and especially sensory atomism, was heralded by his first major work, *An Essay toward a New Theory of Vision*. Although this work was certainly designed to stand on its own as a theory of vision, it was intended to prepare his audience for the immaterialism to come in the *Principles*.

As we've already noted, at the heart of the atomistic conception of substance are the notions of *separation* and *distance*. What makes such a thing a substance is its capacity to exist separately from other atoms, where 'separately' is understood *spatially*. We can conceive of that atom as spatially separated, *existing at a distance*, from any other thing to which it may happen to be currently conjoined, without conceiving of any change in the atom itself,[109] thus providing us with the stable, unchanging foundations of reality.

One of the ways that the *Essay* prepares the way for the immaterialism of the *Principles* is by undermining one of the things that gives the atomistic conception of substance its intuitive appeal. After all, atomism does have an intuitive appeal. Compared with, for instance, Aristotelianism, it presents us with what seems to be a very simple, straightforward conception of what makes something an independently existing substance, a true individual. In the *Three Dialogues*, Hylas famously asks, "What [is] more easy than to conceive a tree or house existing by itself, independent of, and unperceived by any mind whatsoever?"[110] Likewise, one might ask, what is more easy to conceive than a simple atom existing by itself, independently, in space? The intuitive support for that conception of substance is drawn straight from perception. We *see*, with our own two eyes, precisely the kind of independence central to an atom's substancehood. We see objects existing "out there," separately, away from us.[111] It is, thus, no coincidence that just a few lines later, Hylas follows that first question with "[Do] you not think sight suggests something of *outness* or *distance*?" The objection's predecessor is to be found at *Principles* 42,

> [I]t will be objected that we see things actually without or at a distance from us, and which consequently do not exist in the mind, it being absurd that those things which are seen at the distance of several miles, should be as near to us as our own thoughts.[112]

In response to Hylas' second question, Berkeley wields two arguments. The first simply appeals to the phenomenology of dreaming. "[I]n a dream we do oft perceive things as existing at a great distance off, and yet for all that, those things are acknowledged to have their existence only in the mind."[113] But for the second response, Berkeley brings out the big guns. He tells us that "the consideration of this difficulty it was, that gave birth to my *Essay towards a new Theory of Vision*."[114] In that work, he tells us, he had argued that

> distance or outness is neither immediately of it self perceived by sight, nor yet apprehended or judged of by lines and angles, or any thing that hath a necessary connexion with it: but that it is only suggested to our thoughts, by certain visible ideas and sensations attending vision, which in their own nature have no manner of similitude or relation, either with distance, or things placed at a distance. But by a connexion taught us by experience, they come to signify and suggest them to us, after the same manner that words of any language suggest the ideas they are made to stand for.[115]

The immediate objects of sight are "light and colours with their several degrees and variations."[116] The objects of touch are "for example, hard and soft, heat and cold, motion and resistance, and of all these more and less either as to quantity or degree."[117] The immediate objects of sight and touch are "two species entirely distinct and heterogeneous."[118] These being no more than ideas, they are at no distance from the mind. Rather,

> [t]he former are marks and prognostics of the latter.... So that in strict truth the ideas of sight, when we apprehend by them distance and things placed at a distance, do not suggest or mark out to us things actually existing at a distance, but only admonish us what ideas of touch will be imprinted in our minds at such and such distances of time, and in consequence of such or such actions.[119]

The intuitive support for atomism, the "outness" of visual objects, is actively attributed by us as we read distance relations into our ideas. Outness is not passively perceived. Thus, in perception, we do not confront things that enjoy an absolute existence independent of, or rather, "outside" of all minds whatsoever. They are as close to us as our own thoughts.

15. Reflection, Pure Intellect, and Representation

From our present vantage point, we can get our first glimpse of one of the basic links between Berkeley's metaphysics and common sense. We can do this with the unlikely help of Bertrand Russell. In one of his very last discussions on the topic of individuality, "The Principle of Individuation," he begins by defining the fundamental question:

> I shall be concerned in what follows with a very old problem...still, in our day, far from being definitely solved. The problem is this..."what is meant by 'particular'?" or "what sort of objects can have proper names?"[120]

Among the proper subjects of proper names, Russell considers complexes of qualities, substratums, events, and ultimately something he dubs "complexes of compresence." From the Berkelian perspective, what is interesting is what Russell leaves out at consideration. Absent from his list of candidates is the commonsense view of the mob: strictly speaking, proper names are only properly applied to *people*. All others enjoy that privilege only by way of the extension of our activities of naming one another.

This view was one Berkeley hit on very early and developed throughout his career. Already in the first notebook of the *Commentaries*, the young Berkeley writes, "No identity, other than perfect likeness, in any individuals besides persons."[121] Then, some thirty-seven years later, in his last major work, Berkeley writes,

> Upon mature reflection, the person or mind of all created beings seemeth alone indivisible, and to partake most of unity. But sensible things are rather considered as one than truly so, they being in a perpetual flux or succession, ever differing and various.[122]

In Berkeley's metaphysics, the only true individuals are spirits. That is to say, the only true individuals are . . . *individuals*. For this reason, any attempt to attribute to Berkeley a bundle account of spirits turns the very basics of his metaphysics upside down. Spirits are not bundles. They are that which does the bundling. The category of *spirit*, not *idea*, is where we must look for the ground of identity: unity and simplicity. This is the basic fact that the influence of the *esse* is *percipi* caricature of Berkeley has so effectively kept us from keeping in focus. Instead, we commonly associate the thesis that only personal identity is strict identity with Butler or with Reid, all the while never seeing its far more developed and fundamental role in Berkeley's philosophy.[123]

While the removal of the caricature clears away many obstacles, there is still more work to do. We have established that spirits are the only true substances and that our only concept of substance is identical to the concept *spirit*. And we have also seen that this in turn means that it is our knowledge of the nature of spirits that supplies us with our grasp of the nature of identity, simplicity, unity, and being.

However, since spirits cannot be perceived by sense, this means that our concept *substance* cannot be acquired from perception. The concept *spirit* must by acquired by way of reflection on our selves. Since reflection is the means by which we acquire this concept, reflection cannot be a form of inner sense. If it were, we would find Berkeley in Hume's position, searching inside for something substantial but finding only a flux. The point is one of which Berkeley was keenly aware.

> It will perhaps be said, that we want a sense (as some have imagined) proper to know substances withal, which if we had, we might know our own soul, as we do a triangle. To this I answer, that in case we had a new sense bestowed upon us, we could only receive thereby some new sensations or ideas of sense.[124]

And, as we already know, ideas cannot represent spirits.

> The words *will, soul, spirit*, do not stand for different ideas, or in truth, for any idea at all, but for something which is very different from ideas, and which being an agent cannot be like unto, or represented by, any idea whatsoever.[125]

In light of this, a compelling case can be made that Berkeley must conceive of reflection in much the way that Descartes did, as the inner complement to pure intellect. Reflection must be able to produce something distinct from the familiar ideas of sense, some sort of uniquely non-sensorial, non-imagistic kind of representation capable of representing our imperceptible substantial selves.

Of course, such a reading will have to be squared with Berkeley's general hostility to the Cartesian pure intellect. But this we can do. As we've already noted, in one of his notebook entries, Berkeley declares his hostility to the pure intellect rather directly, "Pure Intellect I understand not." This remark is written sometime in 1708. However, in 1710, the first edition of the *Principles* appears, and strangely, there is no mention at all of the pure intellect. Then, three years later, the first edition of the *Three Dialogues between Hylas and Philonous* is published. In the "First Dialogue," Hylas, looking for a way to defend abstract ideas, appeals to the faculty of the "pure intellect."

> Hylas: But what say you to pure intellect? May not abstracted ideas be framed by that faculty?[126]

The way Philonous' response begins seems to reflect the tone of that 1708 notebook entry.

> Philonous: Since I cannot frame abstract ideas at all, it is plain, I cannot frame them by the help of pure intellect, whatsoever faculty you understand by those words.[127]

It sounds as if the pure intellect is being given the back of Berkeley's hand. But appearances prove misleading. Philonous does not proceed to issue a blanket condemnation of appeals to the pure intellect. Instead, he continues by saying,

> Besides, not to inquire into the nature of pure intellect and its spiritual objects, as virtue, reason, God, or the like; thus much seems manifest, that sensible things are only to be perceived by sense, or represented by the imagination.[128]

This topic of the pure intellect then reappears in 1721 in *De Motu*.

> Pure intellect, too, knows nothing of absolute space. That faculty is concerned only with spiritual and inextended things, such as our minds.[129]

It seems Berkeley is willing to admit this special faculty so long as it is construed as having as its objects only "spiritual things."[130] And so it seems as if the pure intellect, properly understood, is really reflection. Berkeley appears to be a sort of modified Cartesian. He conceives of reflection in the distinctively Cartesian way, i.e., not as "inner sense" but rather as what we might call "reflective pure intellect." This line of interpretation is only strengthened by the notorious addition of the technical term 'notion' to the second edition of the *Three Dialogues* in 1725.

> I say lastly, that I have a *notion* of spirit, though I have not, strictly speaking, an *idea* of it. I do not perceive it as an idea or by means of an idea, but know it by reflexion.[131]

What gave the Cartesian pure intellect its special status was its ability to produce non-imagistic representations. Descartes was happy to call these 'ideas,' but Berkeley has made it clear that our ideas are limited to sense or imagination. Moreover, if an act of reflection results merely in ideas, the best it can hope to capture are snapshots of various passing states of a being, not the being itself. Like the wax, its essence will elude us. It was considerations such as these that caused Malebranche to break with Descartes on the topic of reflection. Risking Cartesian heresy, he argued that the self is *not* known as well as the essence of body because it is known only by what he called "inner sensation."[132] This is no more than a particular kind of *feeling*, a feeling which he then equated with "consciousness." In itself, so to speak, the self is never known to us. Malebranche's view had a clear impact on Locke, and through his influence the inner sense tradition took root. It was then carried on by Hume and Kant and remains prominent right into the present.[133] Berkeley, however, was clearly determined to stand against it.

But can he? On the present interpretation, it seems that an older Berkeley looks back on his younger works and finds himself in a difficult position. His is a spirit-based metaphysics. What he needs is a grasp of spirit *as substance*. But that grasp cannot be had by way of *idea*. Enter 'notions.' Notions, it would seem, are the special "spiritual objects" of the reflective pure intellect. Not being ideas, they allow us a grasp of ourselves *as substance* and give meaning to the word 'spirit.' But this will seem no more than the time-honored dodge of disguising a problem by giving it a name. Making matters worse, nine years after adding the term 'notion' to the second edition of the *Three Dialogues*, the second edition of the *Principles* appears along with a third edition of the *Three Dialogues*. To the second edition of the *Principles*, Berkeley has not only added 'notions,' but he has removed the subtitle "Part I" from the work. The third edition of the *Three Dialogues* has also changed. The prefaces to the first two editions refer to the aforementioned forthcoming "second part" of the *Principles*, but in this third edition, the reference has been removed. On the whole, the picture that emerges is one of a philosopher coming 'round to recognize a problem he could not solve.

Have we traveled all this way only to find ourselves back where we began and no better off? Should we, perhaps, have left the *esse* is *percipi* caricature alone? After all, that caricature had the merit of focusing our attention purely on Berkeley's reductive approach to material substance. And that, not his views about spirits, represents the better part of his known philosophical legacy. From the present perspective, one might feel that the caricature was not so bad after all. In effect, it was the most charitable reading for which one could hope.

Clearly, there is a case to be made for such an interpretation. But there is a better case to be made against it. We are prevented from seeing this by a prejudice that lies even deeper and is, in fact, parent to the *esse* is *percipi* caricature. In effect, having killed Grendel, we find we must now face his mother. In this case, Mom is the representational theory of mind. In Berkeley's time, that theory took the form of the "ideational theory" of the understanding. What both Descartes and those in the inner sense tradition share is a view of cognition according to which understanding consists in the perception of ideas before the mind. In the empiricist tradition, these ideas are strictly imagistic, but in the rationalist tradition, they need not be. Either way, however, the consequence is the same. Reflection is conceived as a representational faculty. Its function is to provide the understanding with ideas. So long as that is the case, the problem remains that in reflection one does not encounter the self *directly* but only by way of representation. How then can we ever encounter the self, as it is in-itself?

But let's suppose something radical. What if Berkeley fully appreciated the problems inherent to the ideational theory and consequently abandoned that view of the mind? If that were the case, then cognition is not the having of ideas before the mind, and it would be a mistake to think of reflection as either "inner sense" or "reflective pure intellect." Apprehension of our being in reflection could be as Berkeley characterizes it, a means of *immediate* knowledge: "[m]y own mind I have an immediate knowledge of."[134]

This would require attributing to Berkeley a rather revolutionary move. In the early modern period, the ideational theory was so well entrenched that its truth was simply assumed, not argued for. But of course, Berkeley's approach to philosophy is nothing if not iconoclastic.[135] As I see it, Berkeley did, in fact, break loose of the ideational theory. But making good on that claim will require a chapter of its own. In the following chapter, I will step back a bit from our present line of investigation and instead approach from the angle of semantic theory. My claim is that Berkeley made the rejection of the ideational theory of meaning one of his primary targets. There is a case to be made that Berkeley regards it as a more fundamental mistake than abstract ideas. In addition, I will argue that the consequences of his rejection of the ideational theory reverberate via the divine language thesis throughout the entirety of his metaphysics.

II

One Berkeley

Protestant Semantics and the Curtain of Words

> Images are what they say, not what they stand for.
> —Dylan Thomas

1. Were There Two Berkeleys? A Dilemma

Although famous for his critique of Locke, Berkeley was a sincere admirer of his work. In one of his early notebooks, the young Berkeley wrote, "Wonderful in Locke that he could, when advanced in years, see at all thro' a mist; it had been so long agathering and was consequently thick."[1] But perhaps not so surprisingly, he immediately followed with "This more to be [wondered at] that he did not see further."[2] And this might well be taken to capture the essence of Berkeley's relationship to Locke and, in particular, to the "historical, plain method" the latter employed.[3]

Scholarly posterity found it fitting to characterize Berkeley as one who appreciated the philosophical power of the "new way of ideas," but he also believed that Locke had not driven it to its logical conclusion.[4] Had Locke managed to "see further," he would have joined Berkeley in rejecting abstract ideas and all that depends upon them. For, as Berkeley would later argue, Locke's own method exposes abstract ideas for the chimeras they are.

> Whether others have this wonderful faculty of abstracting their ideas, they best can tell: for myself I find indeed I have a faculty of imagining, or representing to myself, the ideas of those particular things I have perceived, and of variously compounding and dividing them. I can imagine a man with two heads, or the upper parts of a man joined to the body of a horse. I can consider the hand, the eye, the nose, each by itself abstracted or separated from the rest of the body. But then whatever hand or eye I imagine, it must have some particular shape or colour.... [However] I cannot by any effort conceive the Abstract Idea...described [by Locke].[5]

So it would seem, and is commonly thought, that in this matter Berkeley stands by Locke's approach.[6] His central quarrel with Locke is that he simply failed to see all of its consequences.

> Of late many have been very sensible of the absurd opinions and insignificant disputes which grow out of the abuse of words. And, in order to remedy these evils, they advise well, that we attend to the idea signified, and draw off our attention from the words

which signify them. But how good soever this advice may be they have given others, it is plain they could not have a due regard to it themselves so long as they thought that ... the immediate signification of every general name was a determinate abstract idea.[7]

Granted, Berkeley thinks Locke has made a most unfortunate mistake, because the countenancing of abstract ideas has "had a chief part in rendering speculation intricate and perplexed, and to have occasioned innumerable errors and difficulties in almost all parts of knowledge."[8] But ultimately, in criticizing them, Berkeley is just following through on what Locke began.

Twenty years later, Berkeley publishes his dialogue *Alciphron*,[9] primarily a work in Christian apologetics. In it, Berkeley's chief dialectical opponent is the book's namesake, the character Alciphron. At the beginning of the concluding dialogue of that work, Berkeley puts the following words into the mouth of Alciphron:

Words are signs: they do or should stand for ideas: which so far as they suggest they are significant. But words that suggest no ideas are insignificant.... Though it is evident that, as knowledge is the perception of the connexion or disagreement between ideas, he who doth not distinctly perceive the ideas marked by the terms, so as to form a mental proposition answering to the verbal, cannot possibly have knowledge.[10]

After a moment's reflection, the alert reader of *Alciphron* might well wonder how the author of the *Principles* can put these words into his *opponent's* mouth? Does Berkeley seriously intend to dispute what Alciphron has said? The answer is yes. Alciphron is a self-described "free-thinker," whom Berkeley dubs, in contrast, a "minute philosopher." He is an atheist who, among other things, uses a basically Lockean theory of meaning to attack a variety of religious doctrines and notions.[11] For instance, of grace he asks,

What is the clear and distinct idea marked by the word 'grace'?... This surely is an easy matter, provided there is an idea annexed to such a term.... after I had read or heard [about grace, I] could make nothing of it, having always found, whenever I laid aside the word 'grace', and looked into my own mind, a perfect vacuity or privation of all ideas.[12]

The same considerations are then applied to other religious notions, such as the doctrine of the Trinity. The conclusion is clear: "by all the rules of right reason, it is absolutely impossible that any mystery, least of all the Trinity, should be the object of man's faith."[13] Alciphron, we might put it, is simply doing to Bishop Berkeley what the Bishop did to Locke.

In response to Alciphron's claim that religious doctrines cannot be the object of a man's beliefs since they are quite literally meaningless, Euphranor, Berkeley's advocate, replies,

I do not wonder you thought so, as long as you maintained that no man could assent to a proposition without perceiving or framing in his mind distinct ideas marked by the terms of it. But although terms are signs, yet having granted that those signs may be significant, though they should not suggest ideas represented by them, provided they serve to regulate and influence our wills, passions, or conduct, you have consequently granted that the mind of man may assent to propositions containing such terms, when it is so directed or affected by them, notwithstanding it should not perceive distinct ideas marked by those terms.[14]

Here is our puzzle: if signs may be significant even though they fail to suggest ideas, why would one be moved by Berkeley's central objection to abstraction, i.e, that the process of abstraction fails to produce a determinate image before the mind? I will assume that it is a consideration such as this that led Anthony Flew to describe the situation in the following manner:

[I]n the *Alciphron* we find a revolutionary and historically premature insight. But that, of course, is not to say that Berkeley himself saw how far he had moved; or that he himself appreciated how drastically the development of this insight might affect some of his own most cherished and distinctive philosophical moves. On the contrary: the claim that it was historically premature should suggest the very opposite.[15]

This is where Flew closes his discussion. He doesn't go on to specify which of Berkeley's "most cherished and distinctive philosophical moves" the semantic insights expressed in *Alciphron* would undercut, nor why they would be undercut, but I suggest he has in mind the following: Berkeley, it seems, is faced with a dilemma. He can abandon his critique of abstract ideas—realizing, of course, that as Berkeley sees it, the critique is central to the rest of the claims of the *Principles*—but thereby be in a position to respond to Alciphron's attack on religious notions. Or, Berkeley can maintain the critique of abstract ideas and face the consequences that the Lockean theory produces for his cherished religious commitments. Either way, it seems we have to recognize a fundamental shift in Berkeley's philosophical commitments from the *Principles* to *Alciphron*.

Adding further credence to this interpretation is, once again, Berkeley's notorious introduction of the technical term "notions" to the second edition of the *Principles*.[16] Since spirits are not ideas, and cannot be represented by any idea, we cannot be said to have an "idea of the spirit," however,

it must be owned we have some notion of soul, spirit, and the operations of the mind, such as willing, loving, hating, in as much as we know or understand the meaning of those words.[17]

This must be owned because via reflection we have knowledge of our own mind.[18] One might well think that the introduction of 'notions' is Berkeley's attempt to patch the fissure in his semantic philosophy created by the pressure of this dilemma. If words like 'soul' are to be meaningful, they must be signs of some mental content. And if they are not picturable, then they cannot be ideas.

To me it seems that ideas, spirits and relations are all in their respective kinds, the object of human knowledge and subject of discourse: and that the term idea would be improperly extended to signify every thing we know or have any notion of.[19]

Here we have approached by way of semantic theory, but recalling the discussion of the previous chapter, it will seem that what happened was that Berkeley only slowly came around to the idea of the "pure intellect," at least insofar as the faculty is conceived of as "reflective pure intellect." Thus, the dilemma ultimately results in the late ad hoc positing of "notions" to the second edition of the *Principles*—yet another reason to talk of an early and a late Berkeley.

In what follows, I will argue that Berkeley faces no such dilemma. The appearance of a dilemma is produced by a deep-seated misunderstanding of one of the most innovative features of his philosophy. As we will see, Berkeley can maintain his attack on abstract ideas while defending the meaningfulness of central religious notions, such as grace, the Trinity, and soul, because his attack on abstract ideas does not proceed from an acceptance of Locke's semantic theory. The views about meaning and understanding that Flew calls "revolutionary" and "historically premature," far from undercutting Berkeley's attack on abstract ideas, *are the very views about meaning and understanding that underlie Berkeley's attack*. As we will see, Berkeley's views on the subject of language must be considered exactly as revolutionary as his immaterialism, because they are of a piece with his immaterialism. The concern over Berkeley's introduction of notions evaporates along with the dilemma.

2. Locke's Problem

I believe Berkeley makes his rejection of Locke's ideational semantics clear in the famous "Introduction" to the *Principles*. But, of course, this is the same source that seems to support the opinion that Berkeley is cutting off only a sickly limb of Locke's view rather than digging up the whole by its roots. What is required in order to sort this out is that we must inspect both the overall design as well as the individual arguments of the "Introduction." However, we cannot go to this task immediately. Since, as I claim, the aim of the "Introduction" is to undermine the presuppositions of Locke's semantic theory, we must first get the fundamentals of Locke's semantics on the table.[20]

Locke poses the following question, "How come we by general Terms?"[21] Out of context, this is not the clearest of questions, but it can be made clearer. Locke believes that all things are particular. An instance of a word is a particular, so the question is, how can one particular thing be a sign of many different particular things? Before this can bother you, two things have to happen:

 i. You have to have an account of how anything can be a sign of something else.
 ii. This account must not offer an immediate solution to the question at hand.

With respect to (i), Locke has such a theory: leaving out natural signs, particulars that stand for other particulars are called "words." Words are made signs of ideas by voluntary imposition. We arbitrarily associate a word with an idea. A word thus has as its immediate signification the *idea* with which it is associated. The word lets us talk about the object by way of immediately signifying the idea in our understanding and, in turn, immediately signifying the object itself.

This account makes it seem easy to answer the question of how my use of the word 'Dodd' lets me talk about the building in which I'm now sitting. The answer is that I have an idea, brought about by Dodd Hall. I associate the word 'Dodd' with the idea, so when I utter the sound "Dodd," it immediately signifies my idea of that particular building and, via that idea, refers to Dodd Hall.

But what about a word like 'tree'? From the present perspective, it is an absolutely astonishing sort of thing. I can utter the word 'tree' and, in doing so, talk
about not just one particular tree but all trees, past, present, and future. What
makes it astonishing also makes it problematic. It would seem that what we need is
some object out in the world that causes my idea *tree* and that resembles it. I then
associate the word 'tree' with that idea.

But what kind of object would that be? It cannot be a regular tree. After all, a
regular ol' tree is a particular thing. If it causes an idea in me and I then associate a
word with it, that would just let me talk about that particular tree, but not all trees
everywhere. The object that would cause me to have an idea of all trees everywhere would be a very strange object indeed. Thus, Locke puts the problem this
way: "[f]or since all things that exist are only particulars, how come we by general
Terms, or where find we those general Natures they are supposed to stand for?"[22]

Locke is committed to the doctrine that all things are particular, so saying that
what causes the idea of "tree" is something that is not particular but some sort of
"treeness" just will not do. Down that road lies Platonic forms and, ultimately,
innate ideas. So what kind of thing could this be? It really is hard to imagine. Still,
we *do* have general ideas, reasons Locke. We must have them, Locke believes,
because their existence is shown by our coherent use of general terms. So how do
we come by the necessary general ideas? Locke tries to solve this problem, not by
looking out into the world for some kind of treeness that could be the appropriate
cause, but rather by turning to the power of the mind. Thus, abstraction enters the
scene:

> Words become general, by being made the signs of general ideas: and ideas become
> general, by separating from them the circumstances of Time, and Place, and any other
> ideas, that may determine them to this or that particular Existence. By this way of
> abstraction they are made capable of representing more individuals than one; each
> of which, having in it a conformity to that Abstract Idea, is (as we call it) of that
> sort.[23]

If there cannot be something in the world causing our general ideas, then we must
be doing something to give ourselves these ideas. While it is true that particulars
are involved with causing in us the abstract ideas, they can only do this in concert
with an action of the mind. With the creation of abstract ideas as the product of
the process of abstraction, Locke now has an adequate representation for general
terms to immediately signify and thus can explain their meaningful use via the
representational powers of the abstract idea.

3. Berkeley's Deflationary Strategy

> [Remember]: To be eternally banishing Metaphisics & recalling Men to
> Common Sense.
>
> —Berkeley[24]

Berkeley's response to Locke's theory of abstract ideas is *not* to offer one of his own. Rather his aim is to defuse the problem that motivated Locke to posit abstract ideas in the first place. This is typical of Berkeley. It is characteristic of him to employ a deflationary strategy against philosophical problems. As Berkeley's widow put it in a letter to their son: "had he *built* as he has *pulled down* he had been then a *Master builder* indeed, but unto every man his work. Some must remove rubbish."[25] In this context, it is worth drawing attention to the very title of the work in which Berkeley gives us his attack on abstract ideas: A *Treatise concerning the Principles of Human Knowledge*. The "principles" in which Berkeley is primarily interested at the outset are not principles which will provide us with a foundation upon which to build a true metaphysics. This is no Cartesian project. The principles Berkeley is most interested in laying bare are the principles—i.e., the origins, the sources—of *error* in our philosophical thinking.

Toward the very beginning of the "Introduction" to the *Principles*, Berkeley tells us,

> Upon the whole, I am inclined to think that the far greater part, if not the whole, of those difficulties which have hitherto amused philosophers, and blocked up the way to knowledge, are entirely owing to ourselves. That we have first raised a dust, and then complain, we cannot see.[26]

He immediately continues:

> My purpose therefore is, to try if I can discover what those principles are, which have introduced all that doubtfulness and uncertainty, those absurdities and contradictions into the several sects of philosophy.[27]

This is Berkeley's philosophy of philosophy, and we should let it help to guide our understanding of his argumentative strategy. His interest in the issue of abstract ideas is motivated not by the *problem* that Locke poses but by the *solution* Locke offers—and then by the dust that "solution" kicks up. Locke is moved to posit his abstract ideas in order to solve a problem that *his* prior semantic theory creates. Berkeley's strategy is to uncover and then undermine Locke's motivation to this semantic theory. He does this by focusing his attack on abstract ideas.

Berkeley's attacks on abstract ideas are always three pronged. Whether he is attacking abstract ideas in general or some particular abstract idea, e.g., *matter*, he proceeds by first arguing that the existence of said item is impossible. Second, he argues that even if we were to allow for such a thing to exist, we would have no good reason to countenance its existence because there is no work for it to do. Finally, he offers an error theory exposing the motivation that led to the positing of the abstract idea. His approach is summed up at §21 of the "Introduction" to the *Principles*.

> We have, I think, shewn the impossibility of Abstract Ideas. We have considered what has been said for them by their ablest patrons; and endevoured to shew they are no use for those ends, to which they are thought necessary. And lastly, we have traced them to the source from whence they flow.[28]

Keeping this strategy in mind will help to clarify the nature of Berkeley's famous attack on Locke's theory and to allow a fresh look at it.

4. The "Killing Blow"

> [Remember]: to bring the killing blow at the last e.g. in the matter of
> Abstraction to bring Locke's general triangle at the last.
>
> —Berkeley[29]

It is the first objection to abstract ideas, the one that the young Berkeley called his
"killing blow," that has garnered the most interest and the most criticism. His
approach is to simply check and see if it is possible to do this act of "abstracting"
about which Locke talks; he finds that he cannot and that it is not. Berkeley allows
that he has observed many particular things that share some common feature. The
task then, as Berkeley understands it, is for the mind to single out that aspect
that these particulars have in common. So, if the common aspect of the particulars
that we are considering is extension, then our job is to form an idea of extension
which is neither "line, surface, solid, nor has any figure or magnitude, but is an idea
prescinded from all these."[30] But this, Berkeley tells us, he cannot do.

Is this just some failure peculiar to Berkeley? After all, powers of imagination
vary from person to person. Robert Benchley once complained that his imagination ceased collecting images at the age of eight. Consequently, when he finally got
around to reading *Chanson de Roland*, all the battles occurred on the streets of his
childhood home in Worcester, Massachusetts.[31] But this really is not about one's
powers of imagination; any such limitations peculiar to Berkeley (or Benchley) are
beside the point. Locke claimed that our use of general terms requires abstract
ideas and, thus, the ability to abstract. Berkeley can use general terms, so he simply
checks to see if he has either such an idea or such an ability. According to Locke's
theory, he should. Berkeley's initial objection ("Introduction," §10) is that he has
no ability to conceive of such a thing, and so he has no ability to perform this task
of abstraction despite his ability to sensibly use general terms.

Is it true that Berkeley, competent user of general terms, cannot conceive of
such a thing? There is a short route to the answer yes by way of the claim that no
one can conceive of Locke's abstract ideas because their description is incoherent.
Sometimes, Locke seems to be committed to the view that the product of abstraction is something which has *inconsistent* properties.

> [G]eneral ideas are fictions and contrivances of the mind, that carry difficulty with
> them, and do not so easily offer themselves, as we are apt to imagine. For example,
> does it not require some pains and skill to form the general idea of a triangle (which
> is yet none of the most abstract, comprehensive, and difficult), for it must be nei-
> ther oblique, nor rectangle, neither equilateral, equicrural, nor scalenon; but all
> and none of these at once. In effect, it is something imperfect, that cannot exist;
> an idea wherein some parts of several different and inconsistent ideas are put
> together.[32]

Whatever powers the mind has, it cannot do the impossible. It cannot produce
something which has inconsistent properties.[33]

At times, Locke says things that, if taken prima facie, would commit him to the existence of such absurd entities. However, this is an uncharitable way to read him on the whole if for no other reason than that, by any standard, Locke is a first-rate thinker. And even though many first-rate thinkers have inadvertently committed themselves to inconsistencies, this would be a glaringly obvious commitment to an inconsistency. Of course, Berkeley did not pass up the opportunity to draw attention to Locke's expository faux pas on this point—but neither should he have. Berkeley's aim after all is to show that in pursuing abstract ideas Locke is actually leading himself down the garden path. The opportunity provided by a passage like this is golden, not to be passed up.[34] Just the same, attributing a deep commitment to that particular conception of the product of abstraction is not his real target.

Here is the nub of the more serious problem. Locke agrees that all things are particular. The natural world is unable to provide the appropriate sort of particular which could be the source of any given abstract idea, so Locke turns to the mind to provide the idea. But, of course, in order to produce something that nature cannot, a mind must have some special sort of power not found in nature. This one kind of particular, a human mind, must have a power to produce another kind of particular, an "abstract idea." But if Locke believed that all the choir of heaven and earth are unable to provide us with this kind of thing, why would a human mind be able to do it? What's so special about it?

Locke has a hard row to hoe. He cannot just blankly appeal to a power of the mind to produce the needed item. If he is going to pursue such a line, then we are owed an account of the nature of this unusual power. Short of that, Locke will be open to the charge that we have been referred to an occult power in order to buttress his preferred empiricist semantics. And that's a very serious problem because in that case one might just as well skip the positing of this occult power and simply claim that the needed abstract ideas are provided by the pure intellect or, worse yet, why not just say they are innate? That is, after all, one way to explain the fact that a person can use general terms, and having them provided innately is no more mysterious a way of getting them than having them put there by an occult power.

Locke's attack on innate ideas, Britain's philosophical declaration of intellectual independence, will come to little if on this point his semantic theory conveniently requires the positing of unexplained powers of the mind. It is not even going to be enough to provide a coherent position; his position is going to have to be compelling. Short of that, the opposition need not wage war; they can put down the revolution with only a police action. Locke, I believe, appreciated this point, and accordingly rose to the challenge. He does offer an account of the power of abstraction, and this account does not require the *compounding* of inconsistent properties into one object. Instead, abstract ideas are to be reached via the *elimination* of detail.

> Ideas become general, by separating from them the circumstances of Time, and Place, and any other ideas, that may determine them to this or that particular Existence. By this way of abstraction they are made capable of representing more individuals than one; each of which, having in it a conformity to that Abstract Idea, is (as we call it) of that sort.[35]

Locke's defenders have frequently attempted to shield him from Berkeley's attack by claiming that Berkeley did not see that this was Locke's settled account of abstraction. But that Berkeley is pursing this (more charitable) reading of the nature of abstraction is rather clearly demonstrated by his explicit and deliberate consideration of this proposed method for producing such an entity. It occupies §§8–10 of the "Introduction."[36] He finds that he can make nothing of it.

Section 8 is designed to draw our attention to the very odd nature of the items that are said to be produced by this power of abstraction when applied to qualities and modes. So, for instance, when the power of abstraction is directed toward providing us with the abstract idea *color*, it "makes an idea . . . which is neither red, nor blue, nor white, nor any other determinate color."[37] And when the power is set to the task of giving us the abstract idea of *extension*, it produces an idea of extension "which is neither line, surface, nor solid, nor has any figure or magnitude but is an idea entirely prescinded from all these."[38]

Section 9 then turns to abstract ideas of "compounded beings."

> For example, the mind having observed that Peter, James, and John, resemble each other, in certain common agreements of shape and other qualities, leaves out of the complex or compounded idea it has of Peter, James, and any other particular man, that which is peculiar to each, retaining only what is common to all; and so makes an abstract idea wherein all the particulars equally partake, abstracting entirely from and cutting off all those circumstances and differences, which might determine it to any particular existence. And after this manner it is said we come by the abstract idea of man or, if you please, humanity or human nature; wherein it is true there is included colour, because there is no man but has some colour, but then it can be neither white, nor black, nor any particular colour; because there is no one particular colour wherein all men partake. So likewise there is included stature, but then it is neither tall stature nor low stature, nor yet middle stature, but something abstracted from all these. And so of the rest.[39]

The first step of Berkeley's examination of the power of abstraction (§§8 and 9) is designed to highlight that the posited power is highly suspect due to the bizarre nature of its product—not to mention the strained Ptolemaic complexity of the processes by which these products are produced. After drawing this out, Berkeley then explains why this pursuit was doomed to failure in the first place.

> To be plain, I own my self able to abstract in one sense, as when I consider some particular parts or qualities separated from others, with which though they are united in some object, yet, *it is possible they may really exist without them.* But I deny that I can abstract one from another, or conceive separately, those qualities which *it is impossible should exist so separated.*[40]

Locke is of the opinion that nature is unable to provide the kind of particular his semantic theory requires because it is repugnant to him that such things should exist.[41] But if it is repugnant that such things should exist, then *it is repugnant that such things should exist.* Nothing Locke tells us about this power of abstraction explains why putting them "in the mind" changes that fact. Why should the mind be made into a metaphysical halfway house for ontologically challenged entities? Hume would later seize upon this in his rejection of abstract ideas.

[It] is a principle generally receiv'd in philosophy, that everything in nature is individual, and that 'tis utterly absurd to suppose a triangle really existent, which has no precise proportion of sides and angles. If this therefore be absurd in *fact and reality*, it must also be absurd in *idea*.[42]

No doubt, the preceding reveals that I regard Berkeley's attack as defensible, but my aim has not been to defend it but, rather, to show that, when properly understood, his attack does not proceed from an acceptance of Locke's semantic theory. As we have just seen, Berkeley's attack at no point requires that he embrace Locke's theory. After outing the odd consequences that these Lockean posits produce, the arguments of §§11–16 move on to pursue the belief that their introduction was driven by any genuine need in the first place. Sections 11 and 12 are designed to show that abstract ideas are not needed to explain how a term can have divided reference. Sections 13 and 14 argue that they are not needed to explain how communication is possible. And §§15 and 16 argue that they are not needed to explain how general reasoning is possible. In short, it is Berkeley's aim to show that these powers and their products are superfluous.

5. The Source of Abstract Ideas

At this point, it is helpful to recall the fact that the original plan of the *Principles* included at least three other parts and that what we have is only Part I. However, the "Introduction" which accompanies Part I was to be the introduction to all the projected parts. The attack on abstract ideas was to be the unifying theme of the whole. Thus, Berkeley considered Part I, his attack on the concept of material substance, to be an application or, at least, a continuation of the attack on abstract ideas.[43] From this perspective, it should be fairly easy to see why.[44] Upon examination, we find that 'matter' is that which "neither acts, nor perceives, nor is perceived: for this is all that is meant by saying it is an inert, senseless, unknown substance; which is a definition entirely made up of negatives."[45] But what do we know of any given abstract idea? The abstract idea of 'triangle' is "neither oblique nor rectangle, neither equilateral, equicrural, nor scalenon."[46] The "Introduction" forces us to ask, what are we to make of such entities? And more to the point, what possible use could such things be to us? As Wittgenstein once put it, "A nothing will do as well as a something about which nothing can be said."[47]

The arguments of the "Introduction" that we have considered so far are designed to press on us the question, what would drive someone to admit such entities (either the power or its products) into one's ontology? This, I believe, is exactly the question the young Berkeley asked himself while reading Locke's account of how it is that we can use general terms. As a direct result, his overall approach in the "Introduction" is deflationary. Locke's semantic theory has raised a dust, and it is because of this that "he did not see further."

I have argued that the success of Berkeley's arguments at no point requires that he embrace Locke's semantics. But, of course, that is not the same as showing that he does not in fact accept them. However, when interpreting a writer, one does not get to attribute substantive philosophical theses to him without good reason.

And those reasons had better be especially strong when it is claimed that accepting them would have the effect of undermining that philosopher's core commitments. The upshot is that the constraints of interpretive charity require that we not assume that Berkeley holds a basically Lockean semantics.

That said, what would establish beyond doubt that Berkeley did not accept Locke's theory is if we found him explicitly rejecting the semantic presuppositions that form the very foundations on which that theory is built. The only thing that would be better than that is if we found that the investigations of the "Introduction" culminated in identifying those semantic presuppositions as driving the doctrine of abstract ideas itself. Now *that* would be interesting. Again, the attack on abstract ideas was to be the unifying theme for all the projected parts of the *Principles*. A whole host of errors in metaphysics, morality, mathematics, etc., were to be shown to have its source in the doctrine of abstract ideas. Therefore, this would mean that Berkeley identifies the belief in ideational semantics as an even more fundamental error than the belief in abstract ideas. And that, I believe, is exactly how the "Introduction" is designed.

The direct attack on abstract ideas ends with §17. That is to say, he has executed the first two prongs of his three-pronged attack against abstract ideas. First, he argued that the existence of such things is impossible. Next, he argued that even if they were not impossible, we would still have no use for them. The last sentence of §17 tells us that

> of all the false principles that have obtained in the world, amongst all which there is none, methinks, hath a more wide influence over the thoughts of speculative men, than this of abstract ideas.[48]

And then, in §§18–20, Berkeley offers his error theory. He traces the error to an assumption about the workings of *language*. He identifies as central a mistaken view about *names*:

> [T]he ablest patrons of abstract ideas, . . . acknowledge that [abstract ideas] are made in order to naming; from which it is a clear consequence, that if there had been no such thing as speech or universal signs, there never had been any thought of abstraction. See B.3 C.6. Sect. 39 and elsewhere of the *Essay on Human Understanding*.[49]

Berkeley does not go on to deny that general terms are names. Rather, he denies the implicit assumption that "every name hath, or ought to have, one only precise and settled signification"[50] for it is this

> which inclines men to think there are certain abstract, determinate ideas, which constitute the true and only immediate signification of each general name. And that it is by the mediation of these abstract ideas, that a general name comes to signify any particular thing.[51]

General terms have divided reference; "they all [signify] indifferently a great number of particular ideas."[52] It is likely here that interpreters have been going wrong. For when Berkeley says that general terms signify "particular ideas," one may think he is endorsing the view of meaning he later attributes to Alciphron, i.e., "that significant names which stand for ideas should, every time they are used, excite in the understanding the ideas they are made to stand for."[53] And consistent with this reading is the interpretation of his attack on abstract ideas as founded upon the complaint that no one can conceive of them (which is then read as 'can picture' such items). But that is not what is happening here. He is employing the use of 'idea' that he will only explicitly introduce in the body of the *Principles* itself, the use by which 'ideas' are identical to the particulars of the natural world, e.g., its tables, chairs, mountains, mothballs, etc.[54] He is not using 'idea' to mean 'image' (i.e., what Berkeley calls "ideas of imagination"). He is using 'idea' for what he calls "ideas of sense." The all-important difference is that *Berkelian ideas of sense are not representations*. In stark contrast to both the Cartesian and Lockean traditions, they are not items that *mediate* between us and the particular objects of the world. They *are* themselves the very items of the world.

The aim of §19 is to "give a farther account of how [a view about] words came to produce the doctrine of abstract ideas."[55] It's here that he identifies two "received opinions" as its source:

> [L]anguage has no other end but the communicating [of] our ideas, and ... every significant name stands for an idea.[56]

Berkeley goes on to argue first against the latter opinion in the remainder of §19 and then against the former in §20. The movement here, from §18 through §20, is pivotal. Again, Berkeley regarded the countenancing of abstract ideas to be the single most prevalent and pernicious source of speculative error. And here, in §18 of the "Introduction," he reveals what he takes to be the source of this doctrine, the reason that philosophers introduce abstract ideas in the first place. The source is identified as being the pair of "received opinions" about language:

> i. Language has no other end but the communicating [of] our ideas.
> ii. Every significant name stands for an idea.

He then offers his error theory, i.e., he explains the connection he sees between these semantic presuppositions and the doctrine of abstraction:

> [I]t being withal certain, that names, which yet are not thought altogether insignificant, do not always mark out particular conceivable ideas, it is straightway concluded that they stand for abstract notions.[57]

Any contemporary philosopher, whether trained in either a broadly analytic or a continental tradition, should be immediately drawn to the following thought: what Berkeley identifies in the "Introduction" as the source of the single most pervasive and pernicious mistake in philosophy is the tacit acceptance ("received opinion") of what is now popularly referred to as the "picture theory of meaning."

After identifying (i) and (ii) as the sources of the worst mistake in philosophy, he then proceeds in the remainder of §19 to argue briefly against (ii) by way of pointing out:

> [I]n reading and discoursing, names being for the most part used as letters are in Algebra, in which, though a particular quantity be marked by each letter, yet to proceed right it is not requisite that in every step each letter suggest to your thoughts that particular quantity it was appointed to stand for.[58]

Section 20 then takes up the argument against (i):

> [T]he communicating of ideas marked by words is not the chief and only end of language, as is commonly supposed. There are other ends, as the raising of some passion, the exciting to, or deterring from an action, the putting the mind in some particular disposition.

He offers the following examples:

> May we not, for example, be affected with the promise of a good thing, though we have not an idea of what it is? Or is not the being threatened with danger sufficient to excite a dread, though we think not of any particular evil likely to befall us, nor yet frame to our selves an idea of danger in abstract?[59]

He then turns to proper names.

> Even proper names themselves do not seem always spoken, with a design to bring into our view the ideas of those individuals that are supposed to be marked by them. For example, when a Schoolman tells me Aristotle hath said it, all I conceive he means by it, is to dispose me to embrace his opinion with the deference and submission which custom has annexed to that name.[60]

That it has so often been assumed that Berkeley basically took over the Lockean theory of meaning and understanding is only made all the more puzzling by the fact that, twenty years later, he repeats and expands upon the point at some length in the concluding dialogue, "Seventh Dialogue," of what was in his lifetime his most widely read work, *Alciphron*. The following is a succinct statement from that work that re-identifies the closely related mistaken views of meaning and understanding that Berkeley sees as driving the doctrine of abstract ideas.

> He who really thinks hath a train of ideas succeeding each other and connected in his mind; and when he expresseth himself by discourse each word suggests a distinct idea to the hearer or reader; who by that means hath the same train of ideas in his which was in the mind of the speaker or writer. As far as this effect is produced, so far the discourse is intelligible, hath sense and meaning. Hence it follows that whoever can be supposed to understand what he reads or hears must have a train of ideas raised in his mind, correspondent to the train of words read or heard.[61]

After identifying the offending semantic presuppositions, as in the "Introduction," he once again goes on to argue that "words may be significant, although they do not stand for ideas"[62] and then, once again, identifies this as the source of the doctrine of abstract ideas.

> The contrary whereof having been presumed seems to have produced the doctrine of abstract ideas.[63]

Here, it becomes even clearer that Berkeley's target is not just the empiricist's version of the picture theory. His target here is the ideational theory in general. He is no more happy with the positing of intermediaries in this realm when they are the unpicturable products of the rationalist's faculty of the pure intellect than when they are the picturable products of the empiricist's faculty of the imagination. He regards the positing of mental intermediaries as productive of the most serious hindrance to speculation (i.e., abstract ideas).

And with that before us, we can also see that there is simply no reason to regard Berkeley's introduction of the technical term 'notion' as introducing more into the ontology than just a term. Remember that we have a notion of soul or spirit, "in so much as we know or understand the *meaning* of those words."[64] No nonpicturable representational entity is being posited for the simple reason that nothing in Berkeley's theory of meaning calls for it. Furthermore, there is no cause to see reflection as the Berkelian version of the pure intellect. On the contrary, as Berkeley tells us, of one's own mind one has *immediate* knowledge.[65] Unlike the pure intellect, reflection is not a faculty for producing representational intermediaries.

Even if we have overlooked how foundational this hostility to intermediaries is to the attack on abstract ideas in the "Introduction," we can easily recognize it in his most famous argument, the attack on material substance. As already noted, Berkeley considered the attack on material substance to be an application of his attack on abstract ideas. This particular abstract idea is directly tied to the pernicious positing of mental intermediaries via the *representational theory of perception*. According to this view, we only have direct (or "immediate") perceptual contact, not with the objects of the natural world as they are in-themselves, but rather with intermediary representational items in the mind. The introduction of intermediaries in this realm leaves us behind the infamous "veil of ideas." The Bishop, of course, attacked this view of perception as one of the main supports of skepticism and atheism. But it is not this mistaken representational intermediary account of perception that leads off the *Principles*. Instead, it is its counterpart, the representational intermediary account of *meaning* and *understanding*. Even in matters of perception and semantics, Berkeley's Protestant sensibilities dominate. Intermediaries are to be shunned.

6. An Application of the Interpretation: Selective Attention and Missing the Point

This approach to Berkeley's views on meaning and understanding sheds light on Berkeley's philosophy as a whole. I would now like to focus on the relationship of his views to the attack on abstract ideas by taking up an objection that John Mackie first raised against this attack in his well-known *Problems from Locke*.

Here's how the objection goes: we might think that, at least with respect to Locke's views about abstraction, Berkeley is upset over nothing. One could admit that if Locke had proposed that what abstraction produced was an image, then Locke's theory would be sunk. For instance, if the product of abstraction were a mental image which had color but no *particular* color, then abstraction would be an ability that no man could have. However, so the argument goes, Locke had no such theory, and so Berkeley's complaints are unwarranted. What Locke really had in mind was a theory of *selective attention*.[66] Here's how it works:

> I see a white piece of paper at a particular time and place, and notice that it resembles in colour other pieces of paper, cups of milk, fields covered with snow, and so on; I pay

attention to the feature in which it resembles these other things and pay no attention to the shape or size of the piece of paper or its surroundings or even to the time at which I see it; I remember this feature and associate the word 'whiteness' with it. . . . I am thus ready to use the same word 'whiteness' with respect to that same feature in any other things at any other places and times, and to apply this predicate expression to them.[67]

The object of our consideration is the feature that these particular objects have in common. But since what we are doing is just selectively paying attention to that feature, we have no need to form an inconsistent or incoherent image.

At this point, Mackie says that Berkeley has badly misread Locke. His claim is that if Berkeley hadn't been in the grip of an image theory of mind, he wouldn't have been led to this reading. We've already seen that Berkeley is not in the grip of such a view, and so we can set this aspect of Mackie's objection aside. His other point is of more interest.

Consider Berkeley's claim that "a word becomes general by being made the sign . . . of several particular ideas."[68] Even if we grant that Berkeley is not positing mental intermediaries here, but rather using 'idea,' as he does, to signify the things themselves, still one might wonder if he hasn't left something key out of the explanation. He says a word becomes general by "*being made the sign* of several particular ideas." But he hasn't told us what this process of sign making involves How is a sign made the sign of several particulars in the way it does in the case of general terms? Locke at least saw the need for some explanation of how this is done. Whether Berkeley liked Locke's solution or not, he should have appreciated that there was a problem.[69] In response to Locke's account of abstraction, Berkeley writes,

> And here it must be acknowledged, that a man may consider a figure merely as triangular, without attending to the particular qualities of the angles or relations of the sides. . . . we may consider Peter so far forth as man, or so far forth as animal without framing the aforementioned Abstract Idea, either of man or of animal, inas much as all that is perceived is not considered.[70]

According to Mackie, what Berkeley offers here is a theory of *general reasoning*. That however, is not the problem Locke set out to solve. What Locke was after was a theory of the meaningful use of general terms. Locke shows how the idea of a feature of a concrete, particular item can be used to represent other similar features. This can be done if we have gone through the process of abstraction with respect to this particular feature. If we have associated a word with this idea, we are then in a position to use this word as a general term. Berkeley, however, sees no difficulty in all this:

> Suppose a geometrician is demonstrating the method of cutting a line in two equal parts. He draws, for instance, a black line of an inch in length; this, which in itself is a particular line, is nevertheless *with regard to its signification* general; . . . And as that particular line becomes general by being made a sign, so the same line, which taken absolutely is particular, by being a sign is made general.[71]

To Berkeley, all this "seems very plain and not to include any difficulty in it."[72] What clearer evidence could there be that Berkeley has missed the point?

This is precisely the danger of taking up a deflationary strategy; one exposes oneself to the charge of missing the point. Often, the problem, whose status as a problem one wants to malign, proves more resilient than one first thought. One pulls up the weed in one spot on one day only to find it growing back again in another spot on the next.

Adapting Mackie's argument, we have an argument that says, okay, let's grant that Berkeley did not hold a picture theory of meaning or understanding. Still, he wrongly interprets Locke as a result of not really appreciating the problem with which Locke was wrestling. Evidence of this is that he fails to see that what Locke is offering is a theory of selective attention. Had he seen the problem with which Locke was struggling, he wouldn't have been so quick to (wrongly) conclude that what abstraction must produce is an inconsistent or in some way incoherent image. If true, this charge is serious.

But I don't think this is true. We must remember that Locke's puzzlement at how words can have general significance is a product of his prior theory of how singular terms have significance. I have reviewed all this previously, so I will not repeat it. The immediate point is that Berkeley does not believe that, even in the case of singular terms, words get their meaning—or that their use becomes meaningful to a speaker/audience—from being associated with a mental content. So when it comes to accounting for the meaningfulness of general terms, he is not immediately faced with the problem (as Locke was) of what kind of idea/entity to make a general term a sign of.

Of course, one might still complain that, although Berkeley is not immediately faced with the problem, there *is* such a problem, and he hasn't offered a theory to deal with it because he failed to see the problem.[73] Again, the charge is that Berkeley has missed the point. What he has offered is a theory of general reasoning (e.g., geometric reasoning), not a theory of the meaningful use of general words.

The first thing that a philosopher with such a complaint must do is to lay the problem, nicely and clearly, at our feet. So far, we have no such thing at our feet. The only problem we have is one created by Locke's theory. Reject Locke's theory from the start, and the problem is not, in any obvious way, before us. That said, I think Mackie does make a valuable attempt to put it before us:

> The problem is, how can I reason generally about white things while using one or two tokens of the type-word 'white'?... what Locke means to say is that a single token of 'is white' may represent or signify many particular white things, and that this signifying or representing consists in the fact that speakers of the language are prepared to apply to any appropriate particulars what they will recognize as other tokens of the same type as this one.[74]

So, even if we think that Berkeley has a solution to the problem of how we reason generally, we still have a further problem. Our general reasoning will involve the use of general terms. What we need is an account of the meaningful use of such terms. General reasoning presupposes such an ability. What we have is a speaker who, in uttering a token of the type word 'white,' can successfully go on to use that word to refer to other instances of white things. And in order to do this, Locke says, objects must have common qualities—in this case, the quality of being white—and speakers need both the ability to recognize white things and they must have undergone the process of abstraction with respect to the quality of whiteness that they have observed in several particular objects.

But in this case, it is the objector who has missed the point. Berkeley is arguing that there is no work for the product of Locke's process of abstraction to do. Berkeley, not holding a picture theory of anything, is already convinced that the attempt to put some kind of intermediary between the understanding and that which is to be understood is at best a superfluous move and at worse a positive obstruction. Again, this is really Berkeley's chief stalking-horse. *The positing of unnecessary intermediaries is a mistake, the most pernicious mistake in philosophy.*

Consider the product of Locke's process of abstraction. Let's call that product α, so as not to prejudice the issue of what sort of thing α is. On the one hand, we might think α is some sort of entity. Now, this is the obvious interpretation. Certainly, given Locke's theory of signification with respect to singular terms, it looks like Locke is trying to create an entity of some sort for general terms to signify. If that's what it is, Berkeley has some very difficult questions for Locke to answer. He is going to want to know what sort of entity α is. In particular, he is going to want to know what sort of properties α must have in order for it to represent something as both having color and having no particular color, for instance. Berkeley's warm-up objection is that he cannot (and presumably, nobody else can) conceive of such a thing. But this is true whether we take α to be an image or some other kind of entity. Berkeley is shrewdly trying to block anybody who proposes an entity to solve a philosophical problem by asking them to say more about the entity in question. What he will not allow is for a theorist, like Locke for instance, to get himself in a position where what he needs as a result of his philosophical theory is some entity with some pretty unusual properties to solve his problem so he simply hypothesizes a process that—*poof*—creates the necessary entity with its remarkable, but murky, properties. Berkeley first attacks the idea that we have any notion of this process or the product of it.

But let's suppose one could answer Berkeley's demands for an account of this entity. That is, suppose one can produce a coherent account of what α is. Now we face the problem of saying what α's job is. How does α help us to use general terms? The answer here looks pretty bleak for Locke. We want α to help us use the term 'white' correctly. So, first, we must come across a white thing. Next, we must recognize that it is similar to other objects; the account says that we must defer to our abstract idea, α, to be able to refer to the property as 'white.' But why? We already know how to recognize the property. All that is required is that we continue to use 'white' to apply to it. So why not just say that when we recognize the same property, we use the same word we associate with that property? If we say we need to check our use against some entity in the mind to explain how we keep using that word consistently (beyond appealing to our ability to recognize the property when it comes up), we only beg the question of how we know that we are using that proposed entity properly. How do we know that it is properly guiding our use of 'α'? What underlies, or supports, our consistent use of the abstract idea α?

If, on the other hand, we take α to be not an entity but a "process" or an "ability," the objection recurs. Berkeley is going to claim that there is no work for this ability to do and thus no need for this process of abstraction. To see this, consider (again) the following passage from Mackie, taking note of the italicized words:

> I see a white piece of paper at a particular time and place, and *notice* that it resembles in colour other pieces of paper, cups of milk, fields covered with snow, and so on; I *pay attention* to the feature in which it resembles these other things and pay no attention to the shape or size of the piece of paper or its surroundings or even to the time at which I see it; I *remember this feature* and associate the word 'whiteness' with it. . . . I am thus ready to use the same word 'whiteness' with respect to that same feature in any other things at any other places and times, and to apply this predicate expression to them.[75]

Again, we have to assume that the person has the power to recognize the property in question. She must be able to "notice" it as a common feature among particulars. To do this, she certainly must be able to "remember this feature" to the extent that she must realize she has seen that feature in other particulars. So why then must she go to the extra trouble of "paying attention to it"? Hasn't she already "noticed it"? It is hard to see what ability this paying-attention procedure could produce to help explain the consistent use of the word 'white.' What ability could it produce that the abilities of being able to recognize white things and being able to associate the word 'white' with them cannot do?

That Locke hasn't gotten anywhere with this problem, even given Mackie's clarifications, is shown by the following:

> Locke means that we start by observing (and in this sense having ideas of) several different particular [white objects]. . . . We take from these . . . ideas the parts in which they all agree and put these parts together. *[This] just means selectively considering, and associating verbal expressions with those features* in which our different particular [white objects] are alike.[76]

If one were so minded, she might ask the following questions. Now that I have associated the verbal expression 'white' with the features under my selective attention, how do I know that I will continue to use the word 'white' correctly in the future? All I've done so far is associate 'white' with the features I have already selectively considered. What will make sure that in the future, when faced with a white thing, I'll call it 'white.' If the facts that I will recognize a white thing when I see it and remember that I call such things 'white' are not enough to explain the ability to use words properly, what more is needed and why is it needed?

As we have already reviewed, Berkeley's attack on any type of abstract idea is always three pronged. First, he will try to show that the existence of the abstract idea in question is impossible. In the case of Locke's abstract ideas, Berkeley employed his killing-blow argument. Once he's done that, his second line of attack is to argue that even if it were possible for abstract ideas to exist, we have no good grounds to countenance their existence because there is no work for them to do. His argument on this front is not limited merely to the claim that abstract ideas are of no use in explaining general reasoning. After the killing-blow objection in §10 of the "Introduction," Berkeley moves on to show that abstract ideas are of no use in explaining:

- How it is possible for a sign to have divided reference (§§11 and 12)
- How communication/understanding is possible (§§13 and 14)
- How general reasoning is possible (§§15 and 16)

Given that, suppose we look out into our language-using community. How will we pick out those unlucky few who lack the power to abstract? Won't they look a lot like you and I?[77]

7. A Competing Interpretation: The Periphery of Language

> The Learning of this People is very defective, consisting only in Morality, History, Poetry, and Mathematicks, wherein they must be allowed to excel. But, the last of these is wholly applied to what may be useful in Life, to the Improvement of Agriculture and all mechanical Arts; so that among us it would be little esteemed. And as to Ideas, Entities, Abstractions and Transcendentals, I could never drive the least Conception into their heads.
>
> —Swift, *Gulliver's Travels*

I turn now to the merits and limitations of a competing interpretation. Independently, Jonathan Bennett and David Berman have advanced interpretations that propose to render consistent the views expressed in *Alciphron* with the views expressed in the *Principles*. This is not done via a partitioning of Berkeley's works into an early and late period à la Flew. Rather, it is done via a partitioning of the linguistic realm.

I begin with Bennett's version. Here is the basic idea: one can render the Berkeley of the "Introduction" and Part I consistent with the Berkeley of *Alciphron* by claiming that he has argued that while one does not *always* need to have some image before one's mind, it seems that one must, at least *sometimes*, have the appropriate image before one's mind.[78] Passages like the following might support such a reading:

> That there are many names[79] in use amongst speculative men which do not *always* suggest to others determinate, particular ideas is what nobody will deny. And a little attention will discover that it is not necessary (even in the strictest reasonings) that significant names which stand for ideas should *every time* they are used, excite in the understanding the idea they are made to stand for.[80]

With one's attention so directed, one might claim that when Berkeley says things like "the mind of man may assent to propositions containing . . . terms" even though not "perceiving or framing in his mind distinct ideas marked by the terms," he is only talking about the "periphery of language."[81] He is not talking about language that's used to communicate claims about facts.

Now, from Berkeley's perspective, it should be noted that there is a welcome aspect to this line of criticism. Most scholarship, as well as the larger philosophical community, has been slow to recognize some of Berkeley's more important philosophical innovations. Passages like the one above are plentiful throughout his writings. As early as the "Manuscript Introduction" to the *Principles*, we find Berkeley writing,

> We are told that the good things which God hath prepared for them that love him are such as eye hath not seen nor ear heard nor hath it enter'd into the heart of man to conceive. What man will pretend to say these words of the inspir'd writer are empty and insignificant? And yet who is there that can say they bring into his mind clear and determinate ideas of the good things in store for them that love God?[82]

Yet, despite this, Ayer's *Language, Truth, and Logic* is still widely considered the birthplace of emotivism.[83] The present interpretation, however, is clearly sensitive to its deeper roots.

However, there is a significant downside too. Rather than seeing this as undermining the attribution of a commitment to the picture theory, it is seen as *supporting* it The idea is that Berkeley is still committed to the basic Lockean view of meaning and understanding because in passages like those above, he is not talking about language that's used to communicate claims about *facts*. Like Ayer's emotivism, Berkeley's does not cover truth-evaluable language. As Bennett puts it,

> Berkeley is right to stress that words may be used 'in propriety of language' for purposes other than *theoretical* ones of stating or mis-stating what is the case about some factual matter, e.g.[,] that one may speak in order to 'raise some passion' in the hearer. But if Berkeley is saying that words can be used meaningfully in the absence of ideas only because words can be used *non-theoretically*, then he . . . has not touched the central error in Locke's thinking.[84]

The idea is that in nontheoretical discourse, for instance, talk of religious mysteries, such as grace and the Trinity, we do not really deal in *truth* and *fact*. Instead, just as we can get someone to behave in a frightened manner by sneaking up behind him and screaming "Boo!" we might also get someone to behave religiously by preaching the Gospel to him. Of course, it is more complicated than that, but the point is that the *understanding* is not really involved here, and such statements have very little to do with truth and facts. Instead, they serve some merely practical function. This, one can allow, is an important, even revolutionary, breakthrough, while at the same time only allowing that these radical views about meaning are applied merely to the "periphery of language." From this perspective, Berkeley has not abandoned the picture theory; it seems he has just tweaked it a bit.

Actually, even according to this interpretation, it must be seen as more than a tweak. What is perhaps most interesting about this line of interpretation is that it extends the activities that Berkeley treats as "practical" or "nontheoretical" so as to include mathematics. The reason for this is because, as we've already seen above, Berkeley writes in the *Principles*,

> [I]n reading and discoursing, names being for the most part used as letters are in Algebra, in which, though a particular quantity be marked by each letter, yet to proceed right it is not requisite that in every step each letter suggest to your thoughts that particular quantity it was appointed to stand for.[85]

Additionally, in *Alciphron*, Euphranor says,

> The algebraic mark, which denotes the root of a negative square hath its use in logistic operations, although it be impossible to form an idea of any such quantity. And what is true of algebraic signs is also true of words or language, modern algebra being in fact a more short, apposite, and artificial sort of language.[86]

According to this line of interpretation, one also has to recognize that Berkeley objected to treating mathematics as *theory*, as giving us a body of knowledge about what is the case and what is not. Now, Berkeley was himself a mathematician of some ability, and he was not interested in maligning it as a discipline. His point is rather that we have to understand that mathematics' true value lies in its practical applications. Mathematics is an instrument we can employ toward our ends. It helps us to build better bridges, count sheep, keep the carriages running on time, etc.

The preceding is Bennett's version of the periphery of language interpretation. Before responding to it, I want to introduce David Berman's version.

8. Berman's Version: Emotive Mysteries and Cognitive Theology

In chapters 1 and 6 of his *George Berkeley: Idealism and the Man*, David Berman provides an illuminating discussion of what he calls Berkeley's "semantic revolution" and the way it figures in the Bishop's defense of belief in religious mysteries.[87] What makes Berman's discussion of interest for our current concerns is that it can be seen as extending and, in effect, strengthening Bennett's interpretation. That is why I want to consider it before beginning my response to the periphery of language interpretation.

Like Bennett, Berman sees Berkeley as confining his semantic revolution to the periphery of language. He agrees that Berkeley makes a distinction between "theoretical" and "practical" uses of language. Disciplines that cannot be presented as "clean, clear theory" can still provide us with useful statements. But those statements merely have practical meaning, and as such they are relegated to the periphery of language. Although Bennett's discussion is, in part, inspired by his consideration of Berkeley's account of religious mysteries, he does not pursue the issue of whether Berkeley thought all religious language was merely practical. However, Berman does. Consideration of his account of religious mysteries leads him to interpret Berkeley's emotivism as parasitic on a basically "cognitive" view of meaning and understanding.

To demonstrate this, Berman takes up the debate between Browne and Berkeley on the question of the "literal" truth of the Bible. Browne defended an analogical interpretation of much of the Bible and objected to Berkeley's insistence on it being read literally. Berman writes:

> Browne criticized Berkeley's natural theology for being too literal and cognitive, and his emotive account of mysteries (in *Alciphron* vii) for not being literal and cognitive enough.[88]

But Berkeley, although he admits that some statements in the Bible are emotive in nature, is committed to what Berman calls "cognitive theology." He defends the *truth* of statements like 'God is either literally wise or not at all' because, as Berkeley put it to Browne, "Between these, there is no medium; God has ends in view, or he has not."[89]
As Berman sees it:

> If we did not believe that God was good and just, or if we had only an analogical and distant idea of these attributes . . . then there would be little point in talking about the Holy Trinity or a future state. For why should a bad man fear a being that is not literally just? Hence Berkeley's emotive account of mysteries rests squarely on his cognitive account of theology.[90]

And

> Since God is at the basis of religion, for Berkeley, any uncertainty or vagueness in our conception of God must affect the stability of the rest of religion.[91]

Thus, Berman concludes, "Our knowledge of God, for Berkeley, is essentially scientific knowledge."[92]

So, Berman finds unity in Berkeley's works (at least up to *Alciphron*). But this unity comes from limiting his noncognitivism about language to a fairly small arena and in such a way that it relies on a foundational commitment to a more traditional empiricist theory of meaning. An interpretation that proposes a division of semantic labor will likely seem desirable to the post–*Language, Truth, and Logic* reader, for not only does the modern reader remember Ayer as the source of noncognitivism, but she also remembers that he used noncognitivism to explain how religious language could be meaningful, while at the same time keeping it outside the realm of respectable, truth-appropriate, "scientific" language. It would seem best for Bishop Berkeley if he maintained that religious discourse is not emotive at its core but is, as Berman interprets it, "essentially scientific." When it comes to talk about religious *mysteries* (things like the Trinity), Berkeley regards religious discourse as noncognitive and thus not truth evaluable. But when it comes to talk about God, his existence, his wisdom, his plans for us, etc., such talk is cognitive and thus truth evaluable. And so, Berman's interpretation can be read as an extension of themes found in Bennett.

I will begin my response to the periphery of language interpretation by presenting some problems for Berman's interpretation.

9. Response to Berman's Version

The central problem I see behind Berman's interpretation lies in not taking noncognitivism seriously enough. This is shown by the way that he runs together 'literal' and 'cognitive.' Noncognitive statements need be no less literal than cognitive ones. I think Berman is drawn to this position because he sees noncognitive language as basically "figurative language." This, in turn, he associates with "vague," "distant," and "uncertain" language. The general implication is that noncognitive discourse is a second-class citizen in the city of language. It is an indirect form of communication at best. In calling it "nonliteral," "figurative," or "analogical," one presents a picture of noncognitive language in which it merely piggybacks on cognitive discourse. Here's the idea: with noncognitive discourse, one gets the right response from someone, not by using statements or words that stand for the relevant idea or ideas—that perhaps not being possible—but rather by introducing an idea or ideas that nonetheless, in the particular context, will bring about the desired response from the subject.

This, however, is just a cognitivizing of noncognitivism. It is to insist that *even in noncognitive uses of language*, the interposition of mediating ideas, or images (i.e., "cognitive content") is necessary But this is exactly what Berkeley rejects.

> But although terms are signs, yet having granted that those signs may be significant, though they should not suggest ideas represented by them, provided they serve to regulate and influence our wills, passions, or conduct, you have consequently granted that the mind of man may assent to propositions containing such terms, *when it is so directed or affected by them*, notwithstanding it should not perceive distinct ideas marked by those terms.[93]

It is the term itself, not the presence of some mediating image or images, that is responsible for providing appropriate conditions for understanding and assent. In the preceding quotation, 'them' is anaphoric on 'terms.' It is hearing, seeing—or in the case of Braille, feeling—the *term*, the symbol token itself, that functions in the regulating and influencing of our conduct. Berkeley's point is that no intermediary in addition to the idea(s) of sense, which is (are) identical to the particular symbol token(s), is necessary.

But perhaps a different line of thought might be at work in Berman's interpretation. He might think that there is only *understanding*, in some technical sense, insofar as there are *ideas*. This objection is suggested by Berman's discussion of *Alciphron*, "Seventh Dialogue," §16. After Euphranor applies noncognitivism to talk of miracles, Alciphron concedes to Euphranor, "I freely own there may be mysteries; that *we may believe where we do not understand*."[94] The (perhaps) implied objection is that we must respect the distinction I introduced earlier, and we must be careful to keep separate Berkeley's theory of *meaning* from his theory of the *understanding*. A statement may be meaningful although it communicates no ideas, but it is only where there are ideas that there is also understanding.

In response, one need only point out that this again relies on the view that noncognitive language must be reducible to the cognitive. But there is another problem here as well: it has the form of confusing the claim that 'All A's are B's' with 'All B's are A's.' All talk of mysteries is noncognitive, but not all noncognitive talk is talk of mysteries. A belief in mysteries is something that one might reasonably describe as "a belief in something we do not understand." But it just does not follow from this that all beliefs arrived at through noncognitive communication are beliefs without understanding.

Berman also claims to find support for his interpretation in *Alciphron*, "Seventh Dialogue," §§27 and 29. He does not quote the relevant parts of those sections. After reviewing them, I am unable to speculate as to what he may have had in mind. However, in the same passage, he does quote from a letter by Berkeley to Sir John James:

Light and Heat are both found in a religious mind duly disposed. Light in due order goes first. It is dangerous to begin with heat, that is with affections.... our affections shou'd grow from inquiry and deliberation.[95]

Unfortunately, Berman does not explain why he thinks this supports his interpretation. And so far as I can see, there is nothing here that a noncognitivist need deny.[96] As displayed in the earlier quotations, Berman tends toward conflating 'analogical,' 'vague,' 'distant,' and 'uncertain' with noncognitive language and the states of mind expressed and communicated by its use. He is clearly of the opinion that noncognitive uses of language cannot result in genuine understanding. Berkeley, however, is not. Again:

[I]n reading and discoursing, names being for the most part used as letters are in Algebra, in which, though a particular quantity be marked by each letter, yet to proceed right it is not requisite that in every step each letter suggest to your thoughts that particular quantity it was appointed to stand for.[97]

In such a case, do we fail to understand? If so, it seems to amount to very little. It seems I might get the right answer anyway. What's more, I may be very good at getting the right answer. I may even be more reliable about it than those who claim to have this ability to "understand" what they're doing when they do an algebra problem. With Berkeley, we might simply reply,

For what is it I pray to understand perfectly, but only to understand all that is meant by the person that speaks?[98]

Still, one might object, maybe there can be said to be understanding in these particular cases in which ideas do not occur only because it is, in principle, possible to bring up the distinct ideas of quantity marked by the terms. But this objection is easily dealt with. Again, from *Alciphron*:

The algebraic mark, which denotes the root of a negative square hath its use in logistic operations, although it be impossible to form an idea of any such quantity. And what is true of algebraic signs is also true of words or language, modern algebra being in fact a more short, apposite, and artificial sort of language.[99]

It is *impossible* to form an idea of the root of a negative square. But perhaps even more to the point, we know that Berkeley holds that

[a]n agent... an active mind or spirit, *cannot* be an idea, or like an idea. Whence it should seem to follow that those words which denote an active principle, soul or spirit do not, in strict and proper sense, stand for ideas. And yet they are not insignificant neither; since I *understand* what is signified by the term 'I' or 'myself', or *know* what it means, although it be no idea, nor like an idea and operates about them.[100]

None of this hinders me from positively knowing things about spirits.

How often must I repeat, that I *know* or am conscious of my own being; and that I my self am not my ideas, but somewhat else, a thinking active principle that perceives, knows, wills, and operates about ideas.[101]

I conclude that Berman has not shown that Berkeley's noncognitivism is parasitic on a more basic commitment to a cognitivist view of meaning and understanding.

10. Responding to Bennett's Version

What goes for religious mysteries goes for the sciences as well. My contention is that Bennett's version of the periphery of language interpretation actually turns Berkeley's view of semantics on its head. Berkeley is not trying to make the point that there are some areas of language that are not about matters of fact and thus merely serve some practical function. He is not saying that we have a distinction here between that which is "clean, clear theory" (i.e., "scientific knowledge" in Berman's version) and that which merely serves some practical function. Rather, Berkeley is claiming that there is nothing *mere* in the least about the practical function of language. Berkeley tells us,

> [T]he true end of speech, reason, science, faith, assent, in all its different degrees, is not merely, or principally, or always, the imparting or acquiring of ideas, but rather something of an active operative nature, tending to a conceived good.[102]

The sciences, all of them, are practical activities. What Berkeley says of mathematics, he says of all disciplines, even religion. What he says of them is not that they contain merely "useful utterances" but that they contain "useful *truths*."[103] The claim is that *all* the sciences—remembering, of course, that they deal with signs as their immediate objects—have a normative, pragmatic end.

> [I]t must be confessed that even the mathematical sciences themselves, which above all others are reckoned the most clear and certain, if they are considered, not as instruments to direct our practice, but as speculations to employ our curiosity, will be found to fall short in many instances of those clear and distinct ideas which, it seems the minute philosophers of this age, whether knowingly or ignorantly, expect and insist upon in the mysteries of religion.[104]

Berkeley is giving expression to the central pragmatist insight, that *belief in the truth must have a close connection with success in action.* Language is a tool that allows us to engage in various activities: scientific, religious, etc. What Berkeley pursues is a conceptual pragmatism (i.e., the view that the grasp of the meaning of words is a matter of the mastery of the employment of signs). More specifically, Berkeley gives two general conditions under which words can be signs:

i. By being the medium for the communication of ideas.
ii. By functioning in the influencing of our conduct and actions.

The second may be accomplished either by

a. forming rules for us to act by

or

a. raising passions, dispositions and emotions in us.[105]

In all these roles, signs are meaningful because they can function successfully in pursuit of our ends. In fact, given his rejection of mental intermediaries and his keenness to emphasize the tight connection between the pragmatic ends of linguistic activities and the meaningfulness of terms, I think it is fair to say that

Berkeley is clearly working not in the ideational semantic tradition but in the contrasting use theory tradition. There is nothing in Berkeley's works to match the sophistication of Sellars' or now Brandom's development of that tradition, but he must be considered one of its progenitors.[106]

11. Language and the Natural Order

So, on the one hand, Flew is right: there is a clear affinity between Berkeley's views and those of the later Wittgenstein. And, on the other hand, Bennett and Berman are right that Berkeley's semantic innovations begin at least as early as the *Principles*. However, both approaches fail to see the proper relationship between Berkeley's innovations and the arguments of the "Introduction" to the *Principles*. And this is no small point. The implications of Berkeley's semantic theory permeate his philosophy in a very deep way. According to Berkeley, the natural world is *linguistically* organized

> [T]he connexion of ideas does not imply the relation of cause and effect, but only of a mark or sign with the thing signified. The fire which I see is not the cause of the pain I suffer upon my approaching it, but the mark that forewarns me of it.[107]

The point of doing science is to help us learn to understand better the language that *constitutes* the natural world. The natural world is nothing more than a vast collection of signs. Whereas Locke excludes natural signs from his account of meaning, Berkeley makes no such exceptions. It is all of a piece. A cloud really is a sign of rain. It is a sign that God communicates to us via our sensations (i.e., "ideas of sense"). The importance of any idea of sense, or even any collection of ideas of sense, lies entirely in its role *as a sign*. My perceptions are only meaningful insofar as I understand what they signify.

> [T]he phenomena of nature, which strike on the senses and are understood by the mind, form not only a magnificent spectacle, but also a most coherent, entertaining, and instructive Discourse; and to effect this, they are conducted, adjusted, and ranged by the greatest wisdom. This Language or Discourse is studied with different attention, and interpreted with different degrees of skill. But so far as men have studied and remarked its rules, and can interpret right, so far they may be said to be knowing in nature. A beast is like a man who hears a strange tongue but understands nothing.[108]

One of the most tempting objections to Berkeley's view of the natural world as a system of signs is that the signs just signify other signs. These signs, in turn, also just signify still more signs. This strikes many people as odd. It seems to them that God cannot possibly be saying anything if all he does is speak in signs which just indicate other signs. But once again, one will only be attracted to this line of objection if one is in the grip of the narrow and implausible ideational theory. Berkeley is not. As he sees it, in speaking to us, God is instructing us in what are ultimately *practical* matters:

> Now the set rules or established methods, wherein the mind we depend on excites in us the ideas of sense, are called the Laws of Nature: and these we learn by experience,

which teaches us that such and such ideas are attended with such and such other ideas, in the ordinary course of things.... This gives us a sort of foresight, which enables us to regulate our actions for the benefit of life. And without this we should be eternally at a loss: we could not know how to act [on] any thing that might procure us the least pleasure, or remove the least pain of sense. That food nourishes, sleep refreshes, and fire warms us; that to sow in the seed-time is the way to reap in the harvest, and, in general, that to obtain such or such ends, such or such means are conducive, all this we know, not by discovering any necessary connexion between our ideas, but only by the observation of the settled laws of Nature, without which we should be all in uncertainty and confusion, and a grown man no more know how to manage himself in the affairs of life, than an infant just born.[109]

Science, at its best, is nothing more (and nothing less!) than a well-managed body of activities that helps us to learn to vaticinate more and more effectively. And in doing so, it does not reveal to us a body of knowledge the contemplation of which is valuable in-itself. The end of science is not the cobbling together of a mind-independent description of "the natural world." God's discourse is not cognitive. It is *expressive* discourse, ultimately aimed at a practical end. Its end is not to *represent* or to convey to us some piece of information in the sense of some idea, image, or bit of "cognitive content," but rather to teach us how to regulate our own behavior. The content of the divine language is expressive of his divine love for us.[110]

Basic to good vaticination is careful attention to which ideas accompany each other and to have some way to indicate that the occurrence of certain ideas of sense should occasion in us the expectation of certain other ideas of sense that will follow.

By sight I have the ideas of light and colours with their several degrees and variations. By touch I perceive, for example, hard and soft, heat and cold, motion and resistance, and of all these more and less either as to quantity or degree. Smelling furnishes me with odours; the palate with tastes, and hearing conveys sounds to the mind in all their variety of tone and composition. And as several of these are observed to accompany each other, they come to be marked by one name, and so to be reputed as one thing. Thus, for example, a certain colour, taste, smell, figure and consistence having been observed to go together, are accounted one distinct thing, signified by the name apple.[111]

We do our best to make use of the order present in nature (i.e., the ideas of sense we receive) by means of introducing words that help us to organize, inculcate, and communicate appropriate expectations. If I say "Lo, a bear!" to my friend, he may expect, upon turning his head in the appropriate direction, to receive certain ideas of sense typical of bear sightings. This may well be of great help to him in getting through the next few minutes of his life. If he knows the meaning of the word 'bear,' he will know what sort of ideas of sense may well be coming his way next.[112] These new ideas of sense, in turn, are only meaningful insofar as he is able to regard them as *signs*. If he is wise in the ways of bears, he will take his ideas of sight, e.g., vivid visual ideas of brown fur and olfactory ideas, like that of a strong musky odor, to be indications of impending extremely painful ideas of sense, ones typical of a mauling. If he is a good vaticinator, he will take these as signs that he ought to either get out of there or make himself appear unappetizing. Thus, the organizing of the ideas of sense into objects by means of the introduction of words is ultimately a practical matter.

> It is evident, things regard us only as they are pleasing or displeasing: and they can please or displease, only so far forth as they are perceived. Farther therefore we are not concerned.[113]

The contrasting attitude is evident in Descartes' work.

> My nature, then, in this limited sense, does indeed teach me to avoid what induces a feeling of pain and to seek out what induces feelings of pleasure, and so on. But it does not appear to teach us to draw any conclusions from these sensory perceptions about things located outside us without waiting until the intellect has examined the matter. For knowledge of truth about such things seems to belong to the [intellect] alone. . . . For the proper purpose of the sensory perceptions given me by nature is simply to inform the mind of what is beneficial or harmful for the composite of which the mind is a part; and to this extent they are sufficiently clear and distinct. But I misuse them by treating them as reliable touchstones for immediate judgements about the essential nature of bodies located outside us; yet this is an area where they provide only very obscure information.[114]

For Descartes, knowledge of the natural world is not ultimately a practical matter ending in concerns about pleasure and pain. Rather, its aim is the grasp of essential natures. When used properly, the intellect's special representational capacities provide us with ideas that accurately represent an object's essential nature.

In stark contrast, Berkeley's bundle account of physical objects is a natural ally of a pragmatic view of science. Names are introduced to refer to collections of ideas, which prove valuable to treat as "belonging to one thing." Their unity is not inherent to them, and so the aim of science is not the uncovering and cataloging of the hidden real essences of the natural world. When it comes to natural objects, then, as Berkeley put it at notebook entry 536, "fruitless the Distinction twixt real & nominal Essences."[115]

We should not, however, make the mistake of thinking that this means that the introduction of words for the purpose of indicating objects is merely a practical matter. There is nothing "mere" about it. What objects we should recognize is not "up to us." Their introduction is guided by norms which are instituted by God.[116] In the case of talk of natural objects, and thus the activities of natural science, the guiding norms are instituted by, and implicit in, the orderly, uniform manner in which God imposes the ideas of sense upon us. Without the regularity of connection between ideas of sense, our language would be impossible. We rely on God's good will toward us to render our experiences intelligible.

The difference between the layperson and the scientist is parallel to the difference between the competent speaker of the language and the linguist. The correct norms for everything are laid down by God. We merely seek to find and follow them.

> There is a certain analogy, constancy, and uniformity in the phenomena or appearances of nature, which are a foundation for general rules: and these are a grammar for the understanding of nature, or that series of effects in the visible world whereby we are enabled to foresee what will come to pass in the natural course of things.[117]

The scientist seeks to make them explicit in the form of rules so that we may better know how to make predictions about the future. But in simply learning a language, we learn a little bit of commonsense science. We learn the predictive practices that helped our ancestors to survive. Our ordinary language is thus a vast and valuable reservoir of predictive success stories. But it is not the last word. There is no reason to think it is either complete or infallible. The activities we call "science" help us to extend and, when done well, improve our ability to collect ideas into predicatively useful collections. These rules in turn can help to constrain and direct our introduction of new useful collections with words like "lepton" and "quark," for instance. Among twentieth-century philosophers, it is J. L. Austin who best reflects the spirit of Berkeley on this front.

> Certainly ordinary language has no claim to be the last word, if there is such a thing. It embodies, indeed, something better than the metaphysics of the Stone Age, namely, as was said, the inherited experience and acumen of many generations of men. But then, that acumen has been concentrated primarily upon the practical business of life. If a distinction works well for practical purposes in ordinary life (no mean feat, for even ordinary life is full of hard cases), then there is sure to be something in it, it will not mark nothing: yet this is likely enough to be not the best way of arranging things if our interests are more extensive or intellectual than the ordinary. And again, that experience has been derived only from the sources available to ordinary men throughout most of civilized history: it has not been fed from the resources of the microscope and its successors. And it must be added too, that superstition and error and fantasy of all kinds do become incorporated in ordinary language and even sometimes stand up to the survival test (only, when they do, why should we not detect it?). Certainly, then, ordinary language is not the last word: in principle it can everywhere be supplemented and improved upon and superseded. Only remember, it is the first word.[118]

The introduction of words may be motivated by all sorts of pursuits, both basic physical needs and, as Austin says, more "intellectual ones." They are designed to suit our needs. But when discussing Berkeley's view, it is important to remember that our needs are ultimately not mundane or even intellectual; they are spiritual. There is nothing mere about practical matters for a Christian philosopher. And while it is true that ultimately the product of scientific practice is knowledge of how we might avoid pain and procure earthly pleasure, it is also true that earthly pleasure and pain are not the ultimate measures of pleasure and pain.

> However mistaken men may be too apt to place their chiefest interest in the slight pleasures & transient enjoyments of this Life in the gratification of some passion, or the gaining of some temporal advantage; yet a man who considers things with any fairness or impartiality will be easily convinced that his chief interest consists in obeying Almighty God, in conforming his life and actions to the will and command of his Creator.... But the spiritual nature of God tho most near and immediately operating on our souls and bodies, is yet invisible to our senses, and ... the Riches of that place where there is no moth nor rust & where thieves do not break thro & steal are placed at a distance from our present state.... men are more powerfully influenced by things which are present and sensible.[119]

Because we are so powerfully influenced by things sensible and immediate, we are tempted to attribute real power to the sensible things themselves. The measure of a successful natural ontology then is no longer the benefit to life, but the uncovering and cataloging of these supposed hidden inner essences of natural objects. The practice of science, like the rest of life, is ripe with temptation.

> [T]his consistent uniform working, which so evidently displays the goodness and wisdom of that governing spirit whose will constitutes the Laws of Nature, is so far from leading our thoughts to him, that it rather sends them a wandering after second causes. For when we perceive certain ideas of sense constantly followed by other ideas, and we know this is not of our doing, we forthwith attribute power and agency to the ideas themselves, and make one the cause of another, than which nothing can be more absurd and unintelligible.[120]

Berkeley is writing in the wake of the great scientific accomplishments of Newton, Harvey, and Boyle. As his own investigations with respect to the potential medicinal powers of tar water amply demonstrate, he saw in science great possibilities for the benefiting of humanity. But pride is the deadliest of the sins, powerful enough to separate the angel Satan from God. One of Berkeley's central concerns is that along with humans' growing pride in our scientific successes comes a temptation to regard knowledge of the natural world as an end in-itself. In so doing, we make an idol of nature. Such mistakes lead people to materialism, which leads people to skepticism, and this in turn to atheism.

12. The "Introduction" and Immaterialism: The Curtain of Words

We now have a clear view of just how tightly connected the central aim of the "Introduction" of the *Principles* is to the immaterialism of Part I; we can see how materialism and the picture theory are two sides of the same coin. In chapter I, we acquired an appreciation of the importance that Berkeley places on the fact that natural objects lack an internal source of unity (i.e., the second sense of 'dependence'). We act toward sensible things *as if* they were one. We do this with the help of names. Philonous makes the connection plain in the *Three Dialogues*.

> [If] in case every variation was thought sufficient to constitute a new kind or individual, the endless number or confusion of *names* would render language impracticable. Therefore to avoid this as well as other inconveniencies...men combine together several ideas...all [of] which they refer to one name, and consider as one thing.[121]

Berkeley's diagnosis is that the mistake of believing that there must be some sort of internal source of unity, a true individual (a substratum substance, a real essence, a substantial form, etc.) which serves as the source and/or support of a natural object's qualities has its rooting in the picture theory, i.e., in the belief that the meaningful use of names requires that they signify one individual thing, *an* idea (e.g., the idea of the wax *itself*). To which Berkeley responds,

> What therefore if our ideas are variable; what if our senses are not in all circumstances affected with the same appearances? It will not thence follow, they are not to be trusted, or that they are inconsistent either with themselves or any thing else, except it be with your preconceived notion of (I know not what) one single, unchanged,

unperceivable, real nature, marked by each name: which prejudice seems to have taken its rise from not rightly understanding the common language of men speaking of several distinct ideas, as united into one thing by the mind.[122]

With this point before us, let's reconsider the famous objection made by Hylas in the *Three Dialogues*.

Hylas: But the same idea which is in my mind, cannot be in yours, or in any other mind. Doth it not therefore follow from your principles, that no two can see the same thing?[123]

The fact that, according to Berkeley, sensible things are not really one thing, but rather are merely "accounted one distinct thing" explains why, instead of being devastated by the objection, Philonous replies, "whether philosophers shall think fit to call a thing the same or no, is, I conceive, of small importance."[124] Failure to appreciate that sensible things are not genuine individuals also explains why so many are struck by his reply, but it is precisely the right reply for Berkeley to put in the mouth of Philonous. The fact that only spirits are genuine individuals means that 'same,' when expressive of numerical identity, does not, strictly speaking, apply here.

That does not mean that it is of no use here at all. The unity, such as it is, of sensible things hangs on the *application of names* in the course of the use of language. The course of language, and thus the introduction of names with respect to sensible things, is driven by the pragmatic concerns of the genuine individuals, the spirits. But our concerns over having identity conditions for nonspiritual "individuals"—i.e., for merely mundane things—are, appropriately enough, finite, in a word, *mundane*. Such concerns are subservient to the ends of language, and thus this is ultimately a pragmatic matter.

Let us suppose several men together, all endued with the same faculties, and consequently affected in like sort by their senses, and who had yet never known the use of language; they would without question agree in their perceptions. Though perhaps, when they came to the use of speech, some regarding the uniformness of what was perceived, might call it the same thing: others especially regarding the diversity of persons who perceived, might choose the denomination of different things. But who sees not that all the dispute is about a word?[125]

Berkeley here imagines a situation where differences among the uses of this word have now come unhitched from any conceivable pragmatic concern. But this is a fictional case. In everyday practice,

men are used to apply the word 'same' where no distinction or variety is perceived, and I do not pretend to alter their perceptions[;] it follows, that as men have said before, several saw the same thing, so they may upon like occasions still continue to use the same phrase.[126]

With respect to sensible things, beyond its usefulness in marking where "distinction or variety is perceived," we cease to have any pragmatic constraints on the use of 'same' because all there is to sensible things is what is perceived. *Their esse is percipi.*

The advocate for real natures, substrata, substantial forms, or "an abstracted notion of identity"[127] has fallen victim to the undeniable lure of the simple denotational theory of meaning: for a name to be meaningful, it *must* denote, and what it must denote is *one single, individual, unitary*, etc., item. When one holds, in addition, an ideational theory of the understanding, this results in one version or another of the ideational theory of meaning. It is precisely this line of thought that leads Descartes to the paradoxical claim that the wax is not perceived by the senses. Since there is no idea of sense or imagination which he can call—i.e., *name*—his idea of "the wax itself," he is compelled to posit a source, the pure intellect, to provide the necessary idea to which the name can then be attached.[128] As for Locke, while he would not go in for radically non-imagistic ideas, he is just as committed to both the ideational theory of understanding and its companion, the ideational theory of meaning. He simply refuses to recognize non-imagistic ideas. But he still needs individual ideas for the names of natural objects to signify. Thus, having repudiated the pure intellect, the strained notion of a faculty of abstraction and its abstract ideas are brought in to fill the gap.

In contrast, Berkeley's introduction of the term 'notions' is not an addition to his ontology. He simply does not need to posit a special species of mental entity for words like 'grace' and spirit' to denote. Notions are introduced for no more than precisely the reason Berkeley gives, i.e., because "the term idea would be improperly extended to signify every thing we know."[129]

Finally, it is the companion doctrines of the ideational theory of the understanding and the ideational theory of meaning that lead to the "embarras and delusion of words" of which Berkeley so famously speaks at the conclusion of the "Introduction."

> Unless we take care to clear the first principles of knowledge, from the embarras and delusion of words, we may make infinite reasonings upon them to no purpose; we may draw consequences from consequences, and be never the wiser. The farther we go, we shall only lose our selves the more irrecoverably, and be the deeper entangled in difficulties and mistakes.[130]

What Berkeley tells us at the end of the "Introduction" is that the way to knowledge requires, not that we lift some supposed veil of ideas, but rather that we must draw the "curtain of words." This curtain, though potentially confounding, is not opaque. It is sheer, lying like lace over the sensory flux, forming patterns, and thereby making individuals appear where, when drawn, there is only an ever-shifting, flowing, sensory plenum.

13. Conclusion: One Berkeley

We have removed the dilemma with which we began. Berkeley's attack on abstract ideas poses no threat to the meaningfulness of words such as 'grace,' 'soul,' and 'Trinity' and therefore no threat to the Bishop's religious convictions. To think otherwise is to fall prey to the mistake that Berkeley was driven to criticize abstract ideas because he was "in the grip of the picture theory of the mind."[131] As we have seen, he does not argue against abstract ideas on the grounds that every meaningful term must be accompanied in the mind by an image. On the contrary, his rejection of any form of the intermediary theory of mind and meaning is what underlies his attack on abstract ideas and thus, in turn, provides the launching point for the introduction of immaterialism. A careful examination of the "Introduction" and *Alciphron* reveals neither an inconsistency nor a fundamental change in Berkeley's philosophy. Quite to the contrary, it reveals the fundamental source of continuity in his work.

III

Knowing Spirits

Shut too in a tower of words, I mark
On the horizon walking like the trees
The wordy shapes of women, and the rows
Of the star-gestured children in the park.
Some let me make you of the vowelled beeches,
Some of the oaken voices, from the roots
Of many a thorny shire tell you notes,
Some let me make you of the water's speeches...
Some let me make you of the meadow's signs;
The signal grass that tells me all I know
Breaks with the wormy winter through the eye.
—Dylan Thomas[1]

1. Knowledge of Other Minds

Thomas Reid, that famed defender of common sense, had this to say about Berkeley:

[T]he opinion of the ablest judges seems to be, that [his principles] neither have been, nor can be confuted; and that he hath proved by unanswerable arguments what no man in his senses can believe.[2]

What is it that "no man in his senses can believe"? One thinks immediately of Hume's answer.

It seems evident, that men are carried, by a natural instinct or prepossession, to repose faith in their senses; and that, without any reasoning, or even almost before the use of reason, we always suppose an external universe, which depends not on our perception, but would exist, though we and every sensible creature were absent or annihilated.[3]

However, on a little reflection, it is no easy task to interpret Berkeley as an appropriate target for this remark. Berkeley, of course, does not deny the existence of an external world independent of our perception. Berkeley is a realist. The dispute is over the *nature* of the stuff that makes up reality. Nor does he approve of the view that we should not repose faith in our senses. All of our sensations are trustworthy, according to Berkeley's view.[4] Where Berkeley's position seems to enter as an appropriate target is in the inference Hume draws from the previous claims, i.e., that these two beliefs amount to or entail a third, that there would be an external world even if every "sensible creature" were annihilated. But while Berkeley becomes an appropriate target at this point, Hume can no longer be interpreted as doing nothing more than presenting something like "common sense." That would be to present atheism as nothing more than common sense. In any reasonably mainstream account, God is an immaterial being, a mind, a spirit. As Berkeley puts it,

> God is a Mind . . . not an abstract idea compounded of inconsistencies, and prescinded from all real things, as some moderns understand abstraction; but a really existing Spirit.[5]

And on any reasonably mainstream theistic account, the existence of *everything* is dependent upon the existence of this mind. We cannot interpret Hume as simply presenting the view of the ordinary person on the street if that means attributing to such a person a belief that everything would exist even though God were, *per impossible*, annihilated. Idealism and the beliefs of ordinary folk (and thereby, one sense of "common sense") make their primary point of contact in theism. To be a theist is to take seriously, in one way or another, the belief that reality ultimately has a spiritual foundation.

That is why Reid is so interesting in this connection. It seems that he was not always of the opinion that no man in his senses could believe Berkeley's principles. In fact, he tells us he once "embrace[d] the whole of Berkeley's system."[6] Nor was it uneasiness for the want of a material world that led him to question it.[7] It was rather uneasiness for the want of other finite spirits like himself.

> I can find no principle in Berkeley's system, which affords me even probable ground to conclude that there are other intelligent beings like myself, in the relations of father, brother, friend, or fellow-citizen.[8]

Reid feels that Berkeley's system gives him sufficient evidence of God's existence but not of other finite minds. Reid is no atheist, and so it is interesting that what drew him to question Berkeley's system was not (at least not primarily) the fact that Berkeley's view of reality does not include material substance. Seemingly, Berkeley's spiritual realism might well have provided Reid with a robust enough sense of external reality if only Berkeley's epistemology of that reality had been robust enough to ensure Reid that he could know that other finite spirits exist.

Now, of course, Berkeley is not alone in having to face the problem of accounting for our knowledge of other minds. Reid's singling him out in this respect is, I believe, motivated by the fact that Berkeley's metaphysics brings the problem to the forefront of attention in ways that others do not.[9] My intention is to exploit this fact as a means toward providing an account of Berkeley's view of the nature of spirits. In this chapter, I provide an interpretation of Berkeley's view of the nature of our knowledge of *other* spirits/minds. This will pave the way toward providing an account of the nature of spirits in chapter IV. In this chapter, we find that Berkeley's idealism requires a rather radical revision of the way we think of our epistemological situation. Our basic epistemological relation to reality must be conceived of as a relation to another mind, and this, I will argue, means that our fundamental epistemological relation to reality must not be conceived of along representationalist lines, but rather along, roughly, noncognitivist lines. That is to say, our basic epistemological link to reality is *attitudinal* in nature. What I mean by this will be made clear in what follows.

2. A Problem about Other Minds

Berkeley regards the "problem of other minds" as a legitimate philosophical prob-lem. However, he does not regard it as insuperable. There are several prima facie problems, but one in particular is brought to the forefront for Berkeley because it falls right out of two characteristic, and even fairly basic, Berkelian theses:

i. Spirits are of a completely different nature than ideas. Spirits are *volitional* in nature, what Berkeley calls "active." An active thing is an appropriate subject for ascriptions of responsibility. Ideas, on the other hand, are not capable of being responsible for anything. They are "passive."
ii. All of our perceptual knowledge must be acquired through the senses, and through our senses we receive only ideas.

Problem: How then is our knowledge of other minds possible?

The natural temptation is to pursue the possibility that our knowledge of other minds is mediated somehow by ideas. The question is, how? As we already know, Berkeley will not attempt to solve this problem by having ideas represent spirits; he has clearly ruled that out. Moreover, given a metaphysics of *activity* and *passivity* and an ontology of *spirits* and *ideas*, he is absolutely right to do so. It is worthwhile to make the reasons for this clear.

First, ideas in no way resemble spirits because they *cannot* resemble spirits. So representation via resemblance is out of the question. Spirits do not look, smell, feel, sound, or taste like any idea, or combination of ideas, because spirits are *that which* look, *that which* smell, *that which* feel, etc.

Second, and more important, ideas cannot *do* anything. Again, Berkeley's is a metaphysics of activity and passivity. Ideas are perfectly inert; they are passive. Among other things, for the Berkelian, this means that, strictly speaking, ideas cannot represent. Spirits alone are active; only spirits act. Representing requires activity. The only kind of activity that the Berkelian recognizes is volitional ac-tivity. In such a metaphysics, spirits must be doing something with ideas in order for ideas to function as representations.

Once the point is put this way, it may seem obvious; nonetheless, it is one of those points that can easily slip from focus. It helps to remember that it applies even for representations involving resemblance. The fact that two things resem-ble one another is a fact that a spirit can exploit in the process of making one a representation of the other. The resemblance of one item, A, to another, B, can sometimes make it easier for a spirit to use A to get some third party to di-rect its thoughts to B. It is, however, neither a necessary nor a sufficient condi-tion for representation. Ideas can only represent because spirits *do* something with ideas.

Representations are, thus, merely a species of *sign*. To avoid falling into the tempting habit of confusing *resembling* with the *power to represent*, it is better to use the terms 'sign' and 'signified' instead of 'representation' and 'represented.' In adopting this terminology, I am merely following Berkeley's lead. Rather than representation, Berkeley prefers to talk of the "sign-signified" relation, and his paradigm examples of this relation are not instances in which A and B resemble one another but rather are instances in which the connection between A and B is perfectly arbitrary. This is the sort of relation we find in language. For instance, to use Berkeley's favorite example, when reading, the signs printed on the page bear no resemblance to what is signified. The connection between the symbols on the page and their meaning is perfectly arbitrary.[10]

3. Berkeley's Approach to the Problem of Other Minds

So it is essential to understanding Berkeley's view of the nature of ideas that we remember that ideas are perfectly impotent. Rather, spirits *use* ideas. Ideas are the instruments by which spirits work their will, so to speak. By using ideas in specific ways, spirits can turn ideas into signs. But turning something into a sign is not a matter of adding any naturalistic property to it. This point not only lays bare the problem of other minds, but it also leads us to the solution of our problem of how we come to know that there are other minds. One of the ways in which ideas may be used is to communicate with other spirits. Berkeley's answer to the problem of other minds is that we have to look for *signs* of *sign use*. There, we will find another mind.

The first thing I will focus on is the issue of what constitutes a *sign* of sign use. Once that is done, I will turn to the issue of what constitutes *sign use*.

4. *Signs* of Sign Use

According to Berkeley's metaphysics, the mere presence of an idea is a sign of a mind distinct from one's own (i.e., another mind). Why? Because

a. When we talk of exciting ideas exclusive of volition we only amuse ourselves with words.[11]

According to Berkeley, the only concept we have of causation is that of volition.

b. The ideas imprinted on [my senses] are not creatures of my will.[12]

We are constantly subject to experiences, and we are *passive* with respect to what we perceive. Our perceptions are something that *happens* to us.

c. There is therefore some other will or spirit that produces them.[13]

Since the perceptions I experience are occurring in me independently of my will, then, by way of (a), it must the case that they are being caused to occur in me by some other agent, some other spirit.

While it is true that no idea, or collection of ideas, is another mind—because minds are of a completely different nature than ideas—still every single idea one perceives is a sign that there is another volitional being, another spirit.[14] Every idea is an indication of activity; every episode of passivity is a sign of activity. So, we can remain faithful to empiricism and it will still follow that, as Berkeley says, "the being of things imperceptible to sense may be collected from effects and signs, or sensible tokens."[15]

5. Signs of *Sign Use*

While every idea passively received by us is a sign of another mind, we do not respond to every perception by acting in a manner appropriate to dealing with a human person. And that's a good thing—otherwise we would frequently find ourselves talking to stacks of waffles and balls of dryer lint.[16] But of course, the human body is just another collection or series of ideas. That's all any natural thing can be in Berkeley's metaphysics. So the question is, when *is* it appropriate to take ourselves to be engaged with another human mind? According to Berkeley, what best convinces us that we are dealing with another mind is that it *talks* to us.

> I find that nothing so much convinces me of the existence of another person as his speaking to me. It is my hearing you talk that, in strict and philosophical truth, is to me the best argument for your being. . . . What I mean is not the sound of speech merely as such, but the arbitrary use of sensible signs, which have no similitude or necessary connexion with the things signified; so as by the apposite management of them to suggest and exhibit to my mind an endless variety of things, differing in nature, time, and place; thereby informing me, . . . and directing me how to act, not only with regard to things near and present, but also with regard to things distant and future. No matter whether these signs are pronounced or written; whether they enter by the eye or the ear: they have the same use, and are equally proofs of an intelligent, thinking, [thing].[17]

A paradigmatic human spirit is a language user. Spirits have the ability to make use of ideas to communicate. So, being confronted with a bit of discourse is convincing evidence that you are dealing with another mind.

Knowing this helps, but it does not immediately solve our problem. We still have to figure out how we come to distinguish occasions when we are confronting a discourse. Our senses can only give us access to ideas. Any discourse we may come across is just another particular collection or series of ideas among the vast and varied mosaic of the natural world. Discourses do not differ intrinsically from any other natural object in that respect. In looking at a die, I see three sides of it first; then, as I turn it, I perceive another side, then another, then another, etc. The same goes for a discourse. When someone speaks to me, I first have the sensation of one sound, then another, then another, etc. The immediate objects of the senses are, in themselves, completely without content, meaningless. As Berkeley writes in *Siris*,

> We know a thing when we understand it; and we understand it when we can interpret or tell what it signifies. Strictly, the sense knows nothing. We perceive indeed sounds by hearing, and characters by sight; but we are not therefore said to understand them. After the same manner, the phenomena of nature are alike visible to all; but all have not alike learned the connexion of natural things, or understand what they signify, or know how to vaticinate by them.[18]

A discourse is just another natural object—just another series of ideas among many. So even though the linguistic organization of ideas requires the activity of a spirit, it is still true that, as Berkeley says, "all acts immediately and properly perceived by sense [are] reducible to motion."[19] In short, there is no natural property that makes something a discourse.

However, although the ideas that make up a bit of discourse are just like all other natural objects in that they are a collection of ideas, they do differ in one very important respect: they admit of a certain kind of *treatment* by a spirit. Ideas so organized are *interpretable*. Again, this is not a natural property of the ideas. Rather, ideas organized into a discourse prove appropriate for a certain kind of activity on the part of a spirit, the *activity of interpretation*. We *act toward* this collection of ideas in a way that is significantly different from the way we act toward the collection that is an apple, or a stack of waffles, etc.

It is the way that ideas are manipulated in language so as to pursue rationally calculated ends that reveals a nonperceptible "principle of thought and action"[20] responsible for so organizing them. And it is the using of ideas as instruments to work our will, to help us achieve communication with other spirits, that turns them into linguistic objects (i.e., signs). As we learn a language, we come to learn the arbitrary connections between words and their meanings. These connections become deeply ingrained, so ingrained, in fact, that we tend to forget that they are not necessary connections:

> [C]onsider how hard it is, for any one to hear the words of his native language pronounced in his ears without understanding them. Though he endeavour to disunite the meaning from the sound, it will nevertheless intrude into his thoughts, and he shall find it extreme[ly] difficult, if not impossible, to put himself exactly in the posture of a foreigner, that never learned the language, so as to be affected barely with the sounds themselves, and not perceive the signification annexed to them.[21]

Treating the collection of ideas that constitutes a discourse as a suitable object of interpretation means we have to consider those ideas, those sensible things, as *being used by a spirit* for the purpose of communication. As Berkeley puts it, "[Y]ou infer . . . from reasonable motions (or such as appear calculated for a reasonable end) a rational cause, soul or spirit."[22] But this "inference" does not end in anything like an ordinary belief, as when, for instance, I see smoke and I take it to be a sign of fire. I take one collection of passive things to be related to another collection of passive things. But when I take a collection of sensible things to be a bit of discourse, I take that collection of passive things to be relating me to something wholly different: a spirit, an active thing. In taking something to be a discourse, I am taking some collection of sensible things to be animated by the *use*, by the *activity*, of a spirit. I am now dealing with another spirit, another responsible being, rather than a mere collection of passive things, a mere object. To deal with an object, I need only be prepared to deal with it on the level of *motion*. But in order for me to treat a collection of sensible ideas as appropriate objects for interpretation, that is, in treating them as mediating a relationship between me and another active being, I must be prepared to interact with a spirit, something which *acts*.

It is also important to keep in mind the distinctive use to which a spirit is putting sensible things when arranging them into a discourse. Often we use sensible things to manipulate other sensible things. I use the baseball bat to make the ball move. But by talking or writing, I use sensible things to get another *spirit* to do something, and what spirits do is *act*. So in taking something to be an instance of talking, or writing, etc., I, as the interpreting agent, must be prepared to engage in an exchange of *actions*. Communication (*commune*-ication) requires that one be prepared to interact (inter-*act*).

6. An Elucidation: Dennett on the "Intentional Stance"

Given an acquaintance with the major trends in the philosophy of mind over the past thirty to forty years, certain aspects of Berkeley's views may seem oddly familiar. Since at least the early 1960s, a cadre of philosophers has been exploring and developing what can be characterized as a normative approach to other minds.[23] Though developed in significantly different ways, they each take their cue from the idea that the beginning of wisdom with respect to understanding the nature of the mental is recognizing a distinction between what Wilfrid Sellars described as the "space of reasons" and the "space of causes."[24]

Daniel Dennett's "intentional stance" is the most compellingly and clearly presented species of this genus, and not coincidentally it is the best known. I suppose it will sound a bit odd to be told that a brief comparison and contrasting with Dennett's view will help to elucidate some of the most important features of Berkeley's. For now, the reader is asked to trust me.

Not all the things we encounter in a day are minds. According to Dennett, any particular thing is a mind only if its behavior yields to a particular sort of predictive strategy. If treating something as a mind proves predicatively valuable, then the attribution of mentality to it is justified; it is correct to do so.

According to Dennett, when we think we may be confronted with a mind, we take up the intentional stance toward it. Taking up the intentional stance toward some entity is a matter of attributing to it beliefs, desires, and "rational acumen." In brief, and in his own words, this involves three "rough and ready principles":

i. A system's beliefs are those it *ought to have*, given its perceptual capacities, its epistemic needs, and its biography.
ii. A system's desires are those it *ought to have*, given its biological needs and the most practical means of satisfying them.
iii. A system's behavior will consist of those acts it *would be rational* for an agent with those beliefs and desires to perform.[25]

6.1. First Point of Comparison

Taking up the intentional stance is distinguished from our other ways of interacting with things by its *evaluative* character. The italicized emphases in the foregoing are Dennett's own. As we see in (i) and (ii) above, attributing intentionality is a matter of attributing to an entity states it *ought* to have.

Here, then, is the first point of contact with Berkeley's view. In taking up the intentional stance toward something, we go from treating the entity in question in a manner appropriate to dealing with a mere *thing* and move toward treating it in a manner appropriate to interacting with an *agent*. We move toward treating it in a way appropriate to dealing with something capable of being held *normatively responsible*. We attribute to it states it *ought* to have. This requires that we go from treating some of its "behaviors" as *motions* of an *object* toward treating them as *actions* of an *agent*. (N.B. One of the terms Berkeley uses as equivalent to 'spirit' is 'agent.')

6.2. Second Point of Comparison

Dennett calls it the intentional *stance*. He describes it as a matter of "taking up an attitude toward something." There is an unmistakable emphasis on *activity* in all this. One is *taking up* the intentional stance *toward* something. I interpret this as intended to emphasize the difference between the way that we know of and about other minds and the way that we know of and about mere things. Seeing something as a mind is a matter of *treating* it as a mind. And treating something as a mind is a matter of *engaging* it in an *evaluative activity*.

Taking up the intentional stance toward something should not be thought of along the lines of just having a mere belief about it. It is not a representation of some aspect of the world. It is not a passive apprehension. It should be thought of more along the lines of having a kind of reaction (re-*action*)—or better, a set of structured reactions. These reactions do not passively represent some fact or facts of the matter; rather, they are *responses*[26] to representations of facts of the matter. In turn, saying of an entity that it is an intentional system should not be thought of along the lines of *describing* some property the entity possesses but rather as the issuing of a *prescription* to others. It recommends a pragmatically valuable strategy for dealing with the entity; it is not a matter of representing or describing the entity as being thus and so.

On this point, such an approach to minds can be compared helpfully with noncognitivism in ethics. The noncognitivist about ethics claims that when we say "killing innocent people is wrong," we are not *describing* a *feature* of the world. Rather, we are *expressing* an *attitude* toward those who would engage in the killing of innocents. In turn, when the attitude is being expressed honestly, we say that we "believe" that killing is wrong; however, the noncognitivist insists that this is not a run-of-the-mill belief. Usually, we think of a belief as a state that *represents* the world as being thus and so. But the noncognitivist insists that this kind of belief is not a representation. Having a belief of this sort is a matter of being of a particular attitude. Accordingly, in uttering honestly "killing innocents is wrong," I am not describing a feature of the world but rather expressing my commitment to the wrongness of such killings and also prescribing this commitment to others. On this view, there simply are no independently existing moral features of the world that could be the object of a description.

To put it somewhat paradoxically, to advocate this sort of approach to minds is to be a noncognitivist about cogitation. Taking S to be an intentional system is not a matter of holding a true or false belief about something in the paradigmatic sense of having a true or false belief for the simple reason that it is not a paradigmatic form of belief. Accordingly, the appropriateness of believing or being of the attitude that S is an intentional system should not be evaluated in the exact same manner that a paradigmatic belief is. The proposal is that the proper way to evaluate it is in terms of its predictive value. The justification is provided not by accuracy of description, but by the pragmatic value of the predictive success that adopting the stance provides. It is right or wrong to treat S as an intentional system only with respect to the pragmatic value an agent can get from successful predictions based on treating something as an intentional system.

In connection with this, it is important to remember that there *is* a fact of the matter about whether there is such value to be had. That is perfectly *objective*. Still, that value is *relative* to the aims of an agent. This is why Dennett says, "The decision to adopt the strategy . . . is not intrinsically right or wrong."[27] That "intrinsically" is important. It can be *wrong* to fail to adopt the strategy. For instance, Dennett would say that the chess player who does not adopt the strategy toward Deep Blue would be making a *mistake*. The key, however, is to see that he is only making a mistake *given that he wants to beat Deep Blue*.[28] If you *want* to beat Deep Blue, you *should* adopt the intentional stance toward it. Thus, Dennett also says, "something is an intentional system only in relation to the strategies of someone who is trying to predict its behavior."[29] The 'should' in 'You should adopt the intentional stance toward S' is a hypothetical imperative. This gives us the second major point of agreement between Dennett's view and Berkeley's. It also gives us our first illuminating point of contrast.

First, the agreement: for Berkeley, like Dennett, being convinced that you are dealing with another mind is not a matter of having a paradigmatic kind of belief about something. In this sense, Berkeley, too, is a noncognitivist about other minds. Just as in Dennett's case, taking oneself to be engaged with another mind is not a matter of representing something as being a certain way. The reason for this should be clear already. According to Berkeley's metaphysics, there is nothing that could serve as a representation of a mind. Minds are unrepresentable. That is the very crux of Berkeley's version of the problem of other minds.

Moreover, in accordance with noncognitivism about the mind, to say 'S is a person' *cannot* be a description of any *natural* object for Berkeley. In Berkeley's case, the reason for this is simply that natural objects are passive things. Activity is not attributable to them. It would be the grossest of category mistakes to take activity to be a property of natural objects. Now, it is true that Berkeley does not share Dennett's or a typical noncognitivist's commitment to naturalism, but that does not in the least threaten his noncognitivism about the mind. The statement 'S is a person' cannot sensibly be taken to be a description of any *nonnatural* thing, either. Active things are persons, and 'S is a person' has no descriptive application with respect to either natural or nonnatural things—and this exhausts the alternatives. So, if we are to take the utterance of "S is a person" as an attempt to convey some information by way of providing a description, then the statement is contentless. Wittgenstein draws our attention to exactly this point in the *Philosophical Investigations*.

Suppose I say of a friend: "He is not an automaton."—What information is conveyed by this, and to whom would it be information? To a human being who meets him in ordinary circumstances? What information could it give him?

"I believe he is not an automaton," just like that, so far makes no sense.[30]

If taken as an attempt to convey information then, for the Berkelian, 'S is a person' misfires just as badly as 'I believe he is not an automaton' does. However, such statements do have a sensible nondescriptive, noninformation-conveying function. If we stop thinking of them as *cognitive* statements and instead think of them as *expressive* utterances, then we can easily imagine sensible uses for them. "Sam is a person" can be uttered quite sensibly to express my indignation at your treatment of Sam. I do not think you are *treating* him rightly. I say, "Sam is a person!" or "Sam is not an automaton!" to you, not to give you some information I believe you do not have, but to get you to change your *attitude* toward Sam. What I say is aimed at getting you to *do* something (i.e., to change the way you act toward Sam).

7. Contrasting Berkeley and Dennett

As deep as the similarities run between Berkeley and Dennett here, the differences run even deeper. The most important of them is the one to which I have already alluded: Dennett is a naturalist; Berkeley is not. For Dennett, the things toward which we take up the intentional stance are natural objects. It's just that to get the sought-after predictive value we seek, we apply to these natural objects precisely that which does not strictly and literally apply to them: a normative principle. That is the point of Dennett's (iii):

> iii. A system's behavior will consist of those acts it *would be rational* for an agent with those beliefs and desires to perform.

To get something valuable (i.e., predictions), we make attributions of mental states to natural objects. But to do this, we have to engage in a bit of pretense. We have to pretend that the entity in question is like a person; we have to pretend that it is rational. This bit of pretense requires the application of an idealization. In order to make the mental state attributions, "[o]ne starts with the ideal of perfect rationality and revises downward as circumstances dictate."[31] However, we never expect these things to live up to that ideal. Downward revision is inevitable and should be regarded as such from the get-go.

Now, we *do* make use of idealizations in science and thus make use of normative principles within the bounds of a purely naturalistic realm. When doing science, we often talk about how something *ought* to behave. We say things like, "A dropped object, like a rock, ought to accelerate toward the center of the earth." However, the 'ought' is derived from the 'is.' We get the proper application conditions of the oughts from carefully observing how in fact bodies have behaved in the past. But more to the point, the oughts do not actually apply to the object whose behavior we are trying to predict. The oughts are for *us*. They tell us what *we* ought to expect from natural objects in such-and-such circumstances. If rocks do not, in fact, behave the way we thought they ought to have, then this is evidence that *our* oughts are out of line with what they ought to be. The rocks aren't out of line; we are.

So, it is not that unusual to impose an idealization on a natural object. We just do so without expecting the object to live up to that idealization. We only expect it will more or less approximate it (and when it is less rather than more, we expect to be able to explain why). Similarly, when I take up the intentional stance toward something, I expect certain things from the entity. If the entity in question fails to live up to predictions made from the intentional stance, I have attributed to it too much rationality. *I* have made a mistake. I *ought* to do something. I ought to adjust my expectations downward.

However, the intentional stance gets us into much deeper normative waters than the common stock of scientific idealization does. This is due to the peculiar sort of idealization we are imposing upon the object of the intentional stance. We assume, for the sake of prediction, that it is *rational*. This assumption is what allows us to attribute to a natural object states *it* ought to have. The oughts involved are not just oughts for us, but also for the object. So, for the purposes of attributing beliefs, desires, etc., we take the "entity" to which we are attributing these states to be an *agent*. And of course, that is what we must do if we are to apply oughts. Strictly speaking, oughts only to apply to responsible things, persons, a.k.a. "agents."

8. The "Personal Stance"

I have been talking as if the class of intentional systems and the class of persons are coextensive. According to Dennett, they are not. All persons are intentional systems, but not all intentional systems are persons. While Dennett pretends to no authority over what constitutes the norms of rationality, he does not believe it includes idealized moral behavior. Instead, he recognizes a distinct version of the intentional stance, which we can call the "personal stance."[32] When we approach something from the personal stance, we attribute to it ideal morality and revise downward as circumstances dictate. But of course, as with the intentional stance, downward revision is inevitable; nothing is actually expected to live up to the ideal of perfect morality.[33]

We are now set to make the contrast between Berkeley and Dennett vivid, while at the same time using Dennett's work as a way to elucidate Berkeley's. While Berkeley would agree with Dennett that no natural object can ever live up to the idealizations involved in the various stances, Berkeley is not a naturalist. The natural world does not exhaust the real. Perfect rationality, perfect morality, *is* instantiated. God realizes these qualities. In Berkeley's philosophy, there is both the natural and nonnatural (i.e., the spiritual). And as we know from our review of Berkelian basics, the natural world is dependent upon the spiritual.

With this in hand, we can think of Berkeley's idealist epistemology as a bit like Dennett's but without the naturalism. According to Berkeley, the necessary precondition of having any kind of knowledge at all is the adopting of the personal stance—not to this or that particular thing but to *reality as a whole*.

A humane spirit or person is not perceived by sense, as not being an idea; when therefore we see the colour, size, figure, and motions of a man, we perceive only certain sensations or ideas excited in our own minds: and these being exhibited to our view in sundry distinct collections, serve to mark out unto us the existence of finite and created spirits like our selves. Hence it is plain, we do not see a man, if by man is meant that which lives, moves, perceives, and thinks as we do: but only such a certain collection of ideas, as directs us to think there is a distinct principle of thought and motion like to our selves, accompanying and represented by it. And after the same manner we see GOD; all the difference is, that whereas some one finite and narrow assemblage of ideas denotes a particular human mind, whithersoever we direct our view, we do at all times and in all places perceive manifest tokens of the divinity: every thing we see, hear, feel, or any wise perceive by sense, being a sign or effect of the Power of GOD; as is our perception of those very motions, which are produced by men.[34]

Berkelian idealism is the view that external reality as a whole is not, as the naturalist would have it, the vast collection of passive objects that constitute the natural world and which we aim to describe. Instead, external reality is an active thing, a mind, a will. It is God. The natural world, the vast collection of ideas of sense, merely provides mediation between us and that will; its status as real is dependent upon the existence of this spirit.

9. The Divine Language

> In the beginning was the pale signature,
> Three syllabled and starry as the smile;
> And after came the imprints on the water,
> Stamp of the minted face upon the moon;
> The blood that touched the crosstree and the grail
> Touched the first cloud and left a sign.
>
> —Dylan Thomas[35]

It is only through adopting the personal stance toward reality as a whole that the natural world becomes intelligible. Why? First, because, as Berkeley frequently reminds us, "General rules . . . are necessary to make the world intelligible."[36] Without the regular rules according to which God applies the ideas of sense to our minds, the natural world would be a blooming, buzzing confusion. However, these connections between events/ideas, considered in themselves, are perfectly arbitrary. There is no necessary connection between them. How then is it that we are able to find order in the world? Berkeley's answer is that the connections between events/ideas, which when considered by themselves are simply arbitrary, are rendered intelligible to us by our ability to approach the natural world as an appropriate object of *interpretation*.

[T]he phenomena of nature, which strike on the senses and are understood by the mind, form not only a magnificent spectacle, but also a most coherent, entertaining, and instructive Discourse; and to effect this, they are conducted, adjusted, and ranged by the greatest wisdom. This Language or Discourse is studied with different attention, and interpreted with different degrees of skill. But so far as men have studied and remarked its rules, and can interpret right, so far they may be said to be knowing in nature. A beast is like a man who hears a strange tongue but understands nothing.[37]

The regularities we rely upon to make sense of nature are *linguistic* regularities. It is Berkeley's view that "[i]deas which are observed to be connected together are vulgarly considered under the relation of cause and effect, whereas, in strict and philosophic truth, they are only related as the sign to the thing signified."[38]

We must adopt the personal stance toward reality because the way that the world is rendered intelligible to us is by our taking up the attitude necessary to treat nature as *interpretable*. Just as finite human minds use the passive things of the natural world as means of communication, so does the infinite mind, which is God.

[The] Author of Nature constantly explaineth himself to the eyes of men by the sensible intervention of arbitrary signs, which have no similitude or connexion with the things signified; so as, by compounding and disposing them, to suggest and exhibit an endless variety of objects, differing in nature, time, and place; thereby informing and directing men how to act with respect to things distant and future, as well as near and present.[39]

The thesis that the intelligibility of nature depends upon its interpretability is one of Berkeley's earliest and remains constant throughout his work. The point is so important to Berkeley that it forms a central theme of his first major publication, *An Essay towards a New Theory of Vision.*[40]

Upon the whole, I think we may fairly conclude, that the proper objects of vision constitute an universal language of the Author of nature, whereby we are instructed how to regulate our actions, in order to attain those things that are necessary to the preservation and well-being of our bodies, as also to avoid whatever may be hurtful and destructive of them. It is by their information that we are principally guided in all the transactions and concerns of life. And the manner wherein they signify, and mark unto us the objects which are at a distance, is the same with that of languages and signs of human appointment, which do not suggest the things signified, by any likeness or identity of nature, but only by an habitual connexion, that experience has made us to observe between them.[41]

This ability to approach the world in a manner appropriate to dealing with a discourse is essential to our nature as responsible things. Our development into personhood tracks our developing ability to be able to take up the personal stance. It is an essential part of the process of becoming a person that we be able to respond appropriately to other persons. Furthermore, essential to being able to take up the personal stance, and thus essential to becoming a person, is a mastery of communication. Again, it is through our ability to respond appropriately to signs of sign use that we solve the "problem of other minds." And, as we already know, being able to communicate requires an ability to interpret. On Berkeley's view, from the womb to the grave, God is communicating with us, training us to be interacting persons, the sorts of things to which ascriptions of responsibility strictly, literally, and justifiably apply.[42] In Berkeley's metaphysics, it would seem that things are much as John 1:1 would have it, "In the beginning was the Word."

10. The Religious Stance: Trust and Faith

I have been calling the Berkelian stance toward reality the "personal stance," but this is misleading. It is characteristic of the personal stance that we do not actually expect ideal rationality or morality from the object of that stance. If we did, we would never regard finite minds as persons. We should contrast the personal stance as it is applied to finite spirits (with its concomitant expectation that the object of the stance will not live up to the idealizations) with a special version of the personal stance in which one does *not* abandon the expectation that the object of the attitude does and will live up to the idealization. I think it only appropriate that this latter stance be called the "religious stance."

With the religious stance comes a subtle but important change in the nature of the attitude one takes toward its object. From the attitude of the personal stance, we attribute states to something and form expectations about how it will behave. We say that, given that S believes that-p and desires that-q, S *ought* to do such and such. In making these predictions about the future behavior of the agent, we adopt an attitude of *trust* toward it. We know that humans do not always live up to what they ought to do, but to treat someone *as a person* is to give him the benefit of the doubt, to trust him, until he proves himself untrustworthy. We act toward him with as much trust as he *deserves*. Trust is defeasible.

In contrast, from the religious stance, our attitude is much like trust, but it is nondefeasible. Trust in this unique form is appropriately called "faith." To be of the religious attitude is to have a sort of ironclad trust toward *reality*. It is to believe that all things will ultimately fall out as they should.

One peculiar, yet certainly fitting, consequence of the preceding considerations is that, in the Berkelian epistemology, *faith* is the foundational attitude upon which all knowledge and, to be sure, our very existence depends. Consider what some have called the implicit "animal faith" we have in the regularity of causation. When considered not as signs but instead as merely a vast succession of passive things, the objects of the natural world exhibit no necessary connection with one another. Here, Berkeley and Hume are in complete agreement. My past and present perceptions provide no basis for valid inferences about how the future will fall out. From a purely passive perspective, their connection with one another is perfectly arbitrary. Nonetheless, we do not *act* as if they were arbitrarily connected. On the contrary, we act as if they were necessarily connected. And, once again, that's a good thing. Our survival depends upon our so acting. We have an implicit trust that things will continue in regular (i.e., interpretable) patterns. But this is no ordinary kind of trust. It is ironclad, nondefeasible trust. We go about our days exhibiting complete confidence in the continued regularity of the course of nature. As Hume put it, "When we have been accustomed to see one object united to another, our imagination passes from the first to the second by a natural transition, which precedes reflection, and which cannot be prevented by it."[43] This kind of trust has an irresistible hold on us. What the Berkelian will now draw your attention to is that this is exactly the form of trust we would have if we were to treat the natural world as a whole as something which is interpretable. An idea, *if treated as a sign*, carries our mind immediately, unhesitatingly, without anything resembling doubt, to that which it signifies. *If considered as a sign*, a sensible thing is *necessarily connected* with that which it signifies and thus is deserving of the implicit "trust" with which our thought moves from the idea of a cause to the expectation of its effect. If not considered as signs, sensible things bear no necessary relation to each other. In and of themselves, there is nothing to justify our attitudes and expectations of necessary connection. We can dig as deeply into the inner core of the "real essences" of objects as we like but in the end will find that there is no naturalistic property that can account for causal necessity. Thus, the divine language thesis opens the door for the development of a uniquely Berkelian take on causal realism, capturing, as it does, *the sense in which objects are only contingently related while at the same time providing justification for our beliefs in their necessary connection*. The latter relies ultimately on the good will of an agent who keeps his *covenants*, whose signs are infallibly reliable—in a word, faithworthy.[44] As Wittgenstein once wrote, "Religious belief and superstition are quite different. One of them results from fear and is a sort of false science. The other is a trusting."[45]

11. Conclusion

We are now armed with a better understanding of what is required of spirits if they are to successfully navigate their way through the world. This, in turn, gives us some idea of just what sort of things spirits must *be* in order to inhabit such a place. With the discussion of this chapter as background, I turn to the task of providing an account of the nature of Berkelian spirits in the next chapter.

IV

Resurrecting Berkelian Spirits

Spirits Are Forensic Unities

> But the Grand Mistake is that we know not what we mean by 'we' or 'selves' or 'mind' etc. 'tis most sure & certain that our Ideas are distinct from the Mind i.e. the Will, the Spirit.[1]

1. The Problem

Since Berkeley left us no detailed account of spirits, one would expect that assessments of the viability of his conception of spirits turn on matters of interpretation. But one would be disappointed. Appraisals of his view typically run the narrow gamut from finding it deeply problematic to finding it outright incoherent. The simple and discouraging fact is that on any currently available interpretation, the experts tend to agree: Berkeley's view faces serious, probably fatal problems. To date, three interpretive options have dominated the discussion. The first takes spirits to be bundles; the second takes spirits to be Cartesian substances; the third takes spirits to be Lockean substratum substances.

We already met the bundle interpretation in chapter I. What we found is that this interpretation of spirits would certainly seem to justify pessimism. Spirits are *simple* substances and the principle and ground of unity in Berkeley's metaphysics. If he conceived of spirits as bundles of any sort, then it certainly seems that his view of them would be not merely problematic but incoherent.

The second option, which is to interpret Berkeley's spiritual substances along Cartesian lines, is both more promising and more popular.[2] Since Cartesian minds are *simple* substances, this approach has the clear advantage of taking the essential unity of spirits seriously. But as advocates for the Cartesian reading acknowledge, this advantage brings with it a particularly nasty problem. While both spirits and Cartesian substances are alike in being simple substances, they differ in that Cartesian minds are "thinking things" and spirits are not—at least, not exactly. When Berkeley is speaking most strictly, he tells us that a "soul or spirit is an active being,"[3] an "incorporeal active substance";[4] it is "one simple, undivided, active being."[5] In short, spirits are not "thinking things" but rather "active things." This difference is also what creates trouble; one will want to know how spirits can be both *simple* and *active* if, in perceiving ideas, they must be *passive*.[6] As Berkeley writes at one point, "That the soul of man is passive as well as active, I make no doubt."[7] It does seem difficult to doubt, but it also seems equally difficult to reconcile with a simple substance view of spirits. As Charles McCracken notes,

> It cannot simply be that 'the substance of a spirit is that it acts, causes, wills, operates'—for that will not explain how a spirit can passively perceive. Nor can it simply be that a spirit is a thing that perceives . . . for that will not explain its capacity to act and will.[8]

So it seems that spirits must be both active and passive in nature and, therefore, not simple. From here on, I will refer to this problem as the "Central Problem."

The third interpretive option fares a bit better against the Central Problem. It advocates that we see spirits as Lockean substratum substances. The chief advantage here is that the will and the understanding can be treated as separate faculties, the former active and the latter passive, but both are then united by a common substratum. As we will see, this does make trouble for understanding the *simplicity* of spirits, but it at least has the advantage of taking Berkeley's claim that spirits are *substances* seriously, more seriously than a bundle interpretation does. Unfortunately, this latter advantage is probably only nominal. The Lockean reading of spirits may initially distance itself from incoherence, but then it courts her close cousin, inconsistency. Berkeley's attack on Lockean material substratum substances is one of the showpieces of his immaterialism. If he conceives of spirits as substratum substances, then it would certainly seem that Philonous is left pinned and wriggling on the wall when, in the "Third Dialogue," Hylas informs him, "Notwithstanding all you have said, to me it seems, that according to your own way of thinking, and in consequence of your own principles, it should follow that you are only a system of floating ideas, without any *substance* to *support* them."[9] And, "To act consistently, you must either admit matter or reject spirit."[10] Consequently, one has to admit that this line of interpretation is not terribly attractive.[11]

In what follows, I propose an alternative interpretation of spirits according to which spirits must be understood as a hybrid of, on the one hand, Cartesian *substances*—but not Cartesian *minds*[12]—and, on the other hand, Lockean *persons*—but not Lockean *substances*. The matchmaker in this somewhat audacious pairing of a Cartesian view of substances with a Lockean view of persons is Berkeley's understanding of the active/passive distinction. The result is a surprisingly harmonious marriage, one that allows us to solve the Central Problem by introducing an important modification in the Cartesian view of the nature of substantial unity.

My first task will be to back up a bit, lay out the attractions of a Cartesian interpretation of Berkelian spirits, and then clarify the distinctive features of Berkeley's view of spirits that must be squared with a Cartesian reading. This will provide us with a list of claims (A–I) that Berkeley either makes explicitly or that can be safely inferred about the nature of spirits. The result will be an elucidation of the chief characteristics of Berkelian spirits. This will then, in turn, provide us with an interpretation of the cardinal distinction of Berkeley's metaphysics, the active/passive distinction. This interpretation of the active/passive distinction reveals the key point of connection between Berkeley's conception of spirits and Locke's conception of persons. I then argue that Berkeley's modified Cartesian view of spirits neatly maps onto Locke's persons, providing an account of spirits as *simple, active substances*. Finally, since this is ultimately a Cartesian interpretation of spirits, I return to and show how this interpretation of spirits allows us to dispense with the Central Problem.

2. Spirits as Cartesian Substances

Why should we think of spirits along Cartesian lines? For starters, there is good reason to think of Berkeley as working within the same overall metaphysical tradition as Descartes. As Berkeley himself puts it,

> Anaxagoras, wisest of men, was the first to grasp the great difference between thinking things and extended things, and he asserted that the mind has nothing in common with bodies. . . . Of the moderns Descartes has put the same point most forcibly. What was left clear by him others have rendered involved and difficult by their obscure terms.[13]

We can see something of Descartes' signature bifurcation of being reflected in Berkeley's distinction between *spirits* and *ideas*. Like Descartes' thinking and extended things, Berkeley's spirits and ideas "have nothing in common but the name."[14] Of course, one important difference lies in Descartes' denial of any priority ordering between mind and body and his subsequent treatment of them as *independent* existents. We might say that Berkeley shares Descartes' stark bifurcation of being but does not interpret that as supporting a *substance* dualism.

This alone makes it natural to think of Berkeley as a Cartesian, only a more austere one who found a way to take the already lean Cartesian ontology and cut it in half, eliminating material substances in favor of an ontology consisting entirely of mental substances. But when we turn to what Berkeley has to say about these remaining substances, we find even more reason to think of him as a kind of Cartesian.

First, both spirits and Cartesian minds are, of course, *immaterial* beings. Second, as we've already touched on, spirits, like Cartesian minds, are *simple substances* and, in fact, echoing Descartes' famous argument from the "Sixth Meditation," Berkeley explicitly infers their natural immortality from the fact that they are unextended and consequently indivisible.[15] Third, for both Descartes and Berkeley, strictly speaking, the mind *is* the soul. So, according to Berkeley, "What I am my self, that which I denote by the term 'I', is the same with what is meant by 'soul' or 'spiritual substance'."[16] A soul is not something one *has* but something one *is*. Fourth, Berkeley is often comfortable using Cartesian language to talk about spirits, sometimes referring to them as "thinking substances"[17] and "thinking things."[18] Fifth, spirits, like Cartesian minds, are *always thinking*—more precisely, *always active*.

This last point brings us to both the key point of similarity and the pivotal point of contrast. Again, the most important feature of a Cartesian substance is that its *being* coincides with its *essence*. In the case of mental substances, *to be* is to be *thinking*. And so, on the Cartesian view, the statements "S is a mind" and "S is not thinking" are inconsistent. Therefore, contra Locke, the mind is always thinking.

Berkeley also identifies a spirit's being with its essence.

> Things are two-fold active, or inactive. The existence of Active things is to act, of inactive, to be perceived.[19]

However, as this quotation reminds us, Berkeley does not take *thought* to be the essence of spirit. It is true that, for all the reasons already given, it is often perfectly acceptable, and likewise expedient, to speak of spirits as "thinking" substances; however, when Berkeley is speaking most strictly, he employs the language of the fundamental categories of his metaphysics. A spirit is an "active being." As far as spirits are concerned, *to be* is *to be active*.

> Substance of a Spirit is that it acts, causes, wills, operates.[20]

Here, we have the principal point of similarity as well as the principal point of contrast between spirits and Cartesian minds.

A. Spirits are *Cartesian substances* in that their *being* and their *essence* coincide.
B. However, spirits are not identical to Cartesian *mental* substances because their essence is *activity*, rather than *thought*.

What this means is that if we are to understand Berkeley's view of spirits, we must understand what distinguishes them from Cartesian minds, and this requires that we focus our attention on just what Berkeley means by "active" and "activity."

The good news is that while Berkeley did not leave us a separate work on spirit, what he left us on this particular topic is illuminating.

C. Activity is *volition*.

Coming to grips with the import of (C) is no trivial task. As we are (so very well) aware, the active/passive distinction is Berkeley's fundamental distinction. So, by identifying activity with volition, Berkeley has placed volition right at the foundation of his philosophy. Moreover, he has done so in such a way as to divide his ontology into the active and the inactive (passive). In other words, the world is divided into the *volitional* and *nonvolitional*. The aim of the rest of this section is to go beyond the ABCs by mapping out Berkeley's understanding of the relationship between volition and a few key, related concepts.

We can begin with a now-familiar point:

D. Only spirits are causes.

I take it that (D) is already well established and need not be labored. It is necessary to begin with it, however, not only because of its fundamental importance but also because it is tightly connected with (E).

E. Causation is volition.

It is Berkeley's view that

> [t]here are no Causes (properly speaking) but Spiritual, nothing active but Spirit.[21]

Since only spirits are causes (D), true causation is the activity of a spirit, and since activity is volition (C), all instances of causation are instances of volition.

The next point, (F), is closely connected in Berkeley's thought with both (D) and (E). We must separate the concepts of *activity* and *motion*, because activity is volition and "[m]otion is one thing and volition another."[22] Unlike volition, motion is *perceivable*, and so we know it to be *passive*.

> There is no other agent or efficient cause than spirit, it being evident that motion, as well as all other ideas, is perfectly inert.[23]

The point was one he was keen to make even as early as the *Commentaries*.

> Silly of Hobbes etc. to speak of ye Will as if it were Motion with which it has no likeness.[24]

And so we have:

> F. Motion is not activity.

Interconnected with (F), as well as (E), is:

> G. Action is volition.

In the "Third Dialogue" between Hylas and Philonous, Berkeley makes it clear that he regards the relationship between *action* and *volition* as an identity.

> I have a mind to have some notion or meaning in what I say; but I have no notion of any action distinct from volition, neither can I conceive volition to be any where but in a spirit: therefore when I speak of an active being, I am obliged to mean a spirit.[25]

Item (G) is also tightly interconnected with (C) and (D). To be active is to *act*, to engage in *actions*, not to merely *move*. Passive things can move, but only agents act. So, for instance, in the "Second Dialogue," we have the following important exchange:

> Hylas: There is indeed something in what you say. But I am afraid you do not thoroughly comprehend my meaning....All I contend for, is that...there is a cause of a limited and inferior nature, which concurs in the production of our ideas, not by any act of will or spiritual efficiency, but by that kind of action which belongs to matter, viz. *motion*.[26]
>
> Philonous: ...I ask whether all your ideas are not perfectly passive and inert, including nothing of action in them?
>
> Hylas: They are.
>
> Philonous: And are sensible qualities any thing else but ideas?
>
> Hylas: How often have I acknowledged that they are not?
>
> Philonous: But is not motion a sensible quality?
>
> Hylas: It is.
>
> Philonous: Consequently it is no action.
>
> Hylas: I agree with you. And indeed it is very plain, that when I stir my finger, it remains passive; but my will which produced the motion, is active.
>
> Philonous: Now I desire to know in the first place, whether motion being allowed to be no action, you can conceive any action besides volition: and in the

second place, whether to say something and conceive nothing be not to talk nonsense: and lastly, whether having considered the premises, you do not perceive that to suppose any efficient or active cause of our ideas, other than spirit, is highly absurd and unreasonable?[27]

This exchange illustrates a number of points. In addition to clarifying *activity* by way of separating it from *motion* (E), we also learn that Berkeley not only identifies *activity* with *volition* but that he treats the terms 'act,' 'activity,' and 'action' as interchangeable. So we have:

H. 'Act,' 'activity,' 'action,' and 'volition' are equivalent terms.

Now, in light of the preceding points and the fact that Berkeley uses the terms 'agent' and 'spirit' interchangeably, it will be no surprise to learn that the other term he uses for spirit is 'will.' We saw this already in what will now be a familiar quotation from chapter I.

So far as I can see, the words *will, soul, spirit,* do not stand for different ideas, or in truth, for any idea at all, but for something which is very different from ideas, and which being an *agent* cannot be like unto, or represented by, any idea whatsoever.[28]

This point must be understood against the backdrop of points (A–H) but with special focus on points (A, B, C). Spirits are Cartesian substances (A), whose essence is activity (B). So spirits are not "thinking things"; they are "active things." Since activity is volition (C), spirits are "volitional things." And so, as Berkeley says, "The soul is the will properly speaking."[29]

I. Spirits are wills.

As with the term 'soul,' the term 'will' does not denote something one *has*. One *is* a will. This is true of both finite spirits (e.g., us) and the Infinite Spirit (i.e., God).

The Spirit, the Active thing, that which is Soul & God is the Will alone.[30]

The last two quotations are, of course, from the *Commentaries*, but the point is at work in the very basics of his mature philosophy. If Berkeley did not identify the mind with the will, he would not be able to dispatch with solipsism so quickly.

But whatever power I may have over my own thoughts, I find the ideas actually perceived by sense have not a like dependence on my will. When in broad day-light I open my eyes, it is not in my power to choose whether I shall see or no, or to determine what particular objects shall present themselves to my view; and so likewise as to the hearing and other senses, the ideas imprinted on them are not creatures of my will. There is therefore some other will or spirit that produces them.[31]

If I were not identical to my will, I would not be able to draw the conclusion that *anything* distinct from myself, let alone another spirit, exists. So, in the *Commentaries*, Berkeley notes the following point:

Locke in his 4th book & Descartes in Med. 6. use the same argument for the Existence of objects viz. that sometimes we see feel etc against our will.[32]

The first passage referred to is from Locke's *Treatise*, IV.xi.5.

I find, that I cannot avoid the having those ideas produced in my mind. For though when my eyes are shut, or windows fast, I can at pleasure recall to my mind the ideas of light, or the sun, which former sensations had lodged in my memory; so I can at pleasure lay by that idea, and take into my view that of the smell of a rose, or taste of sugar. But, if I turn my eyes at noon towards the sun, I cannot avoid the ideas, which the light, or sun, then produces in me. So that there is a manifest difference between the ideas laid up in my memory, (over which, if they were there only, I should have constantly the same power to dispose of them, and lay them by at pleasure) and those which force themselves upon me, and I cannot avoid having. And therefore it must needs be some exterior cause, and the brisk acting of some objects without me, whose efficacy I cannot resist, that produces those ideas in my mind, whether I will or no.

The passage from Descartes to which Berkeley referred is from the "Sixth Meditation," but for present purposes, its content is more clearly stated in the "Third Meditation":

But the chief question at this point concerns the ideas which I take to be derived from things existing outside me: ... I know by experience that these ideas do not depend on my will, and hence that they do not depend simply on me. Frequently I notice them even when I do not want to: now, for example, I feel the heat whether I want to or not, and this is why I think that this sensation or idea of heat comes to me from something other than myself, namely the heat of the fire by which I am sitting.[33]

Both Locke and Descartes are using what Berkeley refers to as the *passivity* of the ideas of sense—the fact that we are passive recipients of our perceptions—to infer the existence of *something* existing external to ourselves, something distinct from ourselves. What distinguishes Berkeley's use of this is that he identifies *causation* with *activity* and *activity* with *volition*, and thus the *self* with the *will*. Therefore, he alone is in the position to infer from the passivity of perception the existence of something distinct from ourselves. Since, I am identical to my *will*, what occurs *independently* of my will implies the existence of something *distinct* from myself. Neither Locke nor Descartes is in the position to draw this inference. Neither identifies activity/causation with volition, and neither identifies the self with the will. At best, all either can infer from the passivity of perception alone is that *something* with causal powers is responsible for these ideas.[34] Since causation is not identified with volition, the possibility is left open that I am, after all, the cause of these passively received ideas. Descartes initially denies this in the quoted passage. "I know by experience that these ideas do not depend on my will, and hence that they do not depend simply on me," but then corrects himself,

[A]lthough these ideas do not depend on my will, it does not follow that they must come from things located outside me. ... there may be some other faculty not yet fully known to me, which produces these ideas without any assistance from external things.[35]

On Berkeley's view, a spirit's very being is volition. So there can be no other "faculties" than the will. But Descartes does not make this identification. For Descartes, volition is just one of the many modes of thought, whereas for Berkeley, thought is one of the modes of volition. (We will return to this latter point soon.)

Furthermore, since according to Berkeley, the only form of causation is volition, only he can immediately derive that the *cause* of his ideas is not just "something" distinct from himself but that it must be a will (i.e., a spirit).[36]

Connected with these last two points is another advantage Berkeley accrues by way of his modification of the Cartesian account of minds. For Descartes, imagining, doubting, wishing, loathing, willing, etc., all are modes of thought; they are all ways of thinking. So where Berkeley identifies the mind with the will, Descartes identifies the mind with the *understanding*. Consequently, of special interest in connection with (I) is that Descartes regards *sensing*, the having of what Berkeley calls "ideas of sense," as modes of thought as well. Now, one problem with this, as Berkeley points out, is that taking sensations to be modes of the mind opens the door to Humeanism, wherein the self is *identified* with its ideas. In contrast, no such temptation is present on Berkeley's view. To recall this chapter's opening quotation:

> But the Grand Mistake is that we know not what we mean by 'we' or 'selves' or 'mind' etc. 'tis most sure & certain that our Ideas are distinct from the Mind i.e. the Will, the Spirit.[37]

Berkeley's identification of mind with the will allows for a very robust bifurcation of being: spirits are *active*. Ideas of sense are *inactive*. And so the self

> is plainly it self no idea, nor like an idea. Ideas are things inactive, and perceived: and spirits a sort of beings altogether different from them.[38]

Sensations just happen to us; we are subject to them; we "suffer" them. No matter what we will, we cannot avoid having some sensation or other. To say that a sensation is "mine" or is "in me" is merely to say that it is one to which I am being subjected. It neither "inheres in me" nor is it a "mode of myself."[39]

In contrast, Descartes' treating our perceptions as modes of the mind, and thus modes of ourselves, tempts precisely the trouble in which Hume found himself. As Hume writes in the "Appendix":

> [H]aving thus loosened all our particular perceptions, when I proceed to explain the principle of connexion, which binds them together, and makes us attribute to them a real simplicity and identity, I am sensible that my account is very defective.[40]

But on Berkeley's view, the self is Hume's sought-for "principle of connexion." The term 'principle' is even one of the names that Berkeley often uses interchangeably with 'spirit,' 'soul,' and 'will.' In fact, he uses it precisely as he is trying to draw people away from the trouble with which Hume would later find himself struggling.

> An active mind or spirit, cannot be an idea, or like an idea. Whence it should seem to follow that those words which denote an active *principle*, soul, or spirit do not, in a strict and proper sense, stand for ideas.[41]

Again, spirits are the source, the principle of unity in Berkeley's philosophy. Hume's extreme version of concept empiricism effectively cuts him off from finding any genuine unity, anything that could play that role. As Berkeley has already argued, no such principle is to be found in the realm of the sensible.[42] Here, then, are the ABCs of spirits:

A. Spirits are *Cartesian substances* in that their *being* and their *essence* coincide.
B. However, spirits are not Cartesian *minds* because their essence is *activity*, not *thought*.
C. Activity is volition.
D. Only spirits are causes.
E. Causation is volition.
F. Motion is not activity.
G. Action is volition.
H. 'Act,' 'activity,' 'action,' and 'volition' are equivalent terms.
I. Spirits are volitional beings; they are wills.

3. An Interpretation of the Active/Passive Distinction

What we are in a position to do now is to bring together these ABCs of spirits and the discussion of the previous chapter to give us something we sorely need, an interpretation of the active/passive distinction.

Now, of course, in chapter III our concerns were primarily epistemological, not ontological. We were interested in uncovering the nature of our knowledge of other minds. What we found was that seeing something as a mind is a matter of *treating* it as a mind. And treating something as a mind is a matter of engaging it in an *evaluative activity*. We did not have much to say about just what minds are. Instead, we followed the contemporary path of starting with the epistemology of the mental. But what our investigation in this chapter has revealed is that, in Berkeley's conception of spirits, we have an ontology that perfectly fits that epistemology.

On Berkeley's view, spirits are essentially evaluative beings. That is to say, it is their very nature to be the proper objects of oughts and shoulds. It is this characteristic that distinguishes them from the mere objects of the world. But this characteristic is not just an attribute in the sense of being a property inhering in or supported by a substance. Rather, it is the *principal attribute* of spirits in the Cartesian sense of "principal attribute." It is the essence, the very being, of a Berkelian spirit. This follows simply from the fact that spirits are volitional beings, and volition is, of course, precisely that which makes something, strictly and literally, an appropriate subject of those sorts of evaluative activities.

Given this and the elucidation provided by the ABCs of spirits, the most sensible reading of the active/passive distinction is the following:

> To be active is to be the sort of thing that is appropriate to evaluate from the point of view of normative responsibility. To be passive is to not be an appropriate subject of responsibility ascriptions.

Passive things do not *act*; they only *move*. For Berkeley, all and only things that are strictly and literally appropriate subjects of responsibility ascriptions are active. We are not, strictly speaking, "thinking things." We are, rather, "responsible things."

What we have found is that Berkeley's basic, irreducible metaphysical distinction, the active/passive distinction, is a *normative* distinction. It divides reality into the responsible and the nonresponsible. For the naturalist, appreciating the significance of this point requires a rather dramatic shift of perspective. For the naturalistic philosopher, the Holy Grail, so to speak, of philosophy is the accommodation of the normative within the natural. The oughts and shoulds of the world must be seen as (in some sense) arising out of a (in some sense) more basic reality that contains no such things. The normative must be reducible to, or supervene upon, etc., the nonnormative. It must be *dependent* upon the natural.

Berkeley's approach is precisely the opposite. It is the normative that is treated as irreducible, basic. The natural world, the world of sense, depends upon it. So, for instance, a naturalist might attempt to accommodate volitions by taking causation as basic and then identify volitions as a certain subset of causal events that meets such-and-such specified conditions. Berkeley, however, takes volition as basic and treats what the naturalist regards as "causal" relations between nonspiritual objects as sign-signified relations, where that relation is treated as a species of normative relation. In short, where the naturalist seeks to cook up the normative out of wholly and irreducibly nonnormative ingredients, Berkeley seeks to cook up the natural world out of wholly and irreducibly normative ingredients.

While a clear understanding of the active/passive distinction is obviously necessary to providing a successful account of spirits, it is not sufficient. We are not yet in place to resolve the Central Problem. Before we can do that, we have to sort out the relationship between spirits and Lockean persons.

4. Spirits as Lockean Persons I: Tipton's Version

At several points in earlier chapters, I have emphasized the ways in which Berkeley, while certainly critical of Locke over key issues, was deeply influenced by Locke and genuinely appreciative of his genius. Now given this and given the fact that Berkeley's is a spirit-based metaphysics in which only *selves* are true substances, it is sensible to suspect that Berkeley would have been a close student of Locke's famous chapter "On Identity and Diversity," where he takes up the issues of the nature of selves and persons and the role of substance in matters of identity.[43]

Now Locke, like many of his past and present readers, takes his central contribution with respect to identity to be the insight that before we can answer the question 'Are α and β one and the same?' we must first know the answer to the question 'The same *what*?' Questions of identity only make sense in the context of some kind or sortal term because identity conditions differ for different kind of things. So, for instance, the large, impressive, Spanish moss–draped tree growing in front of my house is the same *plant* as the little flimsy thing my elderly neighbor planted some fifty years ago, but it is certainly not the same *mass of matter* she planted fifty years ago. The identity conditions for masses of matter are different from the identity conditions for plants. Even if not a single constituent of that original mass remains from fifty years ago, it does not follow that the tree does not remain.

> [Co]nsider wherein an oak differs from a mass of matter, and that seems to me to be in this, that the one is only the cohesion of particles of matter any how united, the other such a disposition of them as constitutes the parts of an oak; and such an organization

of those parts as is fit to receive and distribute nourishment, so as to continue and frame the wood, bark, and leaves, &c. of an oak, in which consists the vegetable life. That being then one plant which has such an organization of parts in one coherent body partaking of one common life, it continues to be the same plant as long as it partakes of the same life, though that life be communicated to new particles of matter vitally united to the living plant, in a like continued organization conformable to that sort of plants.[44]

As Locke's discussion moves forward, such considerations allow him to separate matters concerning sameness of *person* from matters concerning sameness of *substance*. As Locke saw it, substances could be flowing in and out of us qua persons like water drops in a river. What matters to personal identity is *continuity of consciousness*. So, to simplify a bit, if a substantial being (S_1) existing at some point in time (t_1) performs some action at t_1, and, if at some later time (t_2) a substantial being (S_2) remembers performing that action, then S_1 at t_1 and S_2 at t_2 are the same person, even though they are not identical with respect to substance. If S_2 can remember that act as being hers, then S_2 is the appropriate subject of praise or blame. If S_2 is incapable of being able to remember that act as one she committed, then S_2 is not an appropriate subject of praise or blame. Sameness of substance just doesn't figure in as relevant to what we care about when we care about personal identity. It is unity of consciousness that matters. On Judgment Day, one hopes for or fears the continuity of oneself qua conscious being in the afterlife. We have no concern for the fate of substrata.

Working with this aspect of Locke's discussion of identity in mind, I. C. Tipton has attempted to deepen our understanding of the nature of Berkeley's spirits via the possibility of a connection between them and Lockean persons.[45] In support of such a connection, he draws our attention to an early entry, 14, from Berkeley's notebooks:

> Eternity is onely a train of innumerable ideas. Hence the immortality of ye soul easily conceived. or rather the immortality of the person, y^t of ye soul not being necessary ought we can see.[46]

Tipton is clearly onto something. In this entry, Berkeley certainly appears to be thinking along Lockean lines by way of invoking a distinction between "souls" and "persons" and identifying what matters as the status of the "person" after death, as opposed to the "soul." To make the distinction match Locke's, Berkeley's use of 'soul' here must be taken to line up with Locke's spiritual substratum substance. Obviously, this is not how Berkeley will continue to use 'soul,' but of course, this is a notebook entry and an early one at that. It is too early for final decisions about the most perspicuous choice of terms. The important point is the drawing of a decidedly Lockean distinction wherein the status of the person is identified as what matters.

There is one other point relevant to Tipton's interpretation. According to Berkeley, "the being of my self, that is, my own soul, mind or thinking principle, I evidently know by reflexion."[47] Similarly, according to Locke, unlike our spiritual substratum, the being of the self, the person, is known immediately and with certainty. As Locke sees it, "we perceive it so plainly and so certainly, that it neither needs nor is capable of any proof."[48] With this point in place, Tipton is then able to see Berkeley's basic move as being fairly simple. He sheds Locke's spiritual substrata

and identifies spirits with Locke's conception of the person, in which this is understood to be "the conscious thing we are all aware of in all experience, the *esse* of which
is just to be conscious or *percipere*."[49] Tipton then sums up his understanding of the
development of Berkelian spirits out of Lockean persons:

> In the simplest terms the development is from an acceptance of the distinction be-
> tween soul or spiritual substance on the one hand and the person on the other, through
> the rejection of the first to the acceptance of the second as a substance which supports
> ideas in the sense that it perceives them. This move parallels the move he makes in his
> analysis of the objects of sense experience.[50]

But here we have clearly hit a serious problem for Tipton's interpretation. The
aforementioned parallel move with respect to objects of sense experience ends with
an account of them as *bundles*. So if Tipton's characterization of the development of
Berkelian spirits out of Lockean persons is truly parallel to the development of his
analysis of the objects of sense experience, it follows that spirits are going to have to
be bundles of some sort. And in fact, that appears to be Tipton's conclusion. As he
sees it, Berkeley regards spirits as individuals in something like the way a *herd* is an
individual.[51]

The problem that then faces Tipton's interpretation is that whatever metaphysical status herds enjoy, they are not *simple substances*, but Berkeley's spirits are.
A herd may be an "individual" in one loose sense of the term—and, therefore, a
"substance" in one loose sense of the term—but herds are neither individuals nor
substances in the strict sense in which spirits are. Therefore, as with the other versions
of the bundle interpretation, Tipton's must deal with the arguments of chapter I.

That said, it should seem that if Locke's distinction between persons and their
substratum substances is to help shed light on Berkeley's view of spirits, it can, at
best, only shed partial light. It will not help us with the Central Problem because it
does not help us to understand the sense in which spirits are simple substances.

5. Spirits as Lockean Persons II: An Alternate Account

While Tipton's interpretation must be rejected, I still think the basic idea behind it
is sound. Berkeley's view of spirits is, in part, a development of his understanding of
Locke's insights about persons. However, to see the relationship between spirits and
Lockean persons properly, we must first review the basic shape of Berkeley's attack
on Locke's *material* substratum substances and then see what does happen if we
pursue parity with respect to persons and spiritual substrata.

With respect to Berkeley's attack on material substrata, it is helpful to remember that Locke set the stage for Berkeley's immaterialism by taking the bold
step of stripping from substance many of its traditional roles. However, as we know,
he did not eliminate the category of substance from his metaphysics. Although not
the workhorse it was for others, Locke still saw a need for it.

> [I]f any one will examine himself concerning his notion of pure substance in general,
> he will find he has no other idea of it at all, but only a supposition of he knows not
> what support of such qualities, which are capable of producing simple ideas in us.[52]

The notion of 'support' is invoked to explain the sense in which qualities belong to a substance and thereby belong to one thing. What a substance provides support for are certain "qualities, which are capable of producing simple ideas in us."[53] These qualities are what Locke calls "powers." So, for instance,

> the power of drawing iron, is one of the ideas of the complex one of that substance we call a load-stone; and a power to be so drawn is a part of the complex one we call iron: Which powers pass for inherent qualities in those subjects.[54]

It is via our understanding of its power or powers that we have the "perfectest Idea of any of the particular sorts of substance."[55] But, of course, Berkeley famously argues that no concept of such a substance is to be had. The central problem is that "supporting" is itself an instance of (what Locke would call) a power. So in attempting to explain this concept of "substance," we are referred to our understanding of one kind of power in particular. That in itself is a serious problem because, according to Locke, the role of substance is to supply support for powers. So this power is itself in need of support from a substance, and so on. But even if we were willing to set this aside, we find that our understanding of the power to which we are referred is not up to the task at hand. As Berkeley points out,

> It is evident support cannot here be taken in its usual sense or literal sense, as when we say that pillars support a building: in what sense therefore must it be taken?[56]

There just is not anything special about the power of supporting that suggests it deserves to be classed in an entirely different metaphysical category from, say, the power of drawing iron. Berkeley concludes that, when it comes to the objects of the natural world, we can do without these substratum substances. In its place, he offers a bundle account of such objects.

This is the point at which the parity objection looms. It will seem that consistency demands that Berkeley embrace a bundle account of spirits as well. If sensible objects minus substrata are bundles of some sort, then spiritual objects minus substrata should be bundles as well. And if that's right, it will seem that if there is a connection to be made between spirits and Lockean persons, it cannot be one that takes spirits to be simple substances.

But is it true? What exactly does happen if we proceed to apply Berkeley's attack to spiritual substrata? Are we forced to conceive of Lockean persons as no more than bundles? The answer is no. From the Berkelian perspective, Locke's key insight is that "it is not unity of substance that comprehends all sorts of identity."[57] So when it comes to persons, Locke's fundamental breakthrough is that *personal unity* is not supplied by anything like a relation of inherence in a substratum. Instead, to understand the nature of their unity, we must be sensitive to the sortal under consideration. When it comes to the term 'person,' what Locke tells us is:

> Person is a forensick term, appropriating actions and their merit.[58]

It is here that we find the fundamental point of contact between Lockean persons and Berkelian selves. What Locke tells us is that a mind qua person is that which is the appropriate subject of ascriptions of responsibility. In other words, it is a *responsible thing*. Given the suggested interpretation of the active/passive distinction, a Lockean person is what Berkeley would call an "active thing." And that, in turn, means that to see the proposed reading of the active/passive distinction as the correct reading is to see Berkeley as, once again, standing on the shoulders of Locke and thereby managing to "see farther."

What Berkeley sees is that, in Locke's conception of *person*, there is latent, waiting to be seized upon, a ground-breaking insight about the relationship between the concepts of *unity* and *responsibility*. When Locke tells us, "[i]t is not . . . unity of substance that comprehends all sorts of identity," he is preparing us to see that when we concentrate on the self qua person, we find there is no need to invoke anything like a relation of "being supported by the same substratum" to explain the manner of their unity. Instead, we have an understanding of the unity of persons independent of such obscure metaphysical notions. It is found in our common practical understanding of the sense in which *actions belong to an agent*. All normal adults have had to master the practices of recognizing, parceling out, and accepting ascriptions of responsibility. And because of this, we all understand the sense in which these actions *are mine* because *I am accountable for them*. Actions do not *depend* upon an agent for their existence in the sense that they partake of some "subsistence" relation with respect to an unknown spiritual substratum. When it comes to persons, the concept of *dependence* at work is the perfectly familiar, normative conception of dependence in terms of *responsibility*.

And that is what we were looking for. We have been trying to come to an understanding of the sense in which spirits are *substances*. In accordance with the independence criterion, we understand a substance to be an "independent existent." This, however, requires an understanding of the natures of 'dependence' and 'independence' here being invoked. What the present interpretation of the active/passive distinction recommends is that these terms be understood normatively. The upshot is that we must take Berkeley's most fundamental and most revolutionary development to be that he treats the kind of normative dependence we find in the category of responsibility as providing the content of our notion of substantial dependence and substantial independence. What we require in the way of an understanding of substantial dependence and independence is an understanding of the sense in which the being of X asymmetrically *depends* upon the being of Y—a sense in which this manner of dependence makes it such that X *belongs* to Y so that, together, they are a genuine unity. Y must also be a termination point for that dependence, in the sense that it must not then depend upon the being of Z in the same way X depends upon Y. That way lays the Lockean regression of substrata.

According to the present interpretation of the active/passive distinction, Berkeley's spirits and their actions meet these needs. To the extent that they are "things," actions are dependent things. The manner of their dependence is "forensick" in nature, i.e., an agent (person, spirit) is accountable for them. That is also the sense in which they *belong* to the person. This action is *mine* because *I am responsible for it*. Persons then, in contrast to actions, are independent beings. Their status as independent existents lies in the fact that they are termination points for responsibility. As all normal adults are fully and often painfully aware, when it comes to responsibility for certain acts, the buck stops here. It stops with us: the person, the responsible thing. Here, the notion of *normative responsibility* is like that of inherence in being regarded as a conceptual primitive, but unlike the latter, the former is a concept we must all come to master because this "responsible thing" is that with which we *identify*. It is our self. Locke's great insight with regard to persons was to see that that with which we identify in the strongest possible sense is something whose being is utterly exhausted by its nature as an accountable thing.

Undeniably, this is, in some sense, a unique take on the nature of substantial unity, but it is certainly a fitting view for a devoutly Christian thinker. From this perspective, we are ultimately forensic entities. Our entire being is exhausted by such facts as that we enter into existence in a state of sin; that through our actions we seek redemption; that we will finally face judgment. The Christian thinker not only takes these to be facts, but also takes these to be the first and last words, the beginning and limit of wisdom with respect to the ultimate nature of our being. If there is anything else to us, it is of no possible concern to us. Berkeley provides us with an ontology that fits such convictions. What matters to personal identity is identical to the metaphysical base for personal identity.

We can now return to the question with which this section began: what happens if we apply Berkeley's attack on Locke's material substrata to Locke's spiritual substrata? First, we know that Berkeley holds that the only genuine substances are spirits. And we know that he holds this because spirits are the only true unities. Now, Locke considered persons to be unities irrespective of their relationship to substrata. When we limit our consideration to Locke's account of persons, we find it is their essential "forensick" nature that supplies their unity. So if we extend Berkeley's attack on material substrata to spiritual substrata, we find that we are left with a unitary being in the form of a Lockean person. So, if one believes, as Berkeley does, that something participates so far of existence as it does of unity, then a Lockean person, considered in-itself, is a substance. It is in this spirit that Berkeley remarks, with approval:

> According to the Platonic philosophy, *ens* and *unum* are the same. And consequently our minds participate so far of existence as they do of unity. But it should seem that personality is the indivisible centre of the soul or mind, which is a monad so far forth as she is a person. Therefore person is really that which exists.[59]

And he continues,

> Upon mature reflection, the *person* or mind of all created beings seemeth alone indivisible, and to partake most of unity. But sensible things are rather considered as one than truly so, they being in a perpetual flux or succession, ever differing and various.[60]

6. How to Turn Lockean Persons into Cartesian Substances

However, as we just mentioned, Locke did not regard persons as substances. Quite to the contrary, he thought one of the chief advantages of his view was that it separated out questions about substantial unity from those about personal unity. And as we saw, while Tipton believed there was a link between Locke's persons and Berkeley's spirits, his understanding of this link only justified talk of them as "substances" in the loose sense—the sense in which a bundle can be called a "sub-stance." It did not yield a view of spirits as *simple* substances.

Now, Bishop Butler took Locke to task for telling us both that a person is a "thinking intelligent being" and that personal identity consists in "the sameness of intelligent being." In light of this, Butler remarks, "The question then is, whether the same rational being is the same substance: which needs no answer, because 'being' and 'substance,' in this place stand for the same idea."[61] Does this show that Lockean persons are substances after all? I don't think so. It helpfully draws at-tention to the fact that although Locke says that persons are not substances, he left it unclear to just what category of being he took persons to belong. The deeper problem is that Locke is simply not in a position to treat persons as *substantial* unities. One particularly important reason for this is that Lockean persons require an additional and distinct sort of unity beyond personal (forensic) unity.[62] The way Locke conceives of persons, they also require the kind of unity supplied by the identity of a *substratum* substance.

The crux of the problem is that Locke attributes more than one faculty to the mind. According to Locke, there are two primary faculties of the mind: will and understanding.[63] But to say something is a "faculty" of the mind is simply to say that it is a "power" of the mind. So if your account of the mind gives it more than one *power*, the nature of the mind is no longer *simple*—it is complex, including as it then would, multiple, distinct powers/faculties. Locke needs the kind of unifying power somehow supposedly supplied by a substratum to explain how multiple dis-tinct powers can be said to belong to a single subject, i.e., to make *one* thing. What this means is that, indirectly, Lockean persons need substratum support because the multiple powers of the mind need substratum support. Thus, Lockean persons can-not be considered substantial unities in-themselves; they require substrata. And so, Locke, while deriding the vagueness of the concept of substratum substance, still insists on deriving substantial unity from substrata.

Berkeley, however, can take Locke's complaints about the notion of substrata to heart because he does not need to invoke any kind of substratum "support" for the powers of the mind for the simple reason that, according to him, there is only *one* legitimate conception of power—*will*.

> To say ye Will is a power. Volition is an act. This is idem per idem.[64]

Appropriately, we find that spirits have only one power: volition. So substrata are not needed to provide a unifying platform to explain how multiple powers can belong to a single subject. In turn, on Berkeley's account, the single power of the mind has no need of a substratum in which to inhere because, on the view that supersedes the congeries account, I am *identical* to my will. Strictly speaking, the will is not to be thought of as a "faculty" of the mind. Since I am identical to my will, it is not something that can be predicated of my mind. I do not *have* a will: I *am* a will (see point I above, §2). This is, for instance, why we find entries like 499a, cor-recting 499. It reads,

> What means 'Cause' as distinguished from 'Occasion'? nothing but a Being which wills when the Effect follows the volition. Those things that happen from without we

are not the Cause of therefore there is some other Cause of them i.e. there is a being that wills these perceptions in us.[65]

The comment on the verso page corrects a subtle but important error.

It should be said nothing but a Will, "a being which wills" being unintelligible.[66]

To be a *being* is to be a *will*. The identification of the mind with the will brings with it a view of the mind in which it is a *simple* substance, for we have come 'round to an essentially Cartesian view of substance, in which the being of something and its essence coincide.

The key move in the dialectic that led from a bundle view of the mind through Locke's conception of the nonsubstantial person and finally to Berkeley's conception of spirits as simple substances can actually be pinpointed in the notebooks. It is a verso-page remark, 194a, and it takes the form of a question directed toward himself.

Query: Whether Identity of Person consists not in the Will.[67]

The normative reading of the active/passive distinction, combined with the identification of the soul with the will, means that Berkeley can reject bundle theories of the self in favor of a simple substance view of the mind. I cannot be identical to any perception or any bundle of perceptions because perceptions are *passive*. They occur independently of my will. They are things that just happen to me. I am not accountable for them, and so they are not part of me.

Consequently, the rejection of a bundle theory of the self is actually built right into the basics of Berkeley's metaphysics by way of his understanding of the active/passive distinction. Notably, at entry 478, Berkeley asks himself an important question: "how is the soul distinguish'd from its' ideas?" He returns to the entry at a later date and provides the answer on the verso page in entry 478a:

The soul is the will properly speaking & as it is distinct from Ideas.[68]

The chief insight Berkeley took from Locke is his conception of a forensic unity. But Berkeley identifies what is traditionally thought of as a "faculty," the will, as just such a unity. To this, he adds the Cartesian insight that being and essence coincide. Locke's forensic unities become Berkeley's simple active substances.

7. The Central Problem and the Elimination of the Understanding

The identification of the mind with the will leads Berkeley to undertake one of the boldest maneuvers in the history of the philosophy of mind: the elimination of the understanding.[69] As we saw in the earlier entries of the notebooks, Berkeley entertains the possibility of what certainly looks like a Humean bundle view of the understanding. So, for instance, we find him writing at entry 614,

The Understanding not distinct from particular perceptions or Ideas.[70]

But after coming to the conclusion that the mind and the will are one and the same, he eliminates the understanding as a distinct faculty. So we find him correcting 614 with the following verso-page entry, 614a:

> The Understanding taken for a faculty is not really distinct from ye Will[.][71]

A spirit is one thing, with one power. As far as Berkeley is concerned, to posit faculties is to engage in abstraction.

> I observe that you very nicely abstract and distinguish the actions of the mind [into] judgment, and will . . . as if they stood for distinct abstract ideas: and that this supposition seems to ensnare the mind into the same perplexities and errors which, in all other instances, are observed to attend the doctrine of abstraction.[72]

But this then brings us right up against the Central Problem. If my being is exhausted by my nature as an active thing, how is it then that I am able to passively receive ideas of sense? Or as Descartes put it,

> There is in me a passive faculty of sensory perception, that is, a faculty for receiving and recognizing the ideas of sensible objects.[73]

Now this, of course, is simply to assert the irreducibility of the understanding. But the implied objection can be developed in the following way:

i. Some things can perceive; others cannot. It would seem that things that can perceive have some ability, power, or (to put it another way) faculty that other things lack.

Now since,

ii. We are the kind of things that enjoy sensory perception (we have what Berkeley calls "ideas of sense").

And since Berkeley is clearly committed to saying that

iii. Having ideas of sense is not the result of one's own activity (i.e., volition).

It follows that

iv. The fact that we have ideas of sense means that we must have some power, some faculty, that is distinct from volition.

So we must, after all, be complex in nature. The best we can reasonably grant Berkeley's spiritual minimalist project is that I must be a complex entity possessing two distinct kinds of powers and thus consisting of at least two faculties (i.e., "the will" and what has traditionally been called the faculty of "the understanding"). We are thrown back to a view of the mind as a complex being, not a simple one.

The appeal of this line of thought is undeniable, and I suspect it has had no small part in keeping Berkeley's readers from wholeheartedly attributing to him the identification of the self with the will.[74] Answering it requires that we first make a negative point and then a positive one.

7.1. Negative Point: What Are "Passive Powers"?

One serious problem with the objection is that, in contrast to the interpretation presented here, we have not been given any explanation of the conceptions of "passivity" or "power," which we are supposed to believe are coming into play here and saving us from our difficulty. Our difficulty was to understand how something that is active could passively receive sensations. A "passive faculty" was introduced to explain this, but it doesn't really explain anything. Rather, what we have here is just one more instance of a classic philosophical mistake: to solve a philosophical problem, one simply posits a new kind of thing. This new thing has some special property or properties in virtue of which the introduction of the entity somehow solves the original problem.[75] Unfortunately, the nature of the entity and its special properties remain critically underdescribed. So until the proponent of passive faculties can give us more than just a name, it can be of no explanatory value.

That this demand can be met in this particular case is especially suspect because appeal to a passive faculty is, at the very least, prima facie incoherent. A faculty is a power. The exercise of a power is its activity. What then is a "passive power," and what is it to *exercise* a passive power? How does something passive become active without changing its essential nature? Ironically, the very concept of the entity appealed to in order to charge Berkelian spirits with incoherence itself appears incoherent.[76] There seems to be no way to cash it out. A passive faculty is simply a rubber check.[77]

7.2. Positive Point: Restating and Tweaking the Objection

Instead of advocating that we must have a passive faculty (i.e., a "faculty of the understanding"), the objection may be reinterpreted as pointing out that, given his conception of power, the Berkelian cannot account for the fact that we have ideas of sense.

But even when reworked in this way, the objection fails to hit its mark. Notice that the objection gets its force from the assumption that, to account for the fact that we have ideas of sense, we must apply the strategy of appealing to the presence of some *power* of the subject. But that is not the only strategy available. Berkeley employs an Augustinian strategy, which proceeds in exactly the opposite direction. He accounts for the fact that we have ideas of sense by appealing to the *limitation* of the subject's single power.

> Body is opposite to spirit or mind. We have a notion of spirit from thought and action. We have a notion of body from resistance. So far forth as there is real power, there is spirit. So far forth as there is resistance, there is inability or want of power; that is, there is a negation of spirit. We are embodied, that is, we are clogged by weight, and hindered by resistance. But in respect of a perfect spirit, there is nothing hard or impenetrable: there is no resistance to the Deity: nor hath He any body: nor is the supreme Being united to the world as the soul of an animal is to its body, which necessarily implieth defect, both as an instrument, and as a constant weight and impediment.[78]

According to our interpretation, the ultimate, irreducible constituents of reality are volitional things—wills. And in this universe of wills, we are "limited and dependent" beings, what he also calls "finite wills." Unlike the infinite will, which is God, we are not infinitely active. We are only finitely active beings. That is to say, we are subject to passivities. But in God, the infinite will, there is no passivity.

> We who are limited and dependent spirits, are liable to impressions of sense, the effects of an external agent, which being produced against our wills, are sometimes painful and uneasy. But God, whom no external being can affect, who perceives nothing by sense as we do, whose will is absolute and independent, causing all things, and liable to be thwarted or resisted by nothing; it is evident, such a being as this can suffer nothing, nor be affected with any painful sensation, or indeed any sensation at all.[79]

The result of the infinite will acting on us, the finite wills, is passivities in the finite wills. These passivities are our ideas of sense—sensations. They are, again, things that just happen to us, no matter what we will. In this way, Berkeley accounts for the undeniable fact that we are receptive beings. He does it not by positing a power but by appeal to the lack or "privation" of power.[80] This lack of power is the consequence of the limitation of the sole power of the mind.

This deepens our understanding of why we need not embrace a congeries account to understand the sense in which minds cannot be separated from their ideas while still being distinct from them.[81] To say that a mind is finite is to say that it is subject to passivities, so ideas and finite minds never come apart. To conceive of a *finite* mind without passivities is a contradiction. One conceives either of God, which is no finite mind, or of an inactive finite mind, which is to not conceive of a mind at all.

Since perception does not require that we posit a "passive power," Berkeley can maintain that the mind is always active.

> While I exist or have any Idea I am eternally, constantly willing, my acquiescing in the present State is willing.[82]

Thus, there is a sense in which even in perception we are still active. Our will, however, is powerless to free us from suffering sensations altogether.

7.3. Understanding as an Activity and the Importance of the Divine Language

Accounting for the fact that we are receptive, perceiving beings is only half the task, however. The understanding's most important job has always been to render the world intelligible. It makes us not merely sentient but sapient beings. Depending on the tradition, this will mean that the understanding has the power to "grasp essential natures" or to "associate ideas," etc. To use a contemporary locution, the understanding is responsible for "cognition." Traditionally, the understanding does this via acts of the understanding. These "acts" are to be distinguished from actions. Acts are not essentially volitional in nature. We have already seen that attributing acts of any nature to a passive faculty is deeply problematic. Just the same, the identification of the mind with the will requires that Berkeley provide a positive reconceptualization of the nature of cognition. It will require that acts of the understanding (whatever they are) be eliminated in favor of full-blooded actions.

Berkeley's active conception of cognition only starts to take shape in the notebooks. To take a particularly vivid example, consider the query of entry 820.

Qu[ery]: may not there be an Understanding without a Will?[83]

He gives his answer in the next entry, 821.

Understanding is in some sort an Action.[84]

However, the response is somewhat timid. He qualifies. Understanding is said to be "in some sort" an action. But "acts," whatever they are, are presumably in "some sort" actions. This will not do. Berkeley needs the activity of understanding to consist of actions, without qualification.

The solution, the breakthrough that will clarify his thinking on this front, is not present in the notebooks. It is the divine language thesis. We need merely recall some key points from chapter III. For Berkeley, any bit of discourse we may come across, divine or otherwise, consists of nothing more than a series of ideas of sense. For instance, to one finite spirit, the discourse of another finite spirit is just another undifferentiated series of such ideas among the vast and varied, flowing, sensory mosaic of the natural world. Discourses do not differ intrinsically from any other natural object in that respect. In looking at a die, I see three sides of it first; then, as I turn it, I perceive another side, then another, then another, etc. The same goes for a discourse. When someone speaks to me, I first have the perception of one sound, then another, then another, etc.[85] There is no natural property that makes something a discourse.[85] However, discourses admit of a certain sort of treatment on the part of a spirit. They yield to *interpretation*. In order for it to be possible to render any given collection of ideas intelligible, an agent must act: it must engage in the activity of interpretation. To recall a quotation cited in that chapter:

> We know a thing when we understand it; and we understand it when we can interpret or tell what it signifies. Strictly, the sense knows nothing. We perceive indeed sounds by hearing, and characters by sight; but we are not therefore said to understand them. After the same manner, the phenomena of nature are alike visible to all; but all have not alike learned the connexion of natural things, or understand what they signify, or know how to vaticinate by them.[86]

Once the divine language thesis is in place, it becomes indispensable to Berkeley's active conception of the understanding. Our immediate objects of sense simply occur to us and are considered in-themselves to be devoid of conceptual content.[87]

> [S]ense knoweth not: and although the mind may use both sense and fancy, as means whereby to arrive at knowledge, yet sense, or soul so far forth as sensitive, knoweth nothing. For, as it is rightly observed in the *Theætetus* of Plato, science consists not in the passive perceptions, but in the reasoning upon them.[88]

It is only as we learn to treat the passively received ideas of sense as standing in sign-signified relationships that they become meaningful. According to Berkeley, even such basic contents of experience as the distance, magnitude, and situation of objects are not immediately "given."

The world of sense is intelligible because it is interpretable. Cognition, so construed, requires action. For while we are not accountable for which ideas of sense occur to us, we are accountable for how we interpret them. It is something we have to learn. We can misinterpret them, make mistakes, and be subject to correction.

Since interpretation is what renders the world intelligible, and since interpretation requires action, it is the divine language thesis that finally allows Berkeley to finish the reduction project and provide an account of spirits as simple, active substances.

Appendix: Samuel Johnson on Spirit

I would like to add one more piece of evidence for the claim that Berkeley identified the soul with the will. It is drawn from the philosophical development of Berkeley's student and friend, the American philosopher Samuel Johnson. In his correspondence with Berkeley, Johnson pressed a number of important questions about Berkeley's conception of spirit. I must quote at length from Johnson's correspondence to illustrate the direction of the development of his views.

> ...These ideas of ours, what are they? Is the substance of the mind the *substratum* to its ideas? Is it proper to call them modifications of our minds? Or impressions upon them? Or what? Truly I can't tell what to make of them, any more than of matter itself. What is the *esse* of spirits?—you seem to think it impossible to abstract their existence from their thinking. *Princ.* p. 143. sec. 98. Is then the *esse* of minds nothing else but *percipere*, as the *esse* of ideas is *percipi*? Certainly, methinks there must be an unknown somewhat that thinks and acts, as difficult to be conceived of as matter, and the creation of which, as much beyond us as the creation of matter. Can actions be the *esse* of any thing? Can they exist or be exerted without some being who is the agent? And may not that being be easily imagined to exist without acting, e.g., without thinking? And consequently (for you are there speaking of duration) may he not be said *durare, etsi non cogitet*, to persist in being, tho' thinking were intermitted for a while? And is not this sometimes fact? The duration of the eternal mind, must certainly imply some thing besides an eternal succession of ideas. May I not then conceive that, tho' I get my idea of duration by observing the succession of ideas in my mind, yet there is a *perseverare* in *existendo*, a duration of my being, and of the being of other spirits distinct from, and independent of, this succession of ideas.[89]

Berkeley is ill when he receives to Johnson's queries and responds with a relatively brief letter, addressing only a few of Johnson's many questions. Disappointingly, the subject of spirits does not loom large in his response. Happily, however, Johnson was not discouraged. In his next letter he pursues some of the questions Berkeley didn't address in his initial response. On the topic of the being and nature of spirits Johnson writes:

> As to the *esse* of spirits, I know Descartes held the soul always thinks, but I thought Mr. Locke had sufficiently confuted this notion, which he seems to have entertained only to serve an hypothesis. The Schoolmen, it is true, call the soul *Actus* and God *Actus purus*; but I confess I never could well understand their meaning[.]...[T]o place the very being of spirits in the mere act of thinking, seems to me very much like making abstract ideas of them.

There is certainly something passive in our souls, we are purely passive in the reception of our ideas; and reasoning and willing are actions of something that reasons and wills, and therefore must be only modalities of that something.[90]

Johnson's questions and objections are quite simply the most thoughtful and probing of those that remain extant to us from Berkeley's own time. But despite this, Berkeley's next letter in response is, once again, relatively brief and, on these points, not terribly illuminating. He apologizes for the brevity of his response, but this time he extends an invitation to Johnson to visit him in Newport and to "pass as many days as you can spend at my house." He adds that 'four or five days' conversation would set several things in a fuller and clearer light than writing could do in as many months."[91]

Johnson took Berkeley up on his offer and, in fact, visited several times and "gladly put himself under Berkeley's instruction."[92] Given the content of Johnson's letters, it is safe to assume that the subject of spirits was a principal point of discussion between the two. So our question is: what was the upshot of those discussions? The sensible place to look for the answer would be Johnson's principal philosophical work, *Elementa Philosophica*, written well after those meetings in Newport. There we find that Johnson has not only been won over to immaterialism, but he has also abandoned his Lockean tendencies with respect to the nature of spiritual substance. His new view is given concise expression in Book I, *Noetica*, chapter II, §20 "Of Unity and Multiplicity, Number and Order."

[B]y how much the less of Composition there is in any Being, by so much the perfecter it is, as being so much the more One. Hence, *spirit being compounded only of Power and Act*, is more perfect than Body, which is compounded of many Parts and Dimensions. And as Power and Act in the Deity intirely coincide, He is the most perfect Being, as being the most simple and intirely one, and therefore is called Pure Act, without any Variety or Multiplicity; a most perfect Unit, consisting of all Reality and Perfection.[93]

The view of the nature of being and spirits that I have attributed to Berkeley in chapters I and IV appears to have found its way into Johnson's work. The most likely point of transmission is Berkeley's farmhouse in Rhode Island.

V

Agency and Occasionalism

The 2 great Principles of Morality. The Being of a God & the Freedom of Man: these to be handled in the beginning of the Second Book.[1]

1. The Problems of Free Will

The philosophical problems that are now commonly associated with free will center around the search for an understanding of how responsible agents could be any part of a naturalistically conceived universe. Since Berkeley presents us with a radically nonnaturalistic view of reality as consisting, at its most basic level, of agents and irreducible normative relations of responsibility, it is reasonable to expect that at least some of these problems will look very different from his perspective. What appear to be serious and complex problems from more familiar perspectives might not be so from Berkeley's, and vice versa.

Mapping the terrain of such problems from a Berkelian perspective represents a massive undertaking. I will not attempt it here. Instead, in this chapter, I will take up just one problem, a particularly nasty one, that has haunted Berkeley's metaphysics from the beginning: the specter of occasionalism. Even though Berkeley did not leave us anything like a detailed action theory, it is widely held that his metaphysics commits him to some version of occasionalism. This is not meant as a compliment. Although at one time occasionalism had a fair share of able defenders, they are now an extremely rare, if not completely extinct, species. A commitment to occasionalism is seen as a problem, despite the fact that occasionalism first came to life as a solution.

I believe that the connection between Berkeley's view of agency and occasionalism has been greatly overblown. My aim in this chapter is to make clear just how deeply incompatible Berkeley's metaphysics is with occasionalism.

2. What Is Occasionalism?

Although occasionalism's roots are older, the classic statement of it comes to us from Malebranche. A (grossly) simplified account of his view will do for present purposes.[2] Malebranche was a substance dualist, and occasionalism gave him an answer to the infamous "interaction problem," i.e., since mind and body are distinct kinds of substances, how can they possibly interact?[3] How can one bring about a change in the other? In piety, Malebranche saw a solution. It requires insisting upon the utter impotence of creation on the one hand and the omnipotence of the Creator on the other. It is not just that God is more powerful than any of his creations: all power is God's alone. Material substances and finite mental substances have no power.

Strictly speaking, substances do not causally interact. For example, when I face the noonday sun with eyes wide open, the blinding sensations that follow are not *caused* by the sun. The sun is merely an "occasional cause." At its presence, it is God's power that produces the appropriate sensations in me. In turn, when I, a mental substance, will the movement of my leg, a material substance, my willing is not the cause of my leg moving. Rather, it is an "occasional cause." It is God's power that brings about a change in the material world, the position of my leg, upon the occasion of my willing the movement of my leg. If God did not accommodate my volitions, my will would be utterly impotent with respect to the position of my leg.

3. Berkeley as an Occasionalist

There are two main lines of argument that support seeing Berkeley as an occasionalist. The first argument is based on textual support. The second proceeds by way of implication, i.e., it proceeds by arguing that certain basic aspects of Berkeley's philosophy imply a commitment to occasionalism.

The textual case is the far weaker of the two, and so it is best to get it out of the way. It draws its main support from entry 107 of the *Philosophical Commentaries*, where Berkeley writes,

> + Strange impotence of men. Man without God. Wretcheder than a stone or tree, he having onely the power to be miserable by his unperformed wills, these having no power at all.[4]

It must be granted that the view expressed here does smack of occasionalism. However, once that is granted, it must also be noted that 107 is a fairly early entry in Berkeley's notebooks, and it is marked by the + sign. As we know, Berkeley used the + sign for entries with which, upon review, he was no longer satisfied for one reason or another. Its presence does not necessarily indicate wholesale rejection of the view expressed. However, this is another instance in which we have good reason to think that the + sign does indicate rejection, at least of any commitment to occasionalism that 107 might have reflected, because later, at entry 548, Berkeley writes,

> We move our Legs our selves. 'tis we that will their movement. Herein I differ from Malbranch.[5]

In context, the tone of entry 548 is that of self-discovery. It strikes the reader that Berkeley has come to understand his own view better and, in doing so, sees wherein the essential difference between Malebranche and him lies. This impression is strengthened by consideration of Berkeley's published works. In these, he repeatedly takes time to distinguish his views from Malebranche's. For instance, Hylas asks,

"But what say you, are not you too of the opinion that we see all things in God? If I mistake not, what you advance comes near it."[6] In replying, Philonous pulls no punches.

> Few men think, yet all will have opinions. Hence men's opinions are superficial and confused. It is nothing strange that tenets, which in themselves are ever so different, should nevertheless be confounded with each other by those who do not consider them attentively. I shall not therefore be surprised, if some men imagine that I run into the enthusiasm of Malbranche, though in truth I am very remote from it. He builds on the most abstract general ideas, which I entirely disclaim. He asserts an absolute external world, which I deny. He maintains that we are deceived by our senses, and know not the real natures or the true forms and figures of extended beings; of all which I hold the direct contrary. So that upon the whole there are no principles more fundamentally opposite than his and mine.[7]

The reply is immediately directed against the charge that Berkeley holds that we "see all things in God," but Berkeley also explicitly, repeatedly, and sometimes vehemently denies any place for Malebranche's occasions. In the *Principles*, §§68–72 are devoted specifically to the consideration and rejection of occasions. For instance, at *Principles* 69, Berkeley writes,

> Let us examine what is meant by occasion: so far as I can gather from the common use of language, that word signifies, either the agent which produces any effect or else something that is observed to accompany, or go before it, in the ordinary course of things. But when it is applied to matter... it can be taken in neither of those senses. For matter is said to be passive and inert, and so cannot be an agent or efficient cause. It is also unperceivable, as being devoid of all sensible qualities, and so cannot be the occasion of our perceptions in the latter sense: as when the burning my finger is said to be the occasion of the pain that attends it. What therefore can be meant by calling matter an occasion?[8]

Occasions also get a hearing in the second of the *Three Dialogues*.[9] In every instance, Berkeley argues that occasions are just another empty abstraction behind which matter attempts to hide. Upon scrutiny, an occasion will always turn out to be an "inert, senseless, unknown substance."[10] It is that which "neither acts, nor perceives, nor is perceived,"[11] an "inactive unthinking being."[12]

Since there is no occasionalism where there are no occasions, and since Berkeley is very clear about rejecting occasions, it would seem that our interpretive constraint from chapter I is once again relevant:

> Constraint 1: When there is a conflict, one should reject early views that the author chose not to publish in favor of later views that the author chose to publish repeatedly.

The textual case for reading Berkeley as an occasionalist runs afoul of Constraint 1, and so I conclude that this first line of argument is very weak.

Constraint 1 can be overridden, however. For this reason, the second line of argument is more formidable. If it can be shown that essential aspects of Berkeley's philosophy force a commitment to occasionalism upon him despite his denials, then we have good reason to set aside our interpretive constraint. Of course, the first hurdle that such an approach must clear is the fact that Berkeley is not a dualist—the point being that occasionalism was brought in to solve the interaction problem produced by substance dualism.[13] One will have to explain, absent substance dualism, what would motivate Berkeley to adopt occasionalism. This hurdle, I believe, can be cleared. Jonathan Bennett has laid out the case rather succinctly. He asks,

> What, for instance, can [Berkeley] say happens when I voluntarily clench my fist?...
> when I clench my fist and watch myself doing it, I am somehow active and yet I
> passively undergo a change of visual state. How can Berkeley fit these two facts to-
> gether? Where can he draw the active/passive line in this case?[14]

According to Berkeley, I am a spirit, an active thing. My body, with its legs, lungs, arms, etc., is merely a collection of ideas; it is a passive thing. The various goings-on of passive things occur independently of my will; they depend upon God's will. If passive things, like my body, are under the sole direction of God's will, how am I ever supposed to be responsible for any of my bodily activities? How can I ever *directly* bring about such a thing as the clenching of my fist or the moving of my legs? Of course, I am free to will such a thing, but that my willing should be followed by the event must depend upon a volition on God's part. If that is the case, then why aren't my volitions merely the "occasion" at which God brings about a change in the position of my limbs? It would seem that one who maintains a metaphysics of activity and passivity faces a serious challenge: providing an account of the volition-upshot relation while not acquiescing in occasionalism. Again, in Bennett's words,

> Berkeley, it seems, must conclude that when I voluntarily clench my fist, I actively
> perform a mental act—a volition—and that the rest of what happens falls outside the
> scope of my activity. That would imply that the modest claim that "We move our legs
> ourselves" is wrong; we do not move our legs; rather we will that our legs should
> move, and then, usually, our legs move.[15]

Such is the case for seeing Berkeley as an occasionalist. It is, on the face of it, a powerful case. Nonetheless, I think it is mistaken. To uncover the mistakes that support it, we need to apply two tools.

i. Berkeley's attack on abstract ideas and, in particular, as it applies to occasions.
   This will be the subject of §5.
ii. Our interpretation of the active/passive distinction from chapter IV. This will
   be the subject of §6.

However, before we make use of either of these tools, a preliminary point should be addressed.

4. A Preliminary Point: Volitions, Wishes, and Hopes

According to Berkeley, causation is activity. However, he also maintains that we can usefully retain the word 'cause' so long as in calling something a cause, we must mean "[c]auses yet do nothing."[16] As he pointedly puts it in one of his notebook entries,

I say there are no Causes (properly speaking) but Spiritual, nothing active but Spirit. Say you, this is only Verbal, 'tis only annexing a new sort of signification to the word Cause, & why may not others as well retain the old one, & call one Idea the Cause of another which always follows it. I answer, if you do so, I shall drive you into many absurditys. I say you cannot avoid running into opinions you'll be glad to disown if you stick firmly to that signification of the Word Cause.[17]

The important point here is that Berkeley will have no more to do with the traditional materialist concept of causation than he will with matter. As far as he is concerned, the materialist's conception of causation was eliminated along with matter. They were a package deal. Instead, the concept of *activity* is taken as understood. An understanding of it is not to be derived from some supposed prior understanding of naturalist cum materialist causation. We must remember that activity is not to be conceived of as some sort of "motion in the soul" that somehow transfers motion or some kind of "motion activity" to an outer object. Nor is it the transfer of "force" or "power." Berkeley regards all such notions as occult.[18]

If we fail to keep this in mind, we will be led to read the direction of explanation in

Causation = Activity

right to left. A prior and independent understanding of causation will be taken as providing an explanation of activity. That is not Berkeley. He understands the equation left to right. The direction of explanation is *from* our grasp of the nature of activity *to* that of causation.[19]

Failing to take this point into account can lead to mistaking Berkelian volitions for congeries of something like *wishing* and *hoping*. Here is how this can come about: with a materialist model of causation in mind, one will look to posit a pair of events in every instance of Berkelian activity. One event will be an "inner" event, a *volition*. This will be followed by an "outer" event, an *upshot*. Once this move is made, the inner event will then quickly become indistinguishable from our ordinary conception of a *wish*. Like a wish, a "volition" will be an inner event that is *about* some outer event. That is to say, like a wish, a volition will have a content. And the content of the volition will be that-ϕ (e.g., that *my leg goes up at time t_n*). The outer event will then be ϕ itself (i.e., the upshot event of *my leg going up at time t_n*). On this model, the volition-upshot relation will bear one similarity to the traditional understanding of the cause-event relation. There will be some kind of "necessary connection" between the former and the latter. The inner event will be necessarily related to the outer event by way of its *content*. However, the account will then be found lacking because although volition and upshot bear one kind of necessary connection to each other, the inner event does not bear the connection of "efficient cause" to the outer event. The inner event simply *precedes* the outer event; it is not what *makes* it occur. Thus, the outer event ϕ will not be one of my *actions* because it will not have been brought about by the inner event. Nor will the inner event be a true volition because it does not bring about the outer event. Like a wish, one makes it and then hopes that it comes true.

But to Berkeley, this will simply seem to be an ill-motivated attempt to construct volitions out of other materials. Naturalists—that is, those who do not believe that the nature of reality is irreducibly normative (i.e., active)—may have a reason to pursue a reductionist line on volitions, but the Berkelian does not.

Wishing is just one of our many different kinds of activities. It is something one has to learn how to do, just as one has to learn how to walk, how to dance, how to make a promise, etc. To wish is to engage in an action. Wishes are somewhat special among our actions in that, normally, they are a fairly safe kind of action in which to engage. Like playing solitaire on a deserted island, wishing is an activity that only directly affects the one who wishes, and even then the impact is minimal.

The same is true of imagining. This point is important from the exegetical angle because imagining is Berkeley's favored example of activity. Unfortunately, it is common for commentators to take it as the *only* kind of activity in which a spirit can engage. The specter of occasionalism is then introduced by way of saying that, according to Berkeley's view, we are "free to will" (usually understood to mean "wish") that our legs move, and via our power of imagination we can even accompany this wish with an image, perhaps providing the volition with its mental content (i.e., an image of our legs moving).[20] However, this will not be enough to bring about the movement of our legs. That requires, among other things, that it be possible to look down and passively receive perceptions of our legs moving. But that, being a passive occurrence, lies outside our power. So, for instance, we find C. C. W. Taylor writing,

> Berkeley's metaphysical system . . . allows no role whatsoever for human agency. The nearest human beings can approach to acting is by exercising their imaginations and by wanting things to happen; but what actually makes anything happen is not the exercise of any finite will but always an act of the Divine will. To adapt Davidson's dictum 'All we ever do is move our wills: the rest is up to God.'[21]

As I see it, there are two problems with this passage. First, when an agent imagines, the agent *is* making something happen; it is making *imagining* happen. Second, imagining is just one kind of activity; it is one of the many actions in which an agent can engage. Berkeley nowhere says that it is our only form of activity, and there is no motivation for him to do so. Like wishing, imagining is unusual in that it is an action that normally has no consequences for anyone beyond the one who engages in it. But this is no reason to reduce all activity to this one.

Principles 28 is often read as implying a reduction of all activity to imagining. Here is the relevant text:

> I find I can excite ideas in my mind at pleasure, and vary and shift the scene as oft as I think fit. It is no more than willing, and straightway this or that idea arises in my fancy: and by the same power it is obliterated, and makes way for another. This making and unmaking of ideas doth very properly denominate the mind active. Thus much is certain, and grounded on experience: but when we talk of unthinking agents, or of exciting ideas exclusive of volition, we only amuse our selves with words.[22]

Now, had Berkeley written "willing is no more than imagining," then we might have some reason to read him as reducing willing to imagining. But he does not. A more charitable reading of the passage is that Berkeley is here making a simple, but rhetorically powerful, point *against* the occasionalists. The occasionalists would have it that, strictly speaking, not all spirits are active—only God is. And accordingly, even in imagining, there is a passive aspect. We will the experiencing of an image and then hopefully God supplies one. But this would seem to conflict directly with experience. "Look," Berkeley says, "I'll *do* something. I'll imagine a tree. There, I did it. It was *no more* than willing." The phenomenology of imagining contradicts the occasionalist view of it. There is nothing passive about the act of imagining. We do not first will an image and then passively receive one. The imagining is exhausted in the willing of it. When the willing ceases, the imagining ceases, because, as Berkeley says, "it is no more than willing." The point mirrors a point he will later make in the first of the *Three Dialogues* about the experience of a great heat and the experience of pain.[23] There are not *two* things here, only one. The experience of a great heat is a pain. Likewise, the act of imagining and the having of the image are one and the same. There are not two things here, only one. This, as Berkeley says, is supported by experience. Anyone can try for himself to separate out two parts in any simple act of imagining.

So, from a phenomenological perspective, imagining is a weak spot in the occasionalist position, and Berkeley exploits it to good effect. The latter is shown by the fact that so many commentators have been prepared to equate imagining and willing. Clearly, they think he has hit a plausible candidate for a genuine activity because, far from it occurring to them to deny it, they embrace imagining as the essence of activity itself. But instead of imagining, Berkeley could have used the example of wishing or even hoping (Locke chooses the activity of recalling memories).[24] These are all equally activities. And if you agree that these activities are entirely under the discretion of your will alone, then you will have to agree that you are *not* a passive thing. You can *do* something. In fact, you can do, at least, several things. You can imagine; you can wish; you can hope. In short, I suggest that we read the passage as saying that imagining alone is *sufficient* to denominate the mind as active.

We now have a good idea of what volitions are not. But this has also moved us toward an understanding of what Berkeley believes volitions are. To see this, however, we need to apply our first tool, Berkeley's attack on abstract ideas, to volition.

5. Volition as an Abstract Idea

Malebranchian occasions come in two basic varieties. First, there are occasions in the role of *matter*, what I will call "material occasions." When I look at the morning star, there is a material planet "out there" (i.e., it has an absolute existence outside of all minds). But that material planet is not what causes the appropriate sensations in me. God does that. Venus is merely the occasional cause of those perceptions. This is an example of a material occasion. Now, occasionalism is designed to get *two* different finite substances, in this case, a mental substance and a material substance, to "interact."[25] Because of this, there are also "mental occasions." When I "will" the clenching of my fist, my volition serves as the occasion for God to bring about a change in the material world, i.e., the movement of my material fist.[26] So, in the

Malebranchian approach to the interaction problem, there are both *material* occasions and *mental* occasions.

Now, as we know, Part II of the *Principles* was to take up the subject of spirits. As we also know, Berkeley told his friend Samuel Johnson that Part II was nearly completed when it was lost while he was traveling in Italy. Importantly, in the same letter, he also tells Johnson that he thinks that if men would attend to what he had to say about abstract ideas, many confusions about the nature of spirits would be cleared up. And that makes perfect sense because, as we already know, while we do not have Part II of the *Principles*, we do have what was to be the introduction to all four projected parts of the *Principles*.[27] The main purpose of the "Introduction" to the whole is to present Berkeley's famous argument against abstract ideas. As he saw it, more than anything else, abstract ideas have had the "chief part in rendering speculation intricate and perplexed, and to have occasioned innumerable errors and difficulties in almost all parts of knowledge."[28] The abstract idea under attack in Part I of the *Principles* is matter. Thus, we find that Malebranche's material occasions come under explicit attack in Part I,[29] and, of course, they are found to be just another manifestation of matter and, thus, nothing but another abstract idea.

Given this and the fact that Part II was to focus on the subject of spirits, it is reasonable to expect that Part II would have found abstract ideas to have had the "chief part in rendering speculation intricate and perplexed, and to have occasioned innumerable errors and difficulties" with respect to our understanding of the nature of spirits as well. That is what he intimates to Johnson. With this in mind, we can reconstruct what Berkeley would have said of mental occasions, i.e., volitions. Berkeley's "Introduction" has given us the argument's formula; we need only plug in the terms. These Malebranchian volitions, these mental occasions, would have gone the way of material occasions. They would have been eliminated as a superfluous posit.

In puzzling over what Berkelian "volitions" could be and how they could be related to "upshots," we have acquiesced in the worst of the metaphysical sins that a Berkelian can commit. We have engaged in abstraction. From out of our perfectly familiar, perfectly particular activities, we have fabricated an abstract metaphysical common core, the volition—the tiniest of all the truncated ghosts in the human machine.

In response to the question "What are Berkelian volitions?" the answer is straightforward. To Berkeley, volitions are the *particular activities* of spirits. One's activities are those things for which one is responsible. What one is responsible for are one's *actions*. In keeping with common sense, my activities are my actions—things like walking, talking, spitting, punching, speaking, etc. And, of course, there are also activities like wishing and imagining. These are all equally actions.

We have been tempted into thinking of the term 'volition' as the name of an abstract something or other (i.e., an "inner mental event"). But a volition is not something over and above and/or distinct from our individual activities. The situation here is exactly the same as that with the word 'man,' to use one of Berkeley's famous examples. 'Man' is not the name of something distinct from individual men. A man is Peter, a man is Paul, etc.[30] Likewise, 'volition' is a term which refers indifferently to any one of our activities. A volition is not something distinct from our individual actions. A volition *is* an action. The term 'volition,' like the terms 'man' or 'triangle,' has divided reference. Berkeley's attack on abstraction applies just as much to activities as it does to ideas. Abstraction in either case will lead us badly astray. It will lead us to posit two things in every action: a volition and an upshot.

Just as Berkeley argues that these outer material occasions are abstractions and utterly unnecessary for the explanation of our sensations, so too are these inner mental occasions unnecessary for the explanation of our actions. Just as there are no material occasions at which God wills sensations in us, neither are there mental occasions. Our volitions are our vast and varied, perfectly familiar, perfectly particular activities.

At this point, we can encapsulate the Berkelian objection to occasionalism. Occasionalists must concede the point that minds can do *something*. It is part of their position that spirits can engage in volition. But, from Berkeley's perspective, in so doing, the occasionalist removes the need to posit occasional causes. Volitions, properly understood, are full-fledged actions.

It is worth pausing to remove one other linguistic source of confusion. One will often hear the term 'mental act' used equivalently with 'volition' when discussing Berkeley (one need look no further than the preceding quotations from Bennett). But what possible meaning could a Berkelian attach to the expression 'mental act'? As contrasted with what? A *material* act? To the Berkelian, the expression 'mental act' is not merely redundant; it is perniciously redundant. It can only serve to confuse. Since no one is sure just what a mental act is supposed to be, it sends one seeking candidate inner events, and this leads one right to the doorstep of activities like wishing, imagining, hoping—all actions that have limited consequences for others and thus are good candidates for inner mental events. One ends up with the reduction of Berkelian actions to a subset of actions. In this way, philosophical monsters are born.

6. Action and Motion

The preceding makes considerable trouble for reading Berkeley as an occasionalist. Still, a reservation may remain. It is rather difficult to render the worry explicit, however. Roughly, it will find expression in something like the following:

> How, according to Berkeley, can it be that I bring about the movement of my legs?

At least as stated, this poses no problem. The proper answer for Berkeley to make is, "Do you mean you do not know how to walk, or kick, or tap dance, or . . . ?" Of course, that is not what the objector means. But the question is, what *does* she mean? If I am walking, my legs will be moving. I (not to mention any properly situated third party) will be able to look down and see that my legs are moving. I will be active in that I am walking, and I will be active insofar as I choose where I turn to look, but I will be passive as I perceive the movement of my legs. But that is as it should be. So we must try again:

The problem is that, according to Berkeley, all I ever perceive is *motion*, not *actions*. Strictly speaking, I cannot see an action.

Correct. But again, that is as it should be. Just as all one ever perceives are ideas, not spirits, all you can strictly see are motions, not actions. Spirits are not, strictly speaking, objects of perception, and neither are their actions.[31] And that is what Berkeley should and does say,

> We may not I think strictly be said to have an idea of an active being, or of an action.[32]

Actions are no more the objects of sensory perception than spirits are. Recalling one of the ABCs of spirits, Berkeley insists that *action* and *motion* are entirely distinct. The motion of a leg toward a ball is not in-itself an act of kicking. Seeing the motion of a leg toward a ball *as an act of kicking* is not a matter of merely having certain sensations. It is a matter of *seeing-as*. It is a matter of how we, spirits, regard that motion—of how we interpret these sensation signs. The act itself is not an object of perception (see chapter III).

Here, I believe, we have gotten at an important point. We will be tempted to break our actions into two parts, a volition and an upshot, so long as we think that motion is a part of action. But this is clearly not Berkeley's view. Motion is not part of an action. We are less tempted to think of motion as being a part of an action in the cases of imagining, wishing, hoping, etc. This makes the case of imagining a good rhetorical device for Berkeley to exploit, but it does not actually mark anything special about these actions. It does not make a difference in kind. According to Berkeley, motion is no more a part of the act of raising my hand than it is a part of my imagining the raising of my hand. The perceivable motion of a hand being raised consists of ideas and is a sign that an act of hand raising has taken place. It is not the action itself.

7. "Events" and the Inescapable Perspectivalness of Spirits

Perhaps even this will not fully satisfy our objector. But at this point, it may well be a result of an implicit commitment to materialism. To see this, it will help if we take up our second tool: our interpretation of the active/passive distinction (i.e., I am active with respect to φ iff I am responsible for φ; I am passive with respect to φ iff I am not responsible for it). In stark contrast to the materialist, Berkeley's is irreducibly a universe of agents in action. Consider these two statements:

i. I raised my hand.
ii. My hand went up.

I use the former to talk about one of *my* acts. I use the latter to talk about, what is to me, an *occurrence*. In the first case, perhaps I volunteered for something; the act is mine. In the second, perhaps you volunteered me; the act is yours. In the first case, I am responsible. In the second case, you, another spirit, are. At this point, we can sharpen up our objector's concern. She will ask,

Responsible for *what*? That's what I'm interested in. Items (i) and (ii) are two different ways of talking about one thing, i.e., the *event* of my arm going up. It is that event that is common to both. It is that event for which either I or you are responsible. What I do not see is how Berkeley can explain how any finite spirit can bring such an event about.

I suspect that this formulation of the worry gets closer to the heart of what bothers the objector. But this formulation of the objection just makes it all the more clear that the objector is appealing to something Berkeley rejects: an abstract idea. Berkeley will want to know what an "event" is. He will want to know if by "the event" you are referring to my act of raising my hand? If not, then you must be referring to a distinct event, i.e., *some other spirit's action*. For Berkeley, (i) and (ii) are not two different ways of talking about one thing: (i) is a particular action in which I engaged; and (ii) is something completely distinct. It is a particular action in which *someone else* engaged. Neither is a description of any responsibility-neutral entity, a "happening," a "pure occurrence."

The point I am trying to draw out here is that spirits are necessarily perspectival. That fact is absolutely basic to a spirit-centered metaphysics. In the famous "unconceived tree" exchange, Philonous brings this point home to Hylas.

> Philonous: I am content to put the whole upon this issue. If you can conceive it possible for any mixture or combination of qualities, or any sensible object whatever, to exist without the mind, then I will grant it actually to be so.
>
> Hylas: If it comes to that, the point will soon be decided. What more easy than to conceive a tree or house existing by itself, independent of, and unperceived by any mind whatsoever? I do at this present time conceive them existing after that manner.
>
> Philonous: How say you, Hylas, can you see a thing which is at the same time unseen?
>
> Hylas: No, that were a contradiction.
>
> Philonous: Is it not as great a contradiction to talk of conceiving a thing which is unconceived?
>
> Hylas: It is.
>
> Philonous: The tree or house therefore which you think of, is conceived by you.
>
> Hylas: How should it be otherwise?
>
> Philonous: And what is conceived, is surely in the mind.
>
> Hylas: Without question, that which is conceived is in the mind.
>
> Philonous: How then came you to say, you conceived a house or tree existing independent and out of all minds whatsoever?
>
> Hylas: That was I own an oversight; but stay, let me consider what led me into it.—It is a pleasant mistake enough. As I was thinking of a tree in a solitary place, where no one was present to see it, methought that was to conceive a tree as existing unperceived or unthought of, not considering that I myself conceived it all the while. But now I plainly see, that all I can do is to frame ideas in my

own mind. I may indeed conceive in my own thoughts the idea of a tree, or a house, or a mountain, but that is all. And this is far from proving, that I can conceive them existing out of the minds of all spirits.[33]

By their very nature, spirits are perspectival. But according to the interpretation I have been presenting, the fundamental nature of that perspectivalness is not *perceptual* perspectivalness. It is a *forensic* perspectivalness, if you will. To be a spirit is to be a responsible thing. To be a *finite* spirit is to be responsible for some things and not others. As a spirit, I take my forensic perspective with me everywhere. I cannot escape it; I cannot separate myself from it. This point is of the first importance, and I suspect that failure to appreciate it drives the objection.

Recently, Simon Blackburn helpfully connected the error that Hylas makes and Philonous corrects with a mistake that he sees in G. E. Moore's work.[34] In *Principia Ethica*, Moore argues for the mind independence of beauty via an "isolation thought experiment." He asks that we conceive of two worlds. The first is filled with green meadows, rushing streams, and blue skies. The second is nothing but cinders and ashes. In neither of these worlds are there any observers. But, as we will all agree, despite the absence of observers, the first world is beautiful, and the second is not. Therefore, Moore concludes, beauty exists independently of minds. But as Blackburn rightly points out,

> Philonous inoculates us against this specious argument of Moore's. It is *we* who accept the invitation to think of these worlds. And *we* bring to them our own aesthetic responses, which no doubt include a love of the countryside and a dislike of cinders and garbage. But we haven't got *behind* those responses or put them into abeyance as we respond to the imagined worlds. On the contrary, it is these *very* responses that we voice in our verdicts.[35]

Of course, Blackburn is here concerned only with aesthetic responses. But from the Berkelian perspective, our aesthetic evaluations are just the tiniest part of the inescapable *evaluative* perspective we bring to everything of which we conceive. For Berkeley, our evaluative perspective is *categorical* in the full sense of that term. In a monistic metaphysics of spirit, where spirit is a forensic concept, *there is no responsibility-neutral perspective* (to put it ironically, there is no traditional "God's eye point of view" on reality). My evaluative perspective goes with me everywhere. If I am responsible for φ, then φ is one of *my* acts; it is something *I* did. If not, φ is something some *other spirit* did. It is some other spirit that is responsible, accountable, answerable for φ. I am not accountable for it. To *me*, it is an occurrence, something that just happened to me. But it is not an occurrence *simpliciter*. It is an act of some agent or other. If it is not the act of some finite agent, then the action is directly attributable to the agent that is God.

The challenge facing the advocate of events is to specify their nature in such a way that 'event' does not turn out to be just another name for an 'occasion.' If you insist that there must be a thing of which both (i) and (ii) are alternate possible descriptions, then you have come back to a form of occasionalism by way of abstraction. Events, instead of occasions, will now be that ever-elusive, evaluative-neutral, spirit-independent "somewhat" that enjoys an absolute existence outside of all minds whatsoever and toward which our volitions are directed. It will be the act of no spirit, conceived of from the perspective of no spirit. If Berkeley were alive today, along with matter and occasions, he would no doubt attack events, so conceived, as just another meaningless abstraction.

8. Conclusion

Much remains to be said about Berkeley's theory of action.[36] However, I think enough has been said here to make serious trouble for those who treat Berkeley's view of agency as a form of or even compatible with occasionalism.

In this chapter, I have had to focus on highlighting some key differences between Berkeley and Malebranche in order to shed some light on the former's view of agency. In the next chapter, I turn to the task of explaining the connection between Berkeley's philosophy and common sense. As we will see, this requires, in part, that I focus on some of their key points of agreement.

VI

Common Sense, the Manifest Image, and Immaterialism

We shall not cease from exploration
And the end of all our exploring
Will be to arrive where we started
And know the place for the first time.
—T. S. Eliot, "Four Quartets"

Although it may, perhaps, seem an uneasy reflexion to some, that when they have taken a circuit through so many refined and unvulgar notions, they should at last come to think like other men: yet, methinks, this return to the simple dictates of Nature, after having wandered through the wild mazes of philosophy, is not unpleasant. It is like coming home from a long voyage: a man reflects with pleasure on the many difficulties and perplexities he has passed through, sets his heart at ease, and enjoys himself with more satisfaction for the future.

—Berkeley, preface to the *Three Dialogues*

1. Back to the Beginning

Finally, we come to the problem with which we began: what is the reader to make of Berkeley's claim that his philosophy is not only consonant with, but even a defense of, common sense? As I said in the introduction, I want to distinguish the task of answering this question from the task of defending Berkeley's views *as* common sense. If my aim were the latter, it would probably be best to proceed as others have by lining up the number of offenses against common sense to which materialism commits us alongside the number of offenses to which immaterialism commits us.[1] But that would not go to the heart of the matter with which I am concerned; it would do little to address a pair of prior problems—both of which are, not coincidentally, suggested by the main title of this work—*A Metaphysics for the Mob*.

The first question to which one wants an answer is the following:

A. In what sense can "the mob" even be said to have a metaphysics

While expressions like 'mob metaphysics' or 'commonsense philosophy' are not exactly oxymorons, they draw whatever charm they possess from playing off a felt tension. One of the hallmarks of philosophical activity is the way that it contrasts with common sense. It is part of the philosopher's job to be reflective about our common stock of beliefs, to attempt to go beyond, beneath, and behind what is taken as common sense and to carefully separate out that which is merely *common* to believe from that which is *sensible* to believe. For this reason alone, it simply is not clear that any philosophical work, never mind Berkeley's, can lay claim on common sense.

But there is still another question that needs answering:

> B. Even if there is something that deserves to be called the "metaphysics of the mob," why should one be particularly keen to show that one's position matches up with it?

Why must this be considered desirable? We have often had to abandon commonly held beliefs for new ones. We have had to come 'round to the beliefs that the sun does not rise or set, that light does not travel instantaneously, and that humans share common ancestry with apes. So if we find that critical reflection supports abandoning some or perhaps even the whole edifice of our commonly held beliefs in favor of a new one, why should this necessarily be regarded as a mark against it?

2. A Sellarsian Framework

Seeing how Berkeley's work deals with questions (A) and (B) will bring us to an understanding of the basic point of contact between common sense and his metaphysics. This, however, means navigating the wine-dark seas of metaphilosophy. To keep the discussion on course, I am going to tie it rather tightly to the mast of a fairly familiar and particularly well-made ship, the metaphilosophy left to us by Wilfrid Sellars in his essay "Philosophy and the Scientific Image of Man." In that work, Sellars provides a view of the fundamental challenge that the philosopher faces. As he saw it:

> The philosopher is confronted by not one complex many-dimensional picture, the unity of which, such as it is, he must come to appreciate, but by two pictures of essentially the same order of complexity, each of which purports to be a complete picture of man-in-the-world.[2]

Sellars' names for those two pictures of man-in-the-world, 'the manifest image' and 'the scientific image,' have acquired currency and, in the process of working their way into our lingua franca, they, quite naturally, have taken on a life of their own. The way in which our current employment of 'the manifest image' has diverged from its origins will matter in a moment, but we can and should begin with what has been preserved. Largely in line with Sellars' intentions, 'the manifest image' has come to name our view of the world as consisting of the sorts of items with which we meet in sense perception. There are two points here. First, the ontology of the manifest image is, as we might put it, ontologically permissive (cf. chapter I, §1). Reality consists of a variety of different kinds of entities, everything from "cabbages to kings."[3] Second, there is an important sense in which the manifest image takes those things to *be* as they *appear* to perception. This is not to say that in the manifest image there is no such thing as perceptual illusion—rather, the point is that, in the manifest image, objects are colored or clear, heavy or light, coarse or smooth, etc. This image of the world then competes with 'the scientific image' of man-in-the-world, and vice versa. The latter is our picture of reality as consisting, at most, of only a few kinds of things, and these things are the postulated entities of physical theory. Importantly, the basic entities of the scientific image are unimaginable because they are *imperceptible*. Within the scientific image, it does not even make sense to think of its basic objects as colored or clear, as smelly or fragrant, as coarse or soft, bitter or sweet, etc.

Now, because the philosopher is confronted by both images and because each image presents itself as a complete picture of man-in-the-world, the philosopher who endorses a given image as real inevitably seeks to subsume its rival. Here, subsumption should not be confused with accommodation. The philosopher who endorses one image as real thereby commits herself, in one way or another, to denying the same of the other image and its objects (cf. chapter I). If one endorses the scientific image as real, then one will be led to account for manifest entities by construing them, in one way or another, as "mere" appearances. That is to say, they will be regarded as appearances to human minds of the genuinely real, imperceptible entities of the scientific image. Many strategies will then present themselves, ranging in ontological hostility toward these mere appearances from the relatively conciliatory attitude of those epiphenomenalisms that tend toward property dualism all the way to the attitudes of the most jackbooted variety of eliminative materialism.

2.1. Berkeley and the Manifest Image

With this in mind, it will be tempting to identify Berkeley as one of the defenders of the manifest image over the scientific image. After all, who more than Berkeley railed against the countenancing of imperceptible posits and those who would thereby "lead us to think all the visible beauty of the creation a false imaginary glare?"[4] From our current perspective, we will see in Berkeley's work a daring attempt to "save the appearances" by advancing an eliminativist stance toward the basic objects of the scientific image. He will appear as the negative image of the contemporary eliminative materialist, shunning what they embrace—the postulated imperceptible entities of physical theory—and embracing what they shun, qualia and irreducible agents. He will, in effect, be an "eliminative immaterialist." In addition, his famous attack on abstract ideas will be seen as an attack on the coherence of any attempt to take our concept *object*, which has its home in perception, and use it without blush to denote *imperceptible* entities. Finally, by identifying Berkeley as a philosopher of the manifest image, we would have what we sought: an account of the connection between his metaphysics and his claim to be defending common sense.

There is a great deal that this sketch of Berkeley as eliminative immaterialist gets right and that I wish to preserve. However, if left as is, it will tend toward the reinforcement of our nemesis, the *esse* is *percipi* caricature. After all, we will, once again, be thinking of Berkeley's metaphysics primarily in terms of his views regarding the *secondary* entities of his ontology, the objects of perception.

The source of our problem here, as we shall see, is that whatever light an eliminative immaterialist characterization of Berkeley casts over his philosophical strategy as a whole, it still fails to reach so far as to illuminate the vital link between such a strategy and the true foundation of the manifest image. As a direct consequence of this, it misses the key connection between Berkeley's metaphysics and common sense. However, to set things right, we don't need to abandon or even really change the account we have given so far; rather, what we need to do is enrich it. The way to do this is to begin by enriching the account of the manifest image in precisely the way that Sellars did.

As Sellars presented it, the difference between the two images of man-in-the-world is defined largely in terms of differences in their basic entities. Our current characterization of the manifest image is designed to reflect popular usage. Consequently, we characterized its basic entities as being simply the familiar objects of sense perception. But this distorts the image in a crucial way. Sellars presents the manifest image as a development of a far more primordial image of man-in-the-world, an image he calls the "original image." It is from the original image that the manifest image inherits two of its most important features.

> i. First, there is an important sense in which the basic entities of the manifest image are not the vast and varied kinds of objects of perception but rather just one particular kind: persons.

This is due to the fact that the manifest image is a development of the original image wherein *all* entities are kinds within the category *person*. Here, human persons are the paradigm for the category *person*. But importantly, other objects, e.g., rivers and trees, are not thought of as differentially limiting enclosures of inhabiting human spirits. In the original image, persons are not conceived as, in some sense, consisting of two things: a visible body and an invisible soul. Rather, being a river or a tree is a *way of being a person*.[5] Two points are important here. First, this means that, within the original image, persons are objects of perception. Second, it means that the sorts of things that are said of rivers and trees, etc., are the sorts of things that are said of persons. But to fully appreciate the importance of this latter point, we need to introduce the second feature that the manifest image inherits from the original image.

> ii. It is the image in terms of which *we* have our origin.

That is to say, it is in terms of the conceptual apparatus common to the manifest and the original images that we come to have a *conception of ourselves*.[6] As Sellars puts it,

> It is the framework in terms of which, to use an existentialist turn of phrase, man first encountered himself—which is, of course, when he came to be man. For it is no merely incidental feature of man that he has a conception of himself as man-in-the-world.[7]

At the very heart of the original image lies the paradox consisting of the fact that "man couldn't be man until he had a conception of himself."[8] Consequently, our conception of the coming into being of man presents itself to us, not as a gradual development from our precursors, but as a kind of all-or-nothing leap into being. For

this reason, Sellars refers to this point as supporting the "last stand of special creation."[9] To be man is to possess a conception of oneself *as man*, but part of the problem
is that the peculiar activity of man, conceptual activity, is an entirely different category of behavior from what our ancestors engaged in; it is an irreducibly *evaluative*
activity and cannot be seen as something we arrived at piecemeal by the simple
cobbling together of prior non-evaluative bits of behavior. Again, as Sellars puts it,

> Anything which can properly be called conceptual thinking can occur only within a
> framework of conceptual thinking in terms of which it can be criticized, supported,
> refuted, in short, evaluated. To be able to think is to be able to measure one's thoughts by
> standards of correctness, of relevance, of evidence. In this sense a diversified conceptual
> framework is a whole which, however sketchy, is prior to its parts, and cannot be
> construed as a coming together of parts which are already conceptual in character. The
> conclusion is difficult to avoid that the transition from pre-conceptual patterns of be-
> haviour to conceptual thinking was a holistic one, a jump to a level of awareness which
> is irreducibly new, a jump which was the coming into being of man.[10]

So when we say, as we did above, that in the original image all objects are *persons*
and that the sorts of things that are said of rivers and trees, etc., are the sorts of
things that are said of persons, this means that one engages all objects as appropriate
targets of what are irreducibly evaluative activities (cf. chapter III, §7).

2.2. Person-Based Ontologies and Common Sense

Thanks to Sellars, we now have a start on answering (A), in what sense does the
mob have a metaphysics? and (B), why should a philosopher be concerned to be
answerable to it? The Sellarsian approach treats these as two sides of the same coin,
for, as points (i) and (ii) make plain, the manifest image and common sense are
united by the common conceptual framework in which *we* qua persons have our
origin and in terms of which we conceive of ourselves as such. This perspective on
ourselves, which the manifest image inherits from the original image, cannot be
regarded as optional; it is essential to us and, thus, is the bedrock of common sense
in the strictest possible meaning of 'common.' Clearly, this gives us a handle on (A),
but it also helps with (B), for the simple reason that the extent to which a philosopher's metaphysics fails to answer this, the core of common sense, is the extent
to which *we* fail to have a place in the proposed metaphysics.[11]

Having enriched our understanding of the foundations of the manifest image
via points (i) and (ii), we have also positioned ourselves to start enriching our picture of Berkeley as an eliminative immaterialist. Most important, we can do so in
such a way as to make clear in what sense he can be considered a defender of
common sense while, at the same time, steering clear of the *esse is percipi* caricature. We are in a better position to do this now because we have found that the key
link between the manifest image and Berkeley's metaphysics lies not in a shared
commitment to save the appearances but rather in the deeper fact that in both
Berkeley's metaphysics and in the manifest image, *the basic entities are persons.*

Now, of course, Berkelian spirits are not objects of perception, and the persons
of the manifest image are. This will matter, and matter deeply, as we proceed;

however, it is important to see that it does not undermine the point immediately at hand. We wanted to know what the basic connection between Berkeley's metaphysics and the manifest image was because we wanted to make sense of Berkeley's claim to be defending common sense. We have found that it is their shared identification of persons as the basic entities of their ontology. By comparison, whether one conceives of persons as perceptible entities or not is a secondary matter. In short, thanks to Sellars' account of both the manifest and the original images, we now have a clearer picture of the basis of the relationship between Berkeley's philosophy and common sense, for by regarding persons as the irreducible, fundamental entities of his ontology, Berkeley is building his metaphysics upon the ancient, adamantine core of our common conceptual inheritance.

3. The Religious Image

However, even though we have uncovered the basic point of contact between a person-based ontology and common sense, this still leaves us to explain two things. First, as just mentioned, even with respect to the basic category *person*, the manifest image and Berkeley disagree sharply. Persons, according to Berkeley, are *spirits*. So we must explain the relationship between common sense and a view of persons as spiritual entities. Second, we must be prepared to explain the relationship between common sense and an eliminativist attitude toward matter. The problem is that it is one thing to have a person-based ontology and quite another to have an immaterialist ontology. Our model for a commonsense metaphysics, the manifest image, also includes entities that are not persons; it recognizes impersonal things as varied in nature as bumblebees and hand grenades. And these impersonal things are not regarded as mere constructions of one sort or another; they are entities in their own right.

To meet both these demands, we must come to see that Berkeley is not a defender of common sense by way of being a philosopher of the manifest image.[12] He works in a tradition and framework not properly delineated by Sellars' discussion. We have to introduce what I will refer to as the "religious image" of man-in-the-world.[13] It, like the manifest image, is a development out of the original image, and because of this it shares those two key features, (i) and (ii), which provide the basic link to common sense. However, the religious image of man-in-the-world is a rival image to the manifest image as well as to the scientific image. It too presents itself as a complete picture of man-in-the-world. Only when we have a clear account of the nature of the religious image and the role of Berkeley's metaphysics in it will we have a clear understanding of the relationship between Berkeley's immaterialism and common sense.

The distinguishing feature of the religious image is that it is irreducibly *supernatural* in orientation. Here, 'supernatural' is being used in the traditional rather than the popular sense. As a first approximation, it is being used to indicate a metaphysical commitment to both a sharp distinction and priority ordering between creation (nature) and Creator. In the religious image, the existence of the natural is distinct from, and fully dependent upon, the existence of the nonnatural, i.e., the spiritual.

We can develop this point by way of contrast because, surprising as it may initially sound, the manifest image is fundamentally *pagan* in orientation. The justification for saying this will emerge as we proceed, but the first thing to note is that describing it as pagan implies that it is polytheistic, recognizing many gods, and so is, in a sense requiring careful qualification, a kind of religious image. However, it does not regard these gods as, strictly speaking, supernatural entities. There is not the same kind of division between a spirit and its associated natural manifestation. So, for instance, the two are not related as Creator and creation. Should the seas all dry up, there is a sense in which Poseidon vaporizes along with the waters. The category *spirit* is not properly a part of the pagan image. This is a function of the way that the manifest image develops out of the original image as opposed to the way that the religious image does.

Even though Sellars' discussion does not properly distinguish the manifest image from the religious image, we can, nonetheless, once again look to tools he left us to clarify the contrast. We just need to look a little further into how the manifest image developed out of the original image (i.e., how the move from an ontology in which all objects are persons to an ontology that is merely person-based is effected). According to Sellars, new objects enter the ontology not via the recognition of a new *category* of being alongside the category *person* but rather via a "depersonalization" of most, but of course not all, of the objects of the original image. Again, human beings are the paradigm persons of the original image and thus the paradigm beings of the manifest image. A conception of other kinds of beings is arrived at by what Sellars refers to as a process of "pruning" or "truncating" the concept *person*.

> In the early stages of the development of the manifest image, the wind was no longer conceived as acting deliberately, with an end in view—but rather from habit or impulse. Nature became the locus of 'truncated persons'; that which things could be expected to do, its habits; that which exhibits no order, its impulses. Inanimate things no longer 'did' things in the sense in which persons do them—not, however, because a *new* category of impersonal things and impersonal processes has been achieved, but because the category of *person* is now applied to these things in a pruned or truncated form. It is a striking exaggeration to say of a person, that he is a 'mere creature of habit and impulse,' but in the early stages of the development of [the] manifest image, the world includes truncated persons which *are* mere creatures of habit, acting out routines, broken by impulses, in a life which never rises above what ours is like in our most unreflective moments.[14]

Depersonalization via pruning is achieved by taking advantage of a pair of distinctions between kinds of action—or, more properly, *ways* of acting.

- Actions which are *in character* as opposed to *out of character*.
- Actions that are done out of *habit* or *impulse* as opposed to actions done *deliberately*.

The paradigm beings of the manifest/pagan image, normal adult humans, engage in the full range of actions. Strictly speaking, a person is something that can act either deliberately or out of habit and who can act in or out of character. Depersonalization can be viewed as the process of constraining the range of inferences one is entitled to make with regard to some entity upon being told that it "did" something. The more far-reaching these constraints, the further we get from our conception of a paradigm personal entity and the more closely we approach the recognition of something like a new category of entity (but, at the same time, the further we get from our conception of a paradigm personal entity, the more we tempt incoherence by straining against the boundaries of the image's basic conception of being).

Now, it should be noted that truncating affects an entity's range of activities—not its range or degree of influence. A man can blow a butterfly off his shoulder, but Astraeus, the wind god, can blow a man off his feet. On the other hand, a man can also build a house, ride a horse, and dig a well. Astraeus cannot or, at least, not unless he can assume the "form" of a man. The pagan gods are not supernatural; they are *superhuman.*

Of course, if we can conceive of entities as having much larger spheres and degrees of influence, then we can also conceive of them as having much more limited ones. A skeptically minded pagan who undertakes to explain the occurrence of events, not in terms of the interventions and interactions of superhuman beings, but rather in terms of the interactions of subhuman beings is still working with entities conceived within the category *person*, for this "scientifically" minded pagan is taking advantage of the ability to think in terms of highly truncated individuals. At the extreme end, the manifest image's conception of subhuman entities is arrived at by moving toward the notion of a being to which the application of the concepts *character* and *deliberation* are less and less useful. As a given entity's behavior is regarded as more and more reliably predictable, it is seen as *always* acting in a blindly *habitual* manner. And where the prospect of a change in the orderly pattern of an entity's habitual activities being effected by either impulses or deliberation is no longer regarded as a going concern, one comes to think of the entity's actions as expressions not of its *character* but merely of its *nature*. So, for instance, it is part of the nature of a subhuman entity, like a rock, to move toward the ground when dropped. Here we are thinking of a thing's nature as a way of "summing up the predictabilities no holds barred"[15] in that it will be the inner nexus of those predictabilities, if you will. Now, with that in mind, we must take care to keep the concepts *character* and *nature* distinct. That is to say,

> we must be careful not to equate the *nature* of a person with his *character*, although his character will be a "part" of his nature in the broad sense. Thus, if everything a person did were predictable (in principle), given sufficient knowledge about the person and the circumstances in which he was placed, and was, therefore, an "expression of his nature," it would not follow that everything the person did was an expression of his *character.*[16]

Even though the concepts of all the various kinds of entities of the manifest image emerge from the concept of that which can have a full-blooded character (i.e., a person), there will be a sense in which the image is coming to recognize new kinds of entities in its ontology. There will be as many different kinds of entities as there are kinds of natures. And one will posit as many different kinds of natures as one needs to see the happenings of the world as the result of just so many different kinds and combinations of blind, habitual actions.

3.1. "The Most Dangerous Error of the Philosophy of the Ancients"

From here, it takes but a very small step to see that Aristotelianism is the paradigm philosophy of the manifest image. As was already intimated, the all-important notion of an object's *form* comes to be the catchall for the internal locus of an entity's nature. To recall the relevant example, it is primarily the fact that Astraeus lacks the *form* of a man that explains why he lacks the *abilities* of a man. Within the framework of the manifest image, the concept of an object's form is intimately tied to that of its "faculties" or "powers." In short, the manifest image presents the natural, perceptible world as home to a vast number of different kinds of powerful individuals.

Given our discussion in chapter I, it will be particularly easy for us to see that it was precisely this view of the world against which Descartes' ontological minimalism was directed. Now, in chapter I, I presented Descartes' project in such a way that it might be tempting to see what Descartes was doing as a kind of whittling down of the number of different kinds of beings that a workable ontology needs to just two: material substances and mental substances.[17] While it is true that Descartes is trying to present a more streamlined ontology, to say that his method for achieving this is simply to show that we can get by recognizing fewer kinds of substances would fail to capture just how radical his proposal was. Descartes is not suggesting that we merely recognize fewer *kinds* of beings; he is suggesting that we must abandon the fundamental *category* of being upon which the manifest/pagan image is built. In its place, we are to introduce two entirely new and distinct categories of being. I pressed the importance of this point in chapter I by emphasizing that, unlike Aristotelian kinds of beings, it simply does not make sense to talk of the difference of *degrees* in the being of matter and the being of mind. The chasm between the two is as deep and dark as that between *being* and *nothingness* and yet is to be conceived as a distinction *within* being. Whether this presents a coherent proposal is a matter to which we will have to return. The immediate point is that, from the Cartesian perspective, we are not merely taking up Occam's razor against the Aristotelian forest of beings, slashing and burning until we come to just two kinds of beings and a corresponding number of forms. The entire framework of explanation in terms of forms, faculties, etc., must be dumped along with the fundamental way in which *being* is conceived. It is Malebranche who did the most to bring the point out. In "Elucidation 10" of *The Search after Truth*, Malebranche replies to an objection raised by "Cartesian gentlemen" who, supposedly, accept the new metaphysics but are still ready to make explanatory appeals that invoke the mind's nature or faculty in an Aristotelian sense.

> I am amazed that the Cartesian gentlemen, who so rightly reject the general terms 'nature' and 'faculty' should so willingly employ them on this occasion. They criticize those who say that fire burns by its nature or that it changes certain bodies into glass by a natural faculty, and yet some of them do not hesitate to say that the human mind produces in itself the idea of all things by its nature, because it has the faculty of

thinking. But with all due respect, these terms are no more meaningful in their mouth[s] than in the mouth[s] of the Peripatetics.[18]

One will recognize in this reply the complaint, later popularized by Voltaire, against the explanatory bankruptcy of appeals to things like the "dormative faculties" of a drug to explain its sedative effects. But there are deeper concerns at work. The conceptual revolution that marks the move from the pagan image of man-in-the-world to the religious image of man-in-the-world centers, in large part, around the concept *power*. Not surprisingly, it is Malebranche who sees the consequences of this most clearly. In a chapter of *The Search after Truth* that he titles "The most dangerous error of the philosophy of the ancients," Malebranche writes,

> [I]f we assume, in accordance with their opinion, that bodies have certain entities distinct from matter in them, then, having no distinct idea of these entities, we can easily imagine that they are the true or major causes of the effects we see. That is even the general opinion of ordinary philosophers; for it is mainly to explain these effects that they think there are substantial forms, real qualities, and other similar entities. If we consider attentively our idea of cause or of power to act, we cannot doubt that this idea represents something divine. For the idea of a sovereign power is the idea of sovereign divinity, and the idea of subordinate power is the idea of a lower divinity, but a genuine one, at least according to the pagans, assuming that it is the idea of a genuine power or cause. We therefore admit something divine in all bodies around us when we posit forms, faculties, qualities, virtues, or real beings capable of producing certain effects through the force of their nature; and thus we insensibly adopt the opinion of the pagans because of respect for their philosophy. It is true that faith corrects us, but perhaps it can be said in this connection that if the heart is Christian, the mind is basically pagan.[19]

The move to what I am calling the religious image requires a shift in the way one understands the relationship between *being* and *power* to one that is directly hostile to the manifest/pagan way of conceiving this relationship. In his insightful *Malebranche and British Philosophy*, Charles McCracken draws our attention to precisely the right point.

> It was Aristotle and his scholastic followers, according to Malebranche, who were guilty of building an entire system of metaphysics and physics on the empty notions of power, force, and faculty.... The belief that nature abounds in forces, powers, and secondary causes is one universally diffused; it is that very 'philosophy of the serpent' that misled the progenitors of our race in paradise. For what led to the Fall of man but the acceptance of this false belief that *something* other than God has the power to cause us joy or sorrow?[20]

This leads to the development of what McCracken labels the "two concepts of nature."

> Two concepts of nature compete with each other, in Malebranche's view. According to one, nature is a dynamic storehouse of powers and forces and causes, which produce all the events our eyes behold (or all those at least that do not depend on the human will). According to the other, natural events, though occurring in a perfectly uniform and invariable way, are connected only by the temporal relations of *before* and *after*. On the latter view, the cause of these events is not some other, earlier event; the cause

is solely the will of God. The former concept of nature, though false, is—because bound up with our fallen nature—almost universally accepted, even by Christians; the latter concept, though true, is almost wholly unknown or ignored.[21]

The development of what McCracken refers to as the "two concepts of nature" is an important part of the development of the religious image, and Malebranche is a key figure in the articulation of the philosophy that endorses this image as real. Malebranche is not, however, the most important figure in many ways. This, I think, is a point Malebranche would not only concede but even upon which he would insist. The most important figure here is Augustine.

3.2. Augustine's Two Problems

Anyone familiar with *The Confessions* will be able to recognize that, within the person of Augustine, we find the conflict between the two competing concepts of nature come to a head. The work presents a searching and powerful account of just what is required of one who would make the move from the pagan image to the religious image. Within those pages, Augustine's struggle focuses on a pair of questions and the concept of *existence*.

> I was ignorant of that other reality, true Being. And so it was that I was subtly persuaded to agree with these foolish deceivers when they put their questions to me: "Whence comes evil?" and, "Is God limited by a bodily shape, and has he hair and nails?" ... In my ignorance I was much disturbed over these things.[22]

The particular group of "foolish deceivers" to which Augustine is referring is the Manichaeans. In one way, the sect represented a kind of reductive, quasi-scientific version of paganism. It saw greater unity in nature than did the advocates for more traditional pagan religions. Ultimately, thought the Manichaeans, we don't need to appeal to a vast pantheon of sometimes competing, sometimes cooperating forces or deities to render the world intelligible. Instead, there is a sense in which one need only recognize two basic forces in nature: one good, the other evil. The position of a human in this world can then be viewed as that of an entity trapped between the two.

Before his conversion to Christianity, Augustine, for a time, counted himself one of the Manichaeans. There are many reasons for this, but certainly one of the things that attracted Augustine was that the Manichaean world view promoted a progressive attitude toward the possibility of seeing nature as an intelligible unity. In the pagan framework, the more one regards the natural world as orderly and predictable, the less need there is to see the various deities as subject to whims and impulses. The less one sees the various deities as acting out of whims and impulses, the more rational and harmonious their interactions will appear. At the same time, the greater the harmony and order one regards nature as displaying, the less conflict one sees in nature. Consequently, there will be less need to posit many distinct deities to explain manifestations of conflict. So, for instance, one possible attitude toward a natural disaster, such as the eruption of a volcano, is seeing it as a kind of *discordance*. It is regarded as something that, in a certain sense, *should not* happen. The pagan can readily accommodate the attitude that regards this event as something that "should not have happened" and yet something that in fact did happen, i.e., the pagan can treat it both as *fully bad* and as *fully real*. Such discordant events are natural manifestations of discord among the deities—perhaps, the result of one of the gods being angered by the actions of another. On the other hand, if one does not view the eruption as a discordant event but instead as the necessary upshot of orderly, perhaps even lawlike governance of the natural world, the less need there is to posit multiple deities.

The Manichaeans, however, understood that no matter how orderly one regards the events of the natural world to be, this is not in itself enough to justify the belief that there is only one god in the Judeo-Christian sense of 'God.' For in the face of manifest evil, how could one advocate the reality of only one deity who is wholly good, omniscient, and omnipotent? The best one can do, the Manichaeans claim, is to recognize two fundamental forces in nature: one good, one evil.

Consequently, Augustine's struggle focuses on the "problem of evil." However, it is the resolution of the second problem that Augustine recounts in the preceding quotation from the *Confessions*—the question of how one is to conceive of the being of God—which provides him with what he needs for his more famous answer to the first: whence comes evil? As Augustine puts it, it was his ignorance regarding "true Being" that was the source of his trouble. His famous solution to the problem of evil is to regard evil as a "privation," as something nonsubstantive. That is to say, it is not a true being but rather a privation of being. But such an approach requires an understanding of the nature of *being*, which, unlike the pagan/manifest conception of being, makes the privation strategy available. That Augustine believes he has come to such a conception is made clear by the way he continues the passage:

> [T]hough I was retreating from the truth, I appeared to myself to be going toward it, because I did not yet know that evil was nothing but a privation of good (that, indeed, it has no being) and how should I have seen this when the sight of my eyes went no farther than physical objects, and the sight of my mind reached no farther than to fantasms? I did not know that God is a spirit who has no parts extended in length and breadth.... And I was entirely ignorant as to what is that principle within us by which we are like God, and which is rightly said in Scripture to be made "after God's image."[23]

The category person must become the category spirit. Importantly, the transformation of the pagan category person to that of spirit is not complete until an irreducibly *evaluative* conception of being is achieved. Here, Augustine looks to Plato for help in developing an ontology to fit a view of reality that regards it as ultimately morally ordered.

> Where there is evil, there is a corresponding diminution of the good. As long, then, as a thing is being corrupted, there is good in it of which it is being deprived; and in this process, if something of its being remains that cannot be further corrupted, this will then be an incorruptible entity and to this great good it will have come through the process of corruption. But even if the corruption is not arrested, it still does not cease having some good of which it cannot be further deprived. If, however, the corruption comes to be total and entire, there is no good left either, because it is no longer an entity at all. Wherefore corruption cannot consume the good without also consuming the thing itself. Every actual entity is therefore good; a greater good if it cannot be corrupted, a lesser

good if it can be. Yet only the foolish and unknowing can deny that it is still good even when corrupted. Whenever a thing is consumed by corruption, not even the corruption remains, for it is nothing in itself, having no subsistent being in which to exist.[24]

Augustine articulates the fundamental conceptual conversion required of one who is to move from the manifest/pagan image to the competing religious image of man-in-the-world. In effect, what he learned from the Manichaeans is that it is not enough to engage in a reductive narrowing down of the number of deities of the pagan image to one or even, through an imaginative combinatorial process, to introduce into the pagan image a new *über* deity, one that would, somehow, render the need for all the others obsolete (just as Berkeley saw that no sensory perception, nor any combination of such by the imagination, would give one the concept of spirit). What is required is a complete transformation of the category *being*. From the perspective of the religious image, the pagan's mistake does not lie in treating person as the primary category of being, but rather in what she takes to be the paradigm of that category. It is not the normal adult human who plays that role. In the religious image, it is God. God is not a being *within* nature but a being distinct from it and, in every way, prior to it. He is in no way limited by physical form. The question about God having hair and nails simply has no place.

3.3. The Promise of Cartesianism

In light of the preceding, it will not appear surprising that Malebranche saw in the Cartesian metaphysics the coming to fruition of the seeds that Augustine had planted. In Descartes' radical bifurcation of being, we have the kind of fundamental reconceptualization of the nature of true being that the religious image requires. Cartesian minds are immaterial spirits, in no way to be confused with pagan persons. And even though Descartes presents a dualistic ontology, the category *spirit* enjoys a privileged position. All beings in the ontology depend on God for their existence, and God, like us, is a mental substance. In addition, God is, of course, the paradigm of the category *spirit*. We are finite spirits, made in his image. In short, it is a super-natural metaphysics built from within the religious image.

In fact, so congenial is the Cartesian metaphysics to the Augustinian conception of being and, correspondingly, to the foundation of the religious image that Augustine more than once anticipates Descartes' famous *cogito* argument. The most telling instance is found in his *The City of God against the Pagans*.

And we indeed recognize in ourselves the image of God, that is, of the supreme Trinity. . . . For we both are, and know that we are, and delight in our being, and our knowledge of it. Moreover, in these three things no true-seeming illusion disturbs us; for we do not come into contact with these by some bodily sense, as we perceive the things outside of us—colors, e.g., by seeing, sounds by hearing, smells by smelling, tastes by tasting, hard and soft objects by touching—of all which sensible objects it is the images resembling them, but not themselves which we perceive in the mind and hold in the memory, and which excite us to desire the objects. But, without any delusive representation of images or phantasms, I am most certain that I am, and that I know and delight in this. In respect of these truths, I am not at all afraid of the arguments of the Academicians, who say, What if you are deceived? For if I am deceived, I am. For he who is not, cannot be deceived; and if I am deceived, by this same token I am. And since I am if I am deceived, how am I deceived in believing that I am? for it is certain that I am if I am deceived. Since, therefore, I, the person deceived, should be, even if I were deceived, certainly I am not deceived in this knowledge that I am. And, consequently, neither am I deceived in knowing that I know. For, as I know that I am, so I know this also, that I know.[25]

Augustine's presentation of the *cogito* argument has the advantage of making clear that while we are certain that we exist from our awareness of ourselves, our being is not the paradigm of the category *spirit*. In fact, our knowledge of our own existence is dependent upon the fact that we find in our own being the "image of God." Still, those who embrace the religious image's conception of spirit will find in the Cartesian account of mental substance a clear philosophical ally.

But what about the Cartesian view of the nonspiritual, i.e., the natural world? Here, too, the pious can find much of which to approve. As far as the Cartesian is concerned, the natural world consists of no more than material substance, and material substance is no more than *extension*. There are two chief reasons for the advocate of the religious image to find this attractive. First, there is the point that Malebranche has already emphasized: if matter is no more than extension, then it is entirely passive, bereft of active pagan powers.

> It is difficult to be persuaded that we should neither fear nor love true powers—beings that can act upon us, punish us with pain, or reward us with pleasure. And as love and fear are true adoration, it is also difficult to be persuaded that we should not adore these beings. Everything that can act upon us as a true and real cause is necessarily above us.... Hence if we assume the false opinion ... that the bodies that surround us are the true causes of the pleasures and ills we feel, reason seems to some degree to justify a religion similar to that of the pagans.[26]

Since matter is no more than extension, neither anything in nature nor even the whole of the natural world are appropriate objects of love or fear; there is nothing in the natural world worthy of our worship.

The other attractive aspect of the Cartesian conception of matter, certainly one that Augustine would have appreciated, is the way it promises to supply a *unified* view of the natural world. The world is the extended plenum. All events in it are harmonious, orderly, perfectly rule governed, in a word, coherent. In fact, because it is no more than extension, we have a perfect science of it in geometry. Such a view fits well with a supernatural metaphysics wherein nature is regarded as the creation of a perfect Creator.

3.4. *The Problematic of Dualism; or, Why Theists Should Be Immaterialists*

We can begin to see where Berkeley's immaterialism fits into the religious image by pressing an overdue question: is the Cartesian metaphysics a viable option for those who endorse the religious image as real? I have emphasized the leap the Aristotelian is asked to make in accepting the Cartesian bifurcation of being by saying that the distinction between the being of *mind* and the being of *matter* is as stark a division as that between *being* and *nothingness*, while at the same time it is to be conceived as a distinction *within* being. But is this a coherent proposal? It might be if the comparisons between mind/matter and being/nothingness were merely an explanatory device, a metaphor of sorts and not to be taken literally. Unfortunately, however, if the account I have been presenting in this chapter is the right way to see the dialectic, then we can expect it will be very difficult to keep the concept *material substance* from collapsing into *nothing*.[27]

The basic problem should already be clear. Simply put, the Cartesian metaphysics is a philosophy within the religious image. As such, its basic category of being is spirit. How then is the concept of a wholly impersonal, nonspiritual substance to be achieved within the religious image? The Cartesians, even if they wanted to, cannot escape this problem by saying that Descartes is not really a philosopher of the religious image. It will not do to say simply that the Cartesian philosophy, by stipulation, recognizes two distinct, independent concepts of substance—and thus two independent categories of being: one mental and one material. The rub is nicely summed up by the Cartesian thesis that God alone is substance in the strictest sense of the term. Within the Cartesian metaphysics, the coherence of the notion *finite* mental substance presupposes the coherence of the category *spirit*. On the other hand, while it makes sense to suppose that the concept of finite spiritual substance might be reachable via a process like truncation, the concept of material substance certainly cannot. At best, that could give us only distinctions of kinds *within* the category of spirit. It will never yield a wholly distinct, nonspiritual category of being.

There are clear signs of instability on the material substance side of Cartesian dualism, and they are exactly where we should expect to find them—in matters regarding the *individuation* of material objects. Once again, we can look to the wax discussion Descartes introduces into the "Second Meditation" to counter the nagging prejudice that corporeal things are better understood than "this puzzling 'I' which cannot be pictured in imagination."[28] Upon reflection, we have found that although we take ourselves to be acquainted with a single thing, this piece of wax, we cannot find our idea of that thing, the wax itself, among the ever-changing wash of sensory ideas. Upon further reflection, we find that neither can we identify the wax with any combination or collection of ideas that our imagination could put together for us. To what idea then does the logically proper name 'this piece of wax' attach? Descartes' proposal is that it is the non-imagistic representational faculty of the pure intellect that lets us grasp the wax itself. It gives us the idea of an *extended thing* to which we attach that name. But does that succeed in giving us a grasp of the wax? Margaret Wilson draws out the central problem:

> The answer Descartes gives to the question, 'what belongs to the wax?'—to be something extended, flexible, mutable—obviously provides no sort of answer at all to the question, 'what makes wax wax?' or 'what makes this thing the same individual?'[29]

Since *all* material things are extended things, simply accounting for the possession of the idea *extension* does not even account for my idea of *wax*, let alone my idea of *this individual* piece of wax. The issue is a fairly familiar one that has contributed to the difficulty of interpreting the notorious wax discussion. Wilson goes on to draw our attention to the crucial point:

> In fact, Descartes has already asserted in the Synopsis that a body that changes "its" shape is in reality no longer the same individual![30]

The passage from the "Synopsis" to which she refers is the following:

> [W]e need to recognize that body, taken in the general sense, is a substance, so that it never perishes. But the human body, in so far as it differs from other bodies [as an individual thing] is simply made up of a certain configuration of limbs and other accidents of this sort; whereas the human mind is not made up of any accidents in this way, but is a *pure substance*. For even if all the accidents of the mind change, so that it has different objects of the understanding and different desires and sensations, it does not on that account become a different mind; whereas a human body loses its *identity* merely as the result of a change in shape of some of its parts.[31]

Notice that material things are here contrasted with "pure substance" and that is because they are not genuine *individuals*. Pure intellect acquaints us with the essence of material being, extension, but thereby reveals that there is only one material substance, "body in the general sense" (i.e., the Cartesian plenum).[32] The wax, in contrast, is not a genuine individual substance because it is not a genuine unity.

The problem is *power* or, rather, the Cartesian thesis that matter utterly lacks it. Cartesian matter is passive. The instability results from the clash of this thesis with the appeal to the "passive power" of matter. We have already looked at some prima facie problems for the notion of passive power in chapter IV. Here, we bring those problems to a head.

On the one hand, the passivity of matter is a point in favor of Cartesian dualism. As Malebranche made clear, it allows a pious view of nature, one in which individuals are stripped of all pagan powers. All interactions between natural objects are entirely and directly under the orderly direction of God's will. This, however, leaves us with the problem of making sense of the claim that matter has something called "passive power."

One possibility is that in calling matter passive, the Cartesian is only denying that bodies stand in transeunt causal relations to one another (i.e., they do not interact with one another). Unfortunately, what we find is that, in the Cartesian metaphysics, there is neither transeunt nor immanent causation. The Cartesian doctrine of continual creation makes plain the serious trouble of attributing any kind of power to the individual. Not only is a body passive with respect to other bodies, it is passive with respect to itself. There is no sense in which earlier or present states of a material body are the cause of later states of it. Once again, we can look to Malebranche for clarification:

> Now observe. God wills that there be a world. His will is all-powerful, and so the world is made. Let God no longer will that there be a world, and it is thereby annihilated. For the world certainly depends on the volitions of the Creator. If the world subsists, it is because God continues to will that the world exist. On the part of God, the conservation of creatures is simply their continued creation. I say, on the part of God who acts. For, on

the part of creatures, there appears to be a difference since, in creation they pass from nothing to being whereas, in conservation, they continue to be. But, in reality, creation does not pass away because, in God, conservation and creation are one and the same volition which consequently is necessarily followed by the same effects.[33]

Here is the problem: we might agree that one body need not be able to act on another body for the concept of material substance to be coherent. After all, Leibniz built an entire metaphysics based on "windowless" monads. But as Leibniz rightly saw, if we are to make sense of the idea of individuals surviving change, then at the very least they must, in some sense, "contain" their own possibilities within themselves. This requires power—*active power*. As pointed out in chapter I, the point of attributing power to the wax seems to be to help make sense of the notion that the wax is a unity. There has to be something about the wax itself that makes it such that *it* (i.e., one and the same individual) *can* (i.e., has the power to) become liquid, that *it can* become blanched, etc. The concepts *individual* and *active power* are inseparable. There must be something about this particular individual that *unites* these possibilities to *it*. It is the attribution of a power to an individual that lets us see the individual as containing or projecting possibilities. If this individual does not "possess" some kind of power, it cannot possess what may come to pass as possible states of itself. The expression 'this piece of wax' will not name a genuine individual but instead will merely name a bundle. "Its" states will be united by nothing more than the *name*. But there is no clear sense in which Cartesian material substances possess any kind of power. It would seem that, strictly speaking, Cartesian material "individuals" are merely fleeting things. Like Berkeley's *ideas*, the slightest change destroys them. In what sense, then, is such a thing a *substance*?

Perhaps none. Perhaps that is the point of the plenum. One might not exactly like the thesis that, strictly speaking, there are no material individuals, but one might still deny that this amounts to immaterialism. There is still something that has an absolute existence distinct from all minds whatsoever; there is the material plenum. It is the general idea of body that represents a substance. "Individual" material things within it are not, strictly speaking, individual substances, but this does not stop matter as such from being a substance.

The viability of this strategy depends upon there being some sense to be made of the attribution of passive power to the material plenum. But what is this power that the plenum holds? Just what exactly is it that matter *does*? In the end, the passivity of matter renders it an ontological extravagance.

As to the opinion that there are no corporeal causes, this has been heretofore maintained by some of the Schoolmen, as it is of late by others among the modern philosophers, who though they allow matter to exist, yet will have God alone to be the immediate efficient cause of all things. These men saw, that amongst all the objects of sense, there was none which had any power or activity included in it, and that by consequence this was like-wise true of whatever bodies they supposed to exist without the mind, like unto the im-mediate objects of sense. But then, that they should suppose an innumerable multitude of created beings, which they acknowledge are not capable of producing any one effect in Nature, and which therefore are made to no manner of purpose, since God might have done every thing as well without them; this I say, though we should allow it possible, must yet be a very unaccountable and extravagant supposition.[34]

Throughout the *Principles* and the *Three Dialogues*, Berkeley relentlessly pursues one proposed positive role for matter after another. The exhaustiveness of his search is one of the more impressive features of his immaterialism. But we need not retrace his hunt here because, at bottom, the problem for the philosopher working within the religious image is really quite simple: *God's power* is sufficient to explain all the phenomena of nature. As Philonous puts it to Hylas,

> Not to insist now on your making sense of this hypothesis [of material substance], or answering all the puzzling questions and difficulties it is liable to: I only ask whether the order and regularity observable in the series of our ideas, or the course of Nature, be not sufficiently accounted for by the wisdom and power of God?[35]

Worse yet, if we do ask Hylas to make sense of his hypothesis, we run up against the problem that without some positive role for matter to play, it becomes indistinguishable from nothing. Think of it this way: suppose one grants that because matter has no power, it is entirely passive. Suppose one also grants that it, therefore, can fill no positive explanatory role. Even so, one might insist that a lack of power does not entail nonexistence. The problem with such a response lies in figuring out just what the content of the idea *material being* is and how we acquire it. Since no amount of "truncating" will lead one from the concept *spiritual being* to that of *material being*, it would seem that the only option left open to the materialist is a process of *negation*. That is to say, one will attempt to achieve the needed idea by way of "abstracting away" the properties appropriate to spirits until one comes to the conception of "being in-itself." But such a process leads to no such place, as Berkeley points out.

> In the last place, you will say, what if we . . . assert, that matter is an unknown somewhat, neither substance nor accident, spirit nor idea, inert, thoughtless, indivisible, immoveable, unextended, existing in no place? For, say you, whatever may be urged against substance or occasion, or any other positive or relative notion of matter, hath no place at all, so long as this negative definition of matter is adhered to. I answer, you may, if so it shall seem good, use the word matter in the same sense, that other men use 'nothing,' and so make those terms convertible in your style. For after all, this is what appears to me to be the result of that definition, the parts whereof when I consider with attention, either collectively, or separate[ly] from each other, I do not find that there is any kind of effect or impression made on my mind, different from what is excited by the term 'nothing.'[36]

Notice that Berkeley need not insist that 'material substance' is meaningless because it denotes neither spirit nor idea. Berkeley can grant it meaning based upon its linguistic role, so long as we see that its role is equivalent to that of the word 'nothing.'

4. Conclusion: Common Sense, Eliminative Immaterialism, and the Religious Image

Finally, we can bring this ship to shore. We have now reached a place where we can make sense of Berkeley's claim that his philosophy is of a piece with common sense. To recap: we took Sellars' manifest image as our starting point for understanding what a commonsense view of reality might be. We found that one important link between the manifest image and common sense was the fact that, in the manifest image, natural objects are regarded as perceivable. However, upon further investigation, we found that it was the fact that the manifest image is a person-based ontology that provided it with its most fundamental link to common sense.[37] It was this feature of the manifest image that gave us a conception of ourselves as having a place in reality. We then pointed out the obvious, i.e., that Berkeley's ontology was also person-based and thereby had a connection to common sense that mirrored the manifest image's connection. As for Berkeley's immaterialism, we suggested that he could be seen as an early modern photo negative of the contemporary eliminative materialist. His mental monism could be seen as a straightforward attempt to streamline the prevailing dualistic ontology by ridding it of a superfluous posit while at the same time maintaining the fundamental link to common sense.

The problem with this interpretation, however, was that it overlooked the fact that Berkeley's view of persons as *spirits* embodies a radical reconceptualization of the manifest image's basic category of being. Because of this, Berkeley could not be considered a philosopher of the manifest image. At this point, I introduced a competing image of man-in-the-world that I dubbed the "religious image." The most important distinguishing feature of this image is that it regards *spirit* as the basic category of being.

From our current perspective, we can easily see that Berkeley's immaterialism has a natural, even an inevitable place in the development of the religious image. There is nothing at all strange about adopting an eliminative attitude toward material substance from within the religious image because that view of reality can make no sense of the idea of material substance, i.e., of an independently existing, absolutely nonspiritual being. Any attempt to introduce such a thing into the ontology undermines the image's conception of the fundamental nature of being and thereby destabilizes the religious image's very conception of reality and humanity's place in it. Berkeley's strategy for denying natural objects the status of substances can then be seen as a working through of the consequences of the Augustinian strategy of treating evil as a privation of being.

Undoubtedly, it will now be pointed out that this account only lines up Berkeley's metaphysics with common sense insofar as the religious image itself is in line with common sense. It will be objected that, while the manifest image is intimately connected to common sense, the religious image is not. When the religious image moved from the manifest image's category *person* to the category *spirit*, it severed the vital link between itself and common sense.

But if for this reason the religious image is denied the status of common sense, then Berkeley would readily reject the notion that his work is a defense of, or even consistent with, common sense. Berkeley is only interested in defending his view as common sense insofar as a commitment to a traditional Judeo-Christian monotheism is considered a part of common sense. It is true that Berkeley claimed to "side in all things with the mob," but the first part of that familiar quotation is almost never reproduced. The whole reads,

All things in the Scripture which side with the Vulgar against the Learned side with me also. I side in all things with the Mob.[38]

Certainly, the great bulk of the "vulgar" are professing monotheists. This is the mob for which Berkeley speaks. As I emphasized in chapter II, Berkeley's overall approach to philosophical problems is largely deflationary in character. As we know, he regards most philosophical perplexity as products of our own making. The problem is that "we have first raised a dust, and then complain, we cannot see."[39] Berkeley works his deflationary strategy from a theistic starting point, a view built upon this fundamental reconceptualization of *person* as *spirit*. Central among his aims is to show that the countenancing of material substance is the worst bit of dust we have yet kicked up. At the same time, however, it is not unaccountable that even committed theists should be drawn to a belief in matter. That is inevitable, given man's fallen nature. As Berkeley writes in one of his earliest notebook entries,

fall of Adam, rise of Idolatry, rise of Epicurism & Hobbism . . . &c expounded by material substances.[40]

Berkeley's point is that no professing theist should believe in material substance. Materialism and idolatry are intertwined, a joint product of our common ailment: our fallen nature. The person who is sincerely committed to the religious image should reject any proposal that would introduce a strong separation between the concepts of existence and spirit in the way that the materialist proposes. From our present perspective, we can see why one might well think it strange that the average person should believe that all the objects of the natural world, its houses, mountains, rivers, trees, etc., have existence independent of all minds whatsoever. God, after all, is a mind, a spirit.

Berkeley's use of 'common sense' must be assumed to include those committed to this conceptual conversion. At the same time, however, we must not forget that a grasp of the true nature of mind (spirit) is something that must be actively pursued if it is to be achieved. Initially, its nature is concealed from us. Berkeley calls on the Platonic philosophy to illustrate his perspective.

It was the Platonic doctrine that human souls or minds descended from above, and were sowed in generation; that they were stunned, stupified, and intoxicated by this descent and immersion into animal nature; and that the soul, in this . . . slumber, forgets her original notions, which are smothered and oppressed by many false tenets and prejudices of sense. Insomuch that Proclus compares the soul, in her descent invested with growing prejudices, to Glaucus diving to the bottom of the sea, and there contracting divers coats of seaweed, coral, and shells, which stick close to him, and *conceal his true shape*.[41]

Again, our task is not primarily constructive; it is not to build but, rather, to tear down. We are "smothered and oppressed by many false tenets and prejudices." To come to a clear conception of the nature of the self, we must strip away our false opinions and prejudices.

[Ac]cording to this philosophy, the *mind of man* is so restless to shake off that slumber, to disengage and emancipate herself from those prejudices and false opinions that so straitly beset and cling to her, to rub off those covers that *disguise her original form*.[42]

But, as Augustine's *Confessions* dramatically chronicles, the move from the pagan to the Judeo-Christian concept of mind requires not merely a conceptual development brought about by careful discursive meditation; it requires conversion. This is an orthodox view, one that Berkeley certainly shared. His respect for the value of philosophy is profound, but we should not confuse his commitment to it as a commitment to the view that unaided reason can generate the kind of conversion that forms the foundation of the religious image. Not even the invaluable insights of the great Plato, who "joined with an imagination the most splendid and magnificent, an intellect not less deep and clear," were all "struck from the hard rock of human reason." Some were rather, "derived, at least in part, by a divine tradition from the author of all things."[43] Left to our own devices, our own nature would remain a mystery to us. What aid even the most profound traditions of philosophy can offer is due to their divine origin.

> Whoever considers a parcel of rude savages left to themselves, how they are sunk and swallowed up in sense and prejudice, and how unqualified by their natural force to emerge from this state, will be apt to think that the first spark of philosophy was derived from heaven.[44]

As Berkeley sees it, the great advantage that his mob enjoys over even the most enlightened pagan philosopher[45] is that of having been raised in the Judeo-Christian tradition, a tradition that, as part and parcel of one's upbringing, communicates the conception of mind as spirit to its members. This, however, does not leave the common person free from the blinding and encumbering effects of "prejudices and false opinions." All members of the mob must work to free themselves and to see themselves aright. They have the great advantage of having been given the concept *spirit* as part of their common conceptual heritage, but to reap its benefits, they must also embrace it. To do this, it is not essential that one be able to give a metaphysician's account of mind as spirit. Here, we must recall Berkeley's philosophy of language. Mastery of a concept is a matter of the mastery of a network of practices. But the word 'spirit' is no ordinary word. In contrast to mundane words like 'toaster,' 'rain,' or even 'quark,' within the word 'spirit' is encapsulated a whole network of implications with global practical import for an agent. Explicitly embracing this conception of the self is manifested by nothing short of a religious form of life. As Berkeley puts it in *Alciphron*, "the true end of . . . faith . . . is . . . something of an active operative nature, tending to a conceived good."[46] Berkeley believes that the more one is clear of the obscuring effects of confusion, superstition, and prejudice (of which materialism is just one source), the more clearly one will see that embracing the religious image's conception of the self is justified by its unmatchable (because infinite) practical value. Moreover, he believes that, once one is no longer burdened by error and prejudice, one will be able to see clearly the value of embracing the uniquely Christian version of the religious image.

> To me it seems the man can see neither deep nor far who is not sensible of his own misery, sinfulness, and dependence; who doth not perceive that this present world is not designed or adapted to make rational souls happy; who would not be glad of getting into a better state; and who would not be overjoyed to find that the road leading thither was the love of God and man, the practising every virtue, the living

reasonably while we are here upon earth, proportioning our esteem to the value of things, and so using this world as not to abuse it. For this is what Christianity requires. It neither enjoins the nastiness of the Cynic, nor the insensibility of the Stoic. Can there be a higher ambition than to overcome the world, or a wiser than to subdue ourselves, or a more comfortable doctrine than the remission of sins, or a more joyful prospect than that of having our base nature renewed and assimilated to the Deity, our being made fellow-citizens with angels, and sons of God? Did ever Pythagoreans, or Platonists, or Stoics, even in idea or in wish, propose to the mind of man purer means, or a nobler end? How great a share of our happiness depends upon hope![47]

Simply put, in Berkeley's philosophy, the two senses of 'idealism,' the popular and the philosophic, converge.

Notes

Introduction

1. *PC*, #405, vol. 1, p. 51.
2. A. C. Fraser's edition of *The Works of George Berkeley* (Oxford University Press, 1871).
3. John Stuart Mill, *Three Essays on Religion* (Holt, 1878), 261.
4. George Pitcher, *Berkeley* (Routledge, 1977), 4.
5. *Enquiry*, II.ii.
6. *The Wit and Wisdom of Bertrand Russell* (Beacon, 1951).
7. *TD*, "First Dialogue," vol. 2, p. 172.
8. Ibid., "Preface," vol. 2, p. 168.
9. *PC*, #405, vol. 1, p. 51.
10. A. C. Fraser, *Berkeley and Spiritual Realism* (Constable, 1908).
11. We will have to revisit this issue in more detail in chapter I.
12. *THN*, I.iv.6.
13. Samuel Johnson was the first president of King's College (now Columbia University) and the "father of American philosophy." His *Elementa Philosophica* (1752) was dedicated to Berkeley.
14. *Works*, "II Berkeley to Johnson," vol. 2, p. 282.
15. For a recent iteration of this line of interpretation see Raymond Martin and John Berresi's *The Naturalization of the Soul: Self and Personal Identity in the Eighteenth Century* (Routledge, 2000), pp. 50–65.
16. See, for example *PC*, #579–81, vol. 1, p. 72.
17. See *TD*, "Third Dialogue," vol. 2, p. 233. I will have more to say about this in chapter II.
18. *NTV*, §13, vol. 1, p. 256.

Chapter I

1. *PC*, #491, vol. 1, p. 62.
2. Such things can even be found in our best reference works. One can find the first in Nicolas Rescher's entry for 'idealism' in *Blackwell's Companion to Metaphysics*, ed. Jaegwon Kim and Ernest Sosa (Blackwell, 1996), and the second in Simon Blackburn's *Oxford Dictionary of Philosophy* (Oxford University Press, 1996).

3. *Works*, vol. 2, p. 41.

4. *P*, §27, vol. 2, p. 52.

5. Ibid., §89, vol. 2, p. 79.

6. As further testament to the power of the caricature, Berkeley's views about existence have remained at the periphery of our vision. One notable exception here is George Pappas. In a series of works, he has elucidated the connection in Berkeley's thought between the attack on abstract ideas and Berkeley's concept of existence. However, Pappas' investigations concern 'existence' as it applies to sensible things (i.e., ideas not spirits). And, of course, as we have just seen, Berkeley's view is that the two share nothing in common but the name. My point is not that Pappas' investigations are, therefore, misguided. Rather, my point is that so focused is our attention on the *esse* is *percipi* thesis that even Pappas isn't moved to mention that he is dealing with the secondary, dependent sense of being in Berkeley's ontology. See his "Abstraction and Existence," *History of Philosophy Quarterly* 19:1 (January 2002): 43–63.

7. *THN*, I.iv.6.

8. *Inquiry into the Human Mind*, chap. 1, §VI, p. 102, in *Philosophical Works of Thomas Reid*, ed. Sir William Hamilton (James Thin, 1850), p. 102. All references to Reid's works will be to this edition. Hereafter abbreviated to the title, section number, and page number.

9. *THN*, I.iv.6.

10. Robert Muehlmann, *Berkeley's Ontology* (Hackett, 1992). See also his "The Substance of Berkeley's Philosophy," in *Berkeley's Metaphysics: Structural, Interpretive and Critical Essays*, ed. Robert Muehlmann (Penn State University Press, 1995), 89–105.

11. Stephen Daniel, "Berkeley's Christian Neoplatonism, Archetypes, and Divine Ideas," *Journal of the History of Philosophy* 39:2 (April 2001): 245.

12. Ian Tipton, "Berkeley's View of Spirit," in *New Studies in Berkeley's Philosophy*, ed. Warren E. Steinkrauss (Holt, Rinehart, and Winston, 1966), 59–71.

13. *PC* #577, 579–81, vol. 1, p. 72. See also Tipton, *Berkeley: The Philosophy of Immaterialism* (Methuen, 1974), chap. 7.

14. For a further critique of Daniel's position, see Marc Hight and Walter Ott's "The New Berkeley," *Canadian Journal of Philosophy* 34:1 (March 2004): 1–24.

15. Muehlmann, *Berkeley's Ontology*, p. 188.

16. Ibid.

17. Ibid., p. 187.

18. *Works*, vol. 1, p. 87.

19. Ibid.

20. *PWD*, vol. 2, pp. 9–10.

21. Malebranche saw that one would have to take advantage of the priority of the infinite substance over the finite ones, hence occasionalism.

22. Nicolas Malebranche, "Dialogue I," in *Dialogues on Metaphysics*, trans. Willis Doney (Abaris, 1980), 27 (hereafter simply *Malebranche*, page number).

23. Ibid.

24. Ibid.

25. On its potential to mislead, see Descartes' response to the second article in "Comments on a Certain Broadsheet," in *PWD*, vol. 2, p. 294.

26. *Malebranche*, p. 27.

27. Ibid.

28. The point continues to be used to great effect. See especially Saul Kripke's *Naming and Necessity* (Harvard University Press, 1972), 144–55.

29. *PWD*, vol. 2, p. 20 (emphasis added).

30. And, of course, at t_2 we have exactly the same synchronic problem.

31. *PWD*, vol. 2, p. 21.

32. Descartes' focus here is on the concept 'material being,' not 'wax.' The full importance of this point, as well as the sense in which I am exploiting Descartes' discussion of the wax rather than merely reconstructing it, will not take center stage until chapter VI.

33. *PWD*, vol. 2, p. 21.

34. *THN*, I.iv.6.

35. Ibid.

36. *PWD*, vol. 2, p. 19.

37. This difficult dialectic is nicely elucidated from the Kantian perspective by Jay Rosenberg in *The Thinking Self* (Temple University Press, 1986), chap. 1.

38. That said, a case might be made that reflection and the pure intellect are not in fact distinct faculties. Notoriously, Descartes holds that the idea 'extension' is innate. It is, thus, in us. So, it would seem, the pure intellect, like reflection, has the self as its object, at least in some sense. Sadly, Descartes says almost nothing at all about the faculty of reflection, and his scattered remarks about the pure intellect are not always enlightening.

39. On this point, see chapter 1 of Don Garrett's *Cognition and Commitment in Hume's Philosophy* (Oxford University Press, 1997).

40. I will say more about this particular point in chapter II.

41. I explore Locke's reasons for attacking innate ideas a bit further in chapter II.

42. The two-part strategy is suggested by the very task with which Locke saw himself as being set. In "Epistle to the Reader," he tells us,

> Were it fit to trouble thee with the history of this Essay, I should tell thee, that five or six friends meeting at my chamber, and discoursing on a subject very remote from this, found themselves quickly at a stand, by the difficulties that rose on every side. After we had awhile puzzled ourselves, without coming any nearer a resolution of those doubts which perplexed us, it came into my thoughts, that we took a wrong course; and that before we set ourselves upon enquiries of that nature, it was necessary to examine our own abilities, and see what objects our understandings were, or were not, fitted to deal with. This I proposed to the company, who all readily assented; and thereupon it was agreed, that this should be our first enquiry.

Locke sets himself the task of defining both the objects and the limits of the understanding. *An Essay concerning Human Understanding*, ed. P. H. Nidditch (Oxford University Press, 1975), "Epistle to the Reader," p. 7 (hereafter simply *Essay*, book number, chapter number, page number).

43. *Essay*, II.ii.1.

44. Ibid., II.i.4.

45. Ibid., II.xi.9.

46. Ibid., III.vi.4.

47. Ibid., III.iii.13.

48. Ibid., III.iii.15.

49. Ibid., II.xxiii.2.

50. Ibid., II.xxiii.1.

51. Ibid., II.xxiii.3.

52. Ibid., II.xxiii.2.

53. Ibid., II.vii.7.

54. Ibid.

55. Though, of course, not as everyone uses the term. Some will allow there are unities which are not simple.

56. And since the faculty of perception itself is not acquired, a good case can be made that the source of the idea of unity is innate, at least as Descartes and Leibniz would interpret 'innate.'

57. *Essay*, I.ii.1.

58. Ibid., II.xxiii.23.

59. Berkeley, S, §266, vol. 5, p. 125.

60. Ibid., p. 124.

61. This is the precisely the point missed by Burnyeat in his influential article "Idealism and Greek Philosophy: What Descartes Saw and Berkeley Missed," *Philosophical Review* 90 (January 1982): 3–40. Throughout, Burnyeat reads Berkeley's central aim as finding the *esse is percipi* thesis in Plato and Aristotle. The catchphrase strikes again! Berkeley's focus is on showing that the priority of mind in the order of being was an ancient theme. He is well aware that the *esse is percipi* thesis is far more original.

62. P, §3, vol. 2, p. 42.

63. *Works*, letter 12, vol. 8, p. 36.

64. P, §1, vol. 2, p. 41.

65. Ibid., P, §3, vol. 2, p. 42.

66. Ibid., P, §4, vol. 2, p. 42.

67. PC, #751, vol. 1, p. 91.

68. P, §3, vol. 2, p. 42.

69. Ibid., §49, vol. 2, p. 61.

70. Ibid. (emphases are Berkeley's).

71. Ibid., §6, vol. 2, p. 43.

72. So, in the introduction, I was careful to qualify these distinctions.

73. TD, "Second Dialogue," vol. 2, p. 215.

74. P, §28, vol. 2, p. 53.

75. TD, "Third Dialogue," vol. 2, p. 235.

76. 'Imagination' is being used to cover the faculty of memory as well.

77. P, §1, vol. 2, p. 41.

78. Ibid., §3, vol. 2, p. 42.

79. Ibid., §12, vol. 2, p. 46.

80. Frege actually cites an early statement of the point by Berkeley in *NTV*, §109, vol. 1, p. 215.

81. For the most recent example of this reading, see Robert Fogelin's *Berkeley and the Principles of Human Knowledge* (Routledge, 2001), 126.

82. Even those who wish to separate Berkeley's aims from Frege's on this issue still misconstrue Berkeley's fundamental concern. See, for example, E. J. Lowe's "Identity, Individuality, and Unity," *Philosophy* 78:305 (July 2003): 321–36.

83. See S, §346, vol. 5, p. 156.

84. Ibid., §347, vol. 5, p. 156.

85. Ibid.

86. PC, #660, vol. 1, p. 80.

87. P, §25, vol. 2, p. 51.

88. Not coincidentally, Reid agrees. See his *Essays on the Active Powers of Man*, I.ii.5, pp. 514–15.

89. P, §89, vol. 2, p. 79.

90. PC, #810, vol. 1, p. 97.

91. P, §102, vol. 2, p. 85.

92. Ibid., §101, vol. 2, p. 85.

93. And for this reason, some have been inclined to identify Lockean substratum substances with Lockean real essences. It seems to me that Locke's work points in this direction,

but it is not clear whether Locke was in command of the issue or not. However, see M. R. Ayers's *Locke: Epistemology & Ontology* (Routledge, 1991), II.i; and Jonathan Bennett's "Substratum," *History of Philosophy Quarterly* 4 (April 1987): 197–215.

94. *S*, §355, vol. 5, p. 160.

95. *TD*, "Third Dialogue," vol. 2, p. 249.

96. *S*, §356, vol. 5, p. 160.

97. *P*, §30, vol. 2, pp. 53–54

98. Ibid., §1, vol. 2, p. 41 (emphasis added).

99. *TD*, "Third Dialogue," p. 249. Emphasis is mine.

100. Daniel Flage, "Berkeley, Individuation, and Physical Objects," in *Individuation and Identity in Early Modern Philosophy: Descartes to Kant*, ed. Kenneth F. Barber and Jorge J. E. Gracia (State University of New York Press, 1994), 135–36 (emphasis added).

101. A. A. Luce, *Berkeley and Malebranche* (Clarendon, 1934), 72.

102. See chapters 3 and 4 of Winkler, *Berkeley: An Interpretation* (Oxford University Press, 1989).

103. *P*, §13, vol. 2, p. 46.

104. *Principles* 13 is prefigured in the notebooks, at entry #670 (vol. 1, p. 82), where in place of the word 'unity,' Berkeley uses 'existence,' providing further evidence for the claim that Berkeley identifies *unum* with *ens*.

105. Wilfrid Sellars, "Philosophy and the Scientific Image of Man," in *Science, Perception and Reality* (Ridgeview, 1961), 26.

106. Sellars, "Science, Sense Impressions, and Sensa: A Reply to Cornman," *Review of Metaphysics* 24 (March 1971): 391–447.

107. The example is borrowed from Hume; however, unlike Berkeley, Hume does countenance sensory simples. *THN*, I.ii.1.

108. But of course, this kind of gunk is not infinitely divisible, for a start.

109. For my part, the image that always comes to mind is one of Max Black's famous indistinguishable spheres. I suspect I'm not alone. Consider the following from E. J. Lowe's recent contribution to the *Oxford Handbook of Metaphysics* (Oxford University Press, 2003) as he elucidates the independent existence conception of substance:

> Roughly, an individual substance is conceived to be an individual object which is capable of independent existence—one which could exist even in the absence of any other such object.... Thus, for example, it seems that [an] individual material sphere could exist as a solitary occupant of space. (p. 79)

110. *TD*, "First Dialogue," vol. 2, p. 200.

111. Cf. Hume's use of Berkeley's theory of vision in *THN*, I.iv.2.

112. The objection is also dealt with in *TD*, "First Dialogue," vol. 2, pp. 201–2.

113. *P*, §42, vol. 2, p. 58.

114. Ibid., §43, vol. 2, p. 58.

115. Ibid.

116. Ibid., §1, vol. 2, p. 41.

117. Ibid.

118. Ibid., §44, vol. 2, p. 58.

119. Ibid., p. 59.

120. Bertrand Russell, "The Principle of Individuation," in *Collected Papers of Bertrand Russell*, ed. John G. Slater (Routledge, 1988), 5:36.

121. *PC*, #192, p. 25. This entry is marked by the + sign. Why is not clear, as is sometimes the case with the + sign. The trouble seems to be with the notion of "perfect likeness." He never makes use of it again.

122. *S*, §347, vol. 5, p. 157.

123. For Butler's use of the view, see his "Dissertation I," first appendix to *The Analogy of Religion*, in *The Works of Joseph Butler*, ed. W.W. Gladstone (Clarendon, 1896). For Reid's use, see his *Essays on the Intellectual Powers of Man*, "Of Identity," Essay III, chapter iv.

124. *P*, §136, vol. 2, p. 103.

125. Ibid., §27, p. 52.

126. *TD*, "First Dialogue," vol. 2, p. 193.

127. Ibid., pp.193–94.

128. Ibid.

129. *DM*, §53, vol. 4, p. 45.

130. See also *S*, §289, vol. 5, p. 134.

131. *TD*, "Third Dialogue," vol. 2, p. 233.

132. Malebranche takes the opposite stance from Berkeley on ideas. The term 'idea' is reserved for the object(s) of the pure understanding. Our sensations, strictly speaking, are not ideas.

133. The doctrine of inner sense was revived in our time by David Armstrong as an account of consciousness. Bill Lycan remains its most able advocate. See his *Consciousness and Experience* (MIT Press, 1996).

134. *TD*, "Third Dialogue," vol. 2, p. 232.

135. Cf. Mill's "Berkeley's Life and Writings," in *Three Essays on Religion* (Holt, 1874), 262.

Chapter II

1. *PC*, #567, vol. 1, p. 71.

2. Ibid.

3. *Essay*, I.i.2.

4. Hume's use and criticism of Berkeley set this reading in motion, but Thomas Reid canonized it. See the latter's *Essays on the Intellectual Powers of Man*, Essay II, chapter X.

5. *P*, Intro. §10, vol. 2, p. 29.

6. See, for instance, George Pitcher, *Berkeley* (Routledge 1977), 71; I. C. Tipton, *Berkeley: The Philosophy of Immaterialism* (Methuen, 1974), 153; Jonathan Bennett, *Locke, Berkeley, Hume: Central Themes* (Oxford University Press, 1971), 52–58; Kenneth Winkler, *Berkeley: An Interpretation* (Oxford University Press, 1989), chap. 2, pp. 10–14.

7. *P*, Intro., §23, pp. 39–40.

8. Ibid., §6, p. 27.

9. The full title reads: *Alciphron; or, The Minute Philosopher in Seven Dialogues Containing an Apology for the Christian Religion, Against Those Who Are Called Free-Thinkers*

10. *A*, "Seventh Dialogue," §2, vol. 3, p. 287.

11. The central point of inspiration for this line of attack was John Toland's notorious *Christianity Not Mysterious* (1696). David Berman reproduces these lines from Berkeley's friend Pope:

> What partly pleases totally will shock
> I question much if Toland would be Locke.

The Works of Alexander Pope, ed. W. Warburton (1757), iii.32, quoted in Berman, *George Berkeley: Idealism and the Man* (Clarendon, 1994), 16.

12. *A*, "Seventh Dialogue," §4, vol. 3, p. 290.

13. Ibid., §8, p. 296.

14. Ibid., pp. 296–97.

15. "Was Berkeley a Precursor of Wittgenstein?" in *Alciphron in Focus*, ed. David Berman (Routledge, 1999), 113.

16. And to the 1734 edition of the *Three Dialogues*.

17. *P*, §27, vol. 2, p. 53.

18. *TD*, "Third Dialogue," vol. 2, p. 232.

19. *P*, §89, vol. 2, p. 80.

20. As we will see, Berkeley's target is broader than the views of just Locke or even of the "empiricists." I should add that Locke's own views about language are richly developed, occupying almost a fifth of the *Essay*. Just the same, the simplifications I make here are innocent.

21. *Essay*, III.iii.6.

22. Ibid.

23. Ibid.

24. *PC*, #751, vol. 1, p. 91.

25. *Works*, vol. 8, p. 388 (emphases in original).

26. *P*, Intro, §3, vol. 2, p. 26.

27. Ibid., §4.

28. Ibid., §21, p. 38.

29. *PC*, #687, vol. 1, p. 84.

30. *P*, Intro., §8, vol. 2, p. 28.

31. Robert Benchley, "Mind's Eye Trouble," in *The Benchley Roundup* (Harper, 1928).

32. *Essay*, IV.vii.9.

33. Even if the mind in question has infinite resources. Even God cannot create items with inconsistent properties.

34. Kenneth Winkler has made the same point, but it bears repeating. See his *Berkeley*, 49–52. Berkeley has often been accused of misreading Locke on this point. See also R. I. Aaron's *John Locke* (Oxford University Press, 1955), 195–96; and E. J. Craig, "Berkeley's Attack on Abstract Ideas," *Philosophical Review* 77 (1968): 425–37.

35. *Essay*, III, iii.6.

36. Cf. "Did Berkeley Blunder in Reading Locke?" appendix to chapter 2 of Winkler, *Berkeley*, pp. 49–52.

37. *P*, Intro. §8, vol. 2, p. 28.

38. Ibid.

39. Ibid., §9, p. 29.

40. Ibid., §10, p. 30.

41. It seems that Locke takes 'all things are particular' to be a necessary truth: "I grant whatever exists is particular, it cannot be otherwise." *The Works of John Locke*, 12th ed. (1823), vol. 8, §45, p. 242. See Winkler, *Berkeley*, p. 38.

42. *THN*, I.i.vii.

43. *P*, §5, vol. 2, pp. 42–43.

44. Others have been puzzled by the connection. See, for instance, Bennett, *Learning from Six Philosophers* (Oxford University Press, 2001), 2:147, and John Mackie, *Problems from Locke* (Oxford University Press, 1975), 121.

45. *P*, §68, vol. 2, p. 70.

46. Ibid., Intro., §13, vol. 2, p. 32.

47. *Philosophical Investigations*, 3d ed., trans. G. E. M. Anscombe and ed. G. E. M. Anscombe and R. Rhees (Macmillan, 1968), #304, p. 102.

48. *P*, Intro vol. 2, pp. 35–36.

49. Ibid., p. 36.

50. Ibid.

51. Ibid.

52. Ibid.

53. Ibid., §19, p. 36. Cf. A, "Seventh Dialogue," §§2–4, vol. 3, pp. 287–91.

54. Berkeley is known to have employed such rhetorical tactics. He comments on this strategy of his explicitly at several places. But to get an appreciation of it, simply consider how late in the *Principles* 'God' occurs despite the centrality of God to his metaphysics.

55. *P*, Intro., §19, vol. 2, pp. 36–37.

56. Ibid.

57. Ibid., p. 37.

58. Ibid. pp. 37–38.

59. Tipton, *Berkeley: Philosophy of Immaterialism* (p. 153), interprets Berkeley as only rejecting the ideational theory insofar as the passions that come before the mind are not images. Such a reading would be justified if Berkeley had said that what happens in this situation is the following: I read or hear something, say the words "Lo, a bear!" Then my mind calls up a memory of having had the passion of fear raised in me. Via the having of this memory, I grasp the meaning of the expression "Lo, a bear!" But that's clearly not Berkeley's point. His point is that words—e.g., certain ink marks on a page—can themselves raise such passions directly. They can have what Austin calls their "perlocutionary" effect without the interposition of intermediary items. Seeing or hearing certain words can raise passions in you every bit as immediately as can seeing a bear running at you full tilt.

60. *P*, Intro., §20, vol. 2, p. 38.

61. A, "Seventh Dialogue," §2, vol. 3, pp. 287–88.

62. Ibid., §5, p. 292.

63. Ibid., p. 293.

64. *P*, §27, vol. 2, p. 53 (emphasis added).

65. *TD*, "Third Dialogue," vol. 2, p. 232.

66. Mackie, *Problems from Locke*, p. 110.

67. Ibid.

68. *P*, Intro §11, vol. 2, p. 29.

69. This objection is reaffirmed in Bennett, *Learning from Six Philosophers*, 2:21–23.

70. *P*, Intro. §16, vol. 2, p. 35.

71. Ibid., §12, vol. 2, p. 32.

72. Ibid., §15, vol. 2, p. 34.

73. Cf. Bennett, *Learning from Six Philosophers*, 2:22.

74. Mackie, *Problems from Locke*, p. 111.

75. Ibid., p. 115.

76. Ibid., p. 116.

77. With apologies to Simon Blackburn. See the conclusion of his "Hume on Thick Connexions," in *Essays in Quasi Realism* (Oxford University Press, 1993), 107.

78. Cf. Jonathan Bennett, *Locke, Berkeley, Hume* (1971), 54.

79. Berkeley uses 'name' ambiguously between singular and general terms. Perhaps this is a source of exegetical confusion.

80. *P*, Intro. §19, vol. 2, p. 36 (emphasis added).

81. The expression is Bennett's (1971), 55.

82. "Manuscript Introduction," in *Works*, vol. 2, p. 137.

83. The situation has started to improve somewhat though. A recent positive sign is that Simon Blackburn's entry on 'emotivism' in the popular reference work the *Oxford Dictionary of Philosophy* credits Berkeley with being the precursor to modern emotivism. Ayer himself, though he credits Berkeley with inspiring the phenomenalism he develops in *Language, Truth, and Logic*, claims that he did not have Berkeley in mind when introducing emotivism there. See Berman, *George Berkeley*.

84. Bennett (1971), 55.

85. *P*, Intro. §19, vol. 2, p. 37.

86. *Alciphron*, D7, §14, vol. iii, p. 307.

87. Berman's intriguing, though admittedly speculative, suggestion is that Berkeley's semantic revolution took shape in the face of criticism of his early paper "Of Infinities," which he presented to the Dublin Philosophical Society in 1707. See also his aptly titled "Berkeley's Semantic Revolution," *History of European Ideas* 7 (1986): 603–7.

88. Berman, *George Berkeley*, p. 143.

89. J. P. Pittion, D. Berman, and A. A. Luce, "A New Letter by Berkeley to Browne on Divine Analogy," *Mind* 78 (1969): 389.

90. Berman, *George Berkeley*, p. 147.

91. Ibid.

92. Ibid., p. 148.

93. *A*, §8, vol. 3, pp. 296–97 (emphasis added).

94. Emphasis is Berman's.

95. *Works*, vol. 7, p. 146.

96. I would add that I think such passages need to be read against other related remarks by Berkeley. Consider, for instance, from his sermon "On Religious Zeal": "Religion, I say, is no such great speculative knowledge which rests merely in the understanding. She makes her residence in the heart, warms the affections and engages the will" (*Works*, vol. 7, p. 16).

97. *P*, Intro. §19, vol. 2, p. 37.

98. "Manuscript Introduction" to the *Principles*, vol. 2, p. 140.

99. *A*, "Seventh Dialogue," §14, vol. 3, p. 307.

100. Ibid., §5, p. 292 (emphases added).

101. *TD*, "Third Dialogue," vol. 2, p. 233.

102. *A*, "Seventh Dialogue," §14, vol. 3, p. 307.

103. Ibid., §7, p. 295.

104. Ibid., §14, p. 308.

105. Ibid., §5, p. 292.

106. Robert Brandom, *Making It Explicit* (Harvard University Press, 1994); Wilfrid Sellars, "Some Reflections on Language Games," *Philosophy of Science* 21 (July 1954): 204–28.

107. *P*, §65, vol. 2, p. 69.

108. *S*, §254, vol. 5, p. 121.

109. *P*, §§30–31, vol. 2, p. 53–54.

110. I say "expressive" rather than "emotive" because the latter is potentially misleading. God's discourse is not emotive because, properly speaking, "emotive" discourse requires emotions. But since emotions, according to Berkeley, are passive, and since God is not subject to passivity because he is purely active, God is not subject to emotional states.

111. *P*, §1, vol. 2, p. 41.

112. N.B. Just as Berkeley says, the formation of the appropriate expectations does not necessarily require that I entertain ideas of imagination that represent possible forthcoming ideas of sense that are likely to occur. Sometimes that's the case, for instance, when one learns a new word in some language. I hear the Welsh word for bear, *aurth*. When I hear it, I match it up in my imagination with a picture of a bear (perhaps, as I remember seeing it in my Welsh language primer next to the entry for *aurth*). But if I become fluent in the language, if I master the use of the term *aurth*, this intermediate step of engaging in an act of imagining will not be necessary. The hearing of an utterance of *aurth* will be enough to get the right response from me. I'll form the proper expectations directly.

113. *TD*, "Third Dialogue," vol. 2, p. 262.

114. *PWD*, vol. 2, pp. 57–58.
115. *PC*, #536, vol. 1, p. 67.
116. See chapter I, §12.
117. *S*, §252, vol. 5, p. 120.
118. J. L. Austin, "A Plea for Excuses," in *Philosophical Papers*, ed. J. O. Urmson and Geoffrey J. Warnock (Oxford University Press, 1961), 175.
119. Sermon III, "On Charity," in *Works*, vol. 7, p. 33.
120. *P*, §32, vol. 2, p. 54.
121. *TD*, "Third Dialogue," vol. 2, p. 245 (emphasis added).
122. Ibid., pp. 245–46.
123. Ibid., p. 247.
124. Ibid., p. 247.
125. Ibid., p. 248.
126. Ibid.
127. Ibid., p. 247.
128. See chapter I, §6.
129. *P*, §89, vol. 2, p. 80.
130. Ibid., Intro. §25, vol. 2, p. 40.
131. Mackie, *Problems from Locke*, p. 110.

Chapter III

1. "Especially when the October Wind," in *The Poems of Dylan Thomas* (New Directions, 1952), 98–99.
2. *Inquiry into the Human Mind* (1764), I.v.
3. *Enquiry* XII.i.
4. For example, a stick does and should look bent when viewed through a medium like water. We wrongly infer that we will have tactile sensations of something bent if we reach in the water.
5. *S*, §323, vol. 5, p. 148.
6. *An Essay on the Intellectual Powers of Man* (1785), II.x.
7. This worry led Reid to rethink his commitment to Berkeley's basic principles. He then attacked the view that "all the objects of my knowledge are ideas in my own mind."

> If I may presume to speak of my own sentiments I once believed this doctrine of ideas so firmly as to embrace the whole of Berkeley's system in consequence of it: till, finding other consequences to follow from it, which gave me more uneasiness than the w[a]nt of a material world, it came into my mind, more than forty years ago, to put the question, What evidence have I for this doctrine, that all the objects of my knowledge are ideas in my own mind? (Ibid.)

8. Ibid.
9. Reid's objection is nicely dealt with in chapter 9 of Winkler, *Berkeley*.
10. One might ask, "Can't a passive thing represent just by way of standing in the right causal relation to something else? Doesn't the moon's reflection on the water represent the moon?" Certainly, but it does so by being a *sign* of the moon. For the Berkelian, causation is a form of activity. And activity is volition, something possible only for spirits. Both the moon and its reflection are ideas that we may have if God wills them in us. Under the right conditions, the idea of the one is a sign that the other idea will (*ceteris paribus*) occur.
11. *P*, §28, vol. 2, p. 53.
12. Ibid., §29, vol. 2, p. 53.

13. Ibid.

14. N.B. A spirit is not the sort of thing with which any sense could give us contact. The problem is not that we lack a sense for perceiving minds. Minds simply are not the right sort of thing for perception:

> It will perhaps be said, that we want a sense (as some have imagined) proper to know substances withal, which if we had, we might know our own soul, as we do a triangle. To this I answer, that in case we had a new sense bestowed upon us, we could only receive thereby some new sensations or ideas of sense. But I believe no body will say, that what he means by the terms soul and substance, is only some particular sort of idea or sensation. We may therefore infer, that all things duly considered, it is not more reasonable to think our faculties defective, in that they do not furnish us with an idea of spirit or active thinking substance, than it would be if we should blame them for not being able to comprehend a round square. (*P*, §136, vol. 2, p. 103)

15. A, "Fourth Dialogue," §4, vol. 3, p. 145.

16. Cf. *PC*, #718, vol. 1, p. 87. "If Matter is once allow'd to exist Clippings of beards & parings of nails may Think." Berkeley is referring to the following passage in Locke's *Essay*:

> There are but two sorts of beings in the world, that man knows or conceives. First, such as are purely material, without sense, perception, or thought, as the clippings of our beards, and parings of our nails. Secondly, sensible, thinking, perceiving beings, such as we find ourselves to be, which, if you please, we will hereafter call cogitative and incogitative beings, which to our present purpose, if for nothing else, are, perhaps better terms than material and immaterial. (IV.x.9)

17. A, "Fourth Dialogue," §7, vol. 3, pp. 148–49.

18. S, §253, vol. 5, p. 120.

19. A, "Fourth Dialogue," §4, vol. 3, p. 146.

20. Ibid., p. 145.

21. *NTV*, §159, vol. 1, p. 235.

22. A, "Fourth Dialogue," §4, vol. 3, p. 145.

23. I have in mind works like Jonathan Bennett's *Rationality* (1964), Daniel Dennett's "Intentional Systems" (1971), and Donald Davidson's "Psychology as Philosophy" (1974), to name some of the earliest and more familiar examples. I say "at least" because we might mark the starting point with Wilfrid Sellars's work, for instance, perhaps as early as the appearance of "A Semantical Solution of the Mind-Body Problem," *Methodos* 5 (1953): 45–82.

24. "Empiricism and the Philosophy of Mind," in Sellars's *Science Perception and Reality* (Ridgeview Publishing Company, 1963), 127–96.

25. Dennett, "Three Kinds of Intentional Psychology," in *The Intentional Stance* (MIT Press, 1987), 49.

26. 'Response' from Latin *respondere*, "answer." From *re-* "back, again" + *spondere* "to promise, pledge" (*Oxford English Dictionary*).

27. Dennett, "Intentional Systems," in *Brainstorms: Philosophical Essays on Mind and Psychology*, ed. Daniel Dennett (MIT Press, 1978), 4.

28. Deep Blue is MIT's famous chess-playing computer.

29. Dennett, "Intentional Systems," pp. 3–4.

30. Part II, §iv (Macmillan, 1968), 178. It is worth noting that Wittgenstein continues with, "My attitude towards him is an attitude towards a soul. I am not of the opinion that he has a soul."

31. Dennett, "True Believers," in *Intentional Systems*, p. 21.

32. "Conditions of Personhood," in Dennett, *Brainstorms*, 267–85. I should mention that the "personal stance" has not occupied much of Dennett's thought since this early and mostly exploratory article. Except where I explicitly attribute certain claims to him about it, the reader should not think that I am expositing his views on the subject in what follows. I am rather taking a cue from some of his early ideas and, frankly, shamelessly exploiting them so as to re-present core aspects of Berkeley's view in a way that will link up with themes more familiar to contemporary philosophy.

33. Ibid., p. 285.

34. *P*, §148, vol. 2, p. 109.

35. "In the Beginning," in *The Poems of Dylan Thomas*, 94.

36. *S*, §256, vol. 5, p. 121.

37. Ibid., §254, p. 121.

38. *NTV*, §13, vol. 1, pp. 256–57.

39. *A*, "Fourth Dialoguue," §12, vol. 3, p. 157.

40. Technically, Berkeley's first publication was a tract on mathematics, *Arithmetica*, but it was probably only circulated at Trinity College.

41. *NTV*, §147, vol. 1, p. 231.

42. What is God saying? God's language is not representational. The natural world is not a representation of something else. The language of nature is not "cognitive." It is expressive practical language aimed at guiding our actions for our benefit. In short, it is expressive of God's divine love for us. See chapter II, §11.

43. *THN*, I.iii.13.

44. So then, should we say, as we do with regard to the intentional stance, that adopting the religious stance is justified by the predictive value we get through taking it up? No, at least, not exactly. Predictions are just one valuable thing a person gets from adopting the religious stance. The person who advocates that we adopt the religious stance is not saying that, if you want to get accurate and thus useful predictions, then you should adopt the religious stance. Instead, that person is saying, if one is to get anything of (genuine) value, then one should adopt the religious stance. It is a stance one should adopt throughout. The 'should' in 'you should adopt the religious stance' is categorical in the deepest possible sense of that term.

45. Wittgenstein, *Culture and Value* (University of Chicago Press, 1984), 72.

Chapter IV

1. *PC*, #847, vol. 1, p. 101.

2. See, for instance, Charles McCracken, "Berkeley's Concept of Mind," *Monist* 71:4 (October 1988): 596–611; McCracken, "Berkeley's Notion of Spirit," *History of European Ideas* 7 (1986): 597–602; Margaret Atherton's "The Coherence of Berkeley's Theory of Mind," *Philosophy and Philosophical Research* 43:3 (1983): 389–401; William Beardsley, "Berkeley on Spirit and Its Unity," *History of Philosophy Quarterly* 18:3 (2001): 258–77.

3. *P*, §139, vol. 2, p. 105.

4. Ibid., §26, p. 52. See also §149, p. 106.

5. Ibid., §27.

6. For developments of this line of objection, see McCracken's "Berkeley's Notion of Spirit"; A. C. Lloyd, "The Self in Berkeley's Philosophy," in *Essays on Berkeley: A Tercentennial Celebration*, ed. John Foster and H. Robinson (Clarendon, 1985), 187–209; C. C. W. Taylor, "Action and Inaction in Berkeley," also in Foster and Robinson, *Essays on Berkeley*, 211–25; Jonathan Bennett, *Learning from Six Philosophers*, vol. 2 (Oxford University Press, 2001), chap. 30, §223, pp. 165–67.

7. *Works*, vol. 2, p. 293.

8. McCracken, "Berkeley's Notion of Spirit," 601.

9. *TD*, "Third Dialogue," vol. 2, p. 233 (emphasis added).

10. Ibid.

11. Jonathan Bennett bites the bullet on this one. He argues that Berkeley's attacks are only directed toward material substratum substances, not substratum per se (Bennett, 2001, §219, p. 155).

12. By denying that they are Cartesian minds, I do not mean they are Cartesian bodies. Rather, as will become clear presently, Berkeley does not accept Descartes' conception of the essential nature of mind, and so his spirits are not Cartesian minds.

13. *DM*, §30, vol. 4, pp. 38–39.

14. *Principles* 89, vol. 2, p. 79. However, it should be noted here that Berkeley's philosophy of language avoids a problem with which Descartes has more trouble. It is difficult for Descartes to maintain the radical distinction between the being of material things and the being of mental things because one might object that both share something in common: existence. The objection invites a Spinozistic response. Berkeley, however, can reject Spinozism and maintain the position that both spirits and minds exist without saying that they share anything in common. On his semantic theory, they need have "nothing in common but the name."

15. See *P*, §141, vol. 2, p. 106.

16. *P* §139, vol. 2, p. 104–5.

17. E.g., *PC*, #270, vol. 1, p. 33, and *P*, §136, vol. 2, p. 104.

18. E.g., *P*, §3, vol. 2, p. 42, and §39, vol. 2, p. 57. *DM*, §25, vol. 4, p. 37.

19. *PC*, #673, vol. 1, p. 82.

20. Ibid., #829, vol. 2, p. 99.

21. Ibid., #850, vol. 2, p. 101.

22. *A*, "Dialogue 7," §16, vol. 3, p. 310.

23. *P*, §102, vol. 2, p. 85.

24. *PC*, #822, vol. 1, p. 98.

25. *TD*, "Third Dialogue," vol. 2, p. 239.

26. Ibid., "Second Dialogue," vol. 2, p. 217.

27. Ibid.

28. *P*, §27, vol. 2, pp. 52–53.

29. *PC*, #478a, vol. 1, p. 60.

30. Ibid., #712, p. 87.

31. *P*, §29, vol. 2, p. 53.

32. *PC*, #790, vol. 1, p. 95.

33. *PWD*, vol. 2, p. 26.

34. Both accept that nothing (except God) exists without a cause of its existence.

35. *Descartes*, vol. 2, p. 27. The point is then reviewed in the "Sixth Meditation":

And despite the fact that the perceptions of the senses were not dependent on my will, I did not think that I should on that account infer that they proceeded from things distinct from myself, since I might perhaps have a faculty not yet known to me which produced them. (*PWD*, vol. 2, p. 52)

36. Actually, it could be many spirits. It will take more argument to establish that the cause of these ideas is a single spirit, God.

37. *PC*, #847, vol. 1, p. 101.

38. *TD*, "Third Dialogue," vol. 2, p. 231.

39. Cf. chapter I, §13.

40. *T,* "Appendix."

41. *P,* vol. 2, §27, p. 52.

42. *Vide,* chap. I.

43. *Essay,* II.xxvii.

44. Ibid., §4.

45. "Berkeley's View of Spirit," pp. 59–71; see also Tipton, *Berkeley: The Philosophy of Immaterialism* (Methuen, 1974), chap. 7.

46. *PC,* #14, vol. 1, p. 9.

47. *TD,* "Third Dialogue," vol. 2, p. 233.

48. *Essay,* IV.ix.3.

49. Tipton, *Berkeley: Philosophy of Immaterialism,* p. 263.

50. Ibid., p. 264.

51. Tipton, "Berkeley's View of Spirit," pp. 68–69.

52. *Essay,* II.xxiii.2.

53. Ibid.

54. Ibid., II.xxiii.7.

55. Ibid., II.xxiii.7.

56. *P,* §16, vol. 2, p. 47.

57. *Essay,* II.xxvii.7.

58. Ibid. §26.

59. *S,* §346, vol. 5, p. 156.

60. Ibid., §347, vol. 5, pp. 156–57.

61. "Dissertation I: Of Personal Identity," appendix 1 to *The Analogy of Religion,* in *The Works of Joseph Butler,* vol. 1, ed. W. E. Gladstone (Clarendon, 1896), 391.

62. I am simplifying for the sake of brevity. There are actually several complicated, overlapping issues here. As we already know, Locke does not share the Cartesian conception of substance, so even if we take responsibility to be the essence of persons, we have not thereby identified persons as substances. Second, Locke regards existence and unity as distinct properties. So he does not identify *ens* with *unum.* Furthermore, because he claims that we have simple ideas of existence and unity, in finding that persons are unitary things, it would seem that we have only identified a quality of something, not its essence. The same goes for existence. Existence is treated as a property of something. (On the latter issue, see Pappas, "Abstraction and Existence.") All these issues are tightly intertwined. This is not the place to attempt to map them all.

63. *Essay,* II.vi.2.

64. *PC,* #621, vol. 1, p. 76.

65. Ibid., ##449, 449a, vol. 1, p. 63.

66. Ibid. (I have added some punctuation to clarify the meaning.)

67. Ibid., #194a, vol. 1, p. 26.

68. Ibid., #478a, vol. 1, p. 60.

69. Even that great minimalist of the mental, Descartes, did not attempt this. In fact, his thinking progresses in the opposite direction. He moves toward identifying the mind with the understanding qua the pure intellect.

70. *PC,* #614, vol. 1, p. 76.

71. Ibid., #614a, vol. 1, p. 76.

72. *A,* "Seventh Dialogue," §17, vol. 3, p. 314. N.B. The point of the passage is to attack faculty positing. It does not signal a change in Berkeley's identification of the mind with the will. Again, it is just as much a mistake to take the will to be a faculty as it is to take the understanding to be a faculty.

73. *PWD,* vol. 2, p. 54.

74. So far as I am aware, only A. C. Lloyd, "The Self in Berkeley's Philosophy," has openly embraced the view that Berkeley identified the soul with the will.

75. Cf. our criticism in chapter II, §6, of Locke's introduction of "abstraction" and "abstract ideas."

76. A similar point is made by Reid. See *Essays on the Active Powers of Man*, I.i.5.

77. N.B. Appealing to an act/action distinction in order to save passive faculties will not help. Content will have to be given to the concept "act" such that it can be something a passive faculty does without changing its essential nature. The introduction of acts to flesh out the concept of a passive faculty will succeed in making the rabbit hole a little deeper, but no better lit.

78. *S*, §290, vol. 5, p. 135.

79. *TD*, "Third Dialogue," vol. 2, pp. 240–41.

80. Berkeley's application of this Augustinian strategy to faculties is no ad hoc maneuver. Just how central it is to immaterialism will be of central concern in chapter VI.

81. That is to say, while still respecting the so-called distinction principle.

82. *PC*, #791, vol. 1, p. 95.

83. Ibid., #820, vol. 1, p. 98.

84. Ibid., #821, vol. 1, p. 98.

85. *Vide*, chap. II.

86. *S*, §253, vol. 5, p. 120.

87. Though Berkeley is often held up as a classic example of a thinker who is victimized by the "myth of the given" (e.g., by Sellars in "Empiricism and the Philosophy of Mind," chap. 6), it should be clear that the divine language thesis alone is enough to put his philosophy fundamentally at odds with that notorious myth.

88. *S*, §305, vol. 5, p. 141.

89. "Philosophical Correspondence I: Johnson to Berkeley," §11, vol. 2, pp. 276–77.

90. Ibid., "III: Johnson to Berkeley," §3, vol. 2, pp. 288–89.

91. Ibid., "IV: Berkeley to Johnson," §3, vol. 2. p. 294.

92. Edwin S. Gaustad, *George Berkeley in America* (Yale University Press, 1979), p. 60. See also Johnson's "Autobiography," vol. 1 of *Samuel Johnson, President of King's College: His Career and Writings*, ed. Herbert Schneider and Carol Schneider (Columbia University Press, 1929), p. 25.

93. Elementa Philosohica, Noetica: Or the First Principles of Human Knowledge, Chap. II, Sect. 20, p. 37 (B. Franklin and D. Hall, 1752).

Chapter V

1. *PC*, #508, vol. 1, p. 63.

2. What follows is a cartoon version of Malebranche's occasionalism. His thinking about causation is sophisticated. The simplifications I employ here are, however, harmless for the purposes of the present discussion.

3. See chapter I, §5.

4. *PC*, #107, vol. 1, p. 18.

5. Ibid., #548, vol. 1, p. 69.

6. *TD*, "Second Dialogue," vol. 2, p. 214.

7. Ibid.

8. *P*, §69, vol. 1, p. 71.

9. See especially the "Second Dialogue," vol. 2, p. 220.

10. Ibid., §69, vol. 1, p. 70.

11. Ibid., §68, p. 70 See also *TD*, "Second Dialogue," vol. 2, p. 222.

12. Ibid., *TD*, "Second Dialogue," vol. 2, p. 220.

13. Again, a gross simplification, but harmless for present purposes. In chapter VI, I will make up for some of this abusive simplification to some degree.

14. Bennett, *Learning from Six Philosophers*, chap. 30, §223, p. 165.

15. Ibid., p. 166.

16. *PC*, #856, vol. 1, p. 102.

17. Ibid., #850, p. 101.

18. On this point, see especially *De Motu*.

19. For this reason, one must be careful when describing Berkeley as an "agent causationist," another perniciously redundant expression when applied to Berkeley. I pursue this point and Berkeley's theory of action in general in greater detail in "Command of the Will" (forthcoming).

20. This reveals an implicit commitment to mistakenly reading Berkeley as holding a picture theory of the understanding.

21. "Action and Inaction in Berkeley," in Foster and Robinson, *Essays on Berkeley*, pp. 211–225.

22. *P*, §28, vol. 2, p. 53.

23. *TD*, "First Dialogue," vol. 2, p. 176.

24. *Essay*, IV.xi.5.

25. Again, a simplification. The target is actually any two created substances, whether they be a mind and a body, two bodies, or two minds.

26. Then those changes in my material fist in turn serve as the occasion of God willing the corresponding perceptions in me of my fist moving.

27. Chapter I, §5.

28. *P*, Intro. §6, vol. 2, p. 27.

29. Material occasions are also the focus of Berkeley's attack on occasions in *Three Dialogues*, as the latter was written as a further defense of Part I of the *Principles*.

30. See *P*, §§9–10, vol. 2, pp. 28–29.

31. See chapter IV.

32. *P*, §142, vol. 2, p. 106.

33. *TD*, "First Dialogue," vol. 2, p. 200.

34. Blackburn, *Think* (Oxford University Press, 1999), 263–64.

35. Ibid.

36. Again, more is attempted in "Command of the Will" (forthcoming).

Chapter VI

1. How well does Berkeley fare on such a count? See George Pappas, *Berkeley's Thought* (Cornell University Press, 2000), especially chaps. 8 and 9.

2. Wilfrid Sellars, "Philosophy and the Scientific Image of Man," in his *Science, Perception, and Reality* (Ridgeview, 1963), 4.

3. Ibid., p. 1.

4. *TD*, "Second Dialogue," vol. 2, p. 211.

5. Sellars (1963), p. 10.

6. Actually, Sellars presents this so that it might be tempting to interpret him as saying that it is within the manifest image, rather than the original image, that "we first encountered ourselves." But this is only because his primary focus is not the original image per se, but rather the development of it, which is the manifest image.

7. Sellars (1963), p. 6.

8. Ibid.

9. Ibid.

10. Ibid.

11. The scientific image is a threat to common sense precisely because its ontology no more brooks irreducibly normative relations than it does our grainless, phenomenal experiences.

12. What Sellars would refer to as a philosopher of the "perennial tradition."

13. Here, I have to be a little unfair to Sellars to stay on course. While Sellars's approach does run together two traditions as both belonging to the "perennial philosophy," it is also true that his account has some of the basic resources needed to properly distinguish them. In fact, I will be exploiting them to help bring the contrasts out in what follows.

14. Sellars (1963), pp. 12–13.

15. Ibid., p. 13.

16. Ibid., p. 12.

17. For a reading of Descartes as a reductionist of this sort, see Thomas M. Lennon's "The Principle of Individuation among the Cartesians," in Barber and Gracia, *Individuation and Identity*, p. 15.

18. Nicolas Malebranche, "Elucidation 10," in *The Search after Truth*, ed. Thomas Lennon and Paul Olscamp (Cambridge University Press, 1997), 622.

19. Ibid., book VI, part II, chap. 3, p. 446.

20. Charles McCracken, *Malebranche and British Philosophy* (Clarendon, 1983), 97.

21. Ibid.

22. Augustine, *The Confessions* (Random House, 1997), book III, chap. 7, par. 12, p. 45.

23. Ibid.

24. Augustine, *Enchiridion* (Westminster, 1955), chap. IV, par. 12.

25. Augustine, *The City of God against the Pagans* (Cambridge University Press, 1998), XI.26.

26. *Malebranche, Search after Truth*, VI.ii.3, pp. 446–47.

27. Recall the Augustinian strategy for dealing with manifest evil. It aligns true being with a wholly good *spirit* and then treats evil as a *privation* of spiritual being. Mind as spirit clearly falls on the left-hand side of the being/nothingness divide. But if matter is wholly distinct from mind, on which side of the divide does it belong?

28. *PWD*, vol. 2, p. 20.

29. Margaret Dauler Wilson, *Descartes* (London and Boston: Routledge & Kegan Paul, 1978), 91–92.

30. Ibid., p. 92.

31. *PWD*, "Synopsis of the Meditations," vol. 2, p. 10 (emphases added).

32. Cf. Thomas M. Lennon, "Descartes' Idealism," in *Philosophy and Culture: Proceedings of the XVII World Congress of Philosophy* (Montmorency, 1988), 4:53–56.

33. *Malebranche, Dialogues on Metaphysics*, "Dialogue VII," p. 153.

34. *P*, §53, vol. 2, p. 63.

35. *TD*, "Second Dialogue," p. 220.

36. *P*, §80, vol. 2, p. 75.

37. Cf. chapter I, §2, "*Esse* Is Not *Percipi*." The marked tendency of readers to focus on what Sellars says about the link between perceivables and the manifest image at the expense of the more fundamental role he gives to persons perfectly mirrors the way Berkeley is commonly misread.

38. *PC*, vol. 1, §405, p. 51.

39. *Works, P*, "Intro." §3, vol. 2, p. 26.

40. *PC*, §17, vol. 1, p. 10.

41. *S*, §313, vol. 5, pp. 144–45.

42. Ibid., §314, vol. 5, p. 145 (emphases added).

43. Ibid., §360, vol. 5, pp. 141–42.
44. Ibid., §301, vol. 5, p. 139.
45. Plato, for instance.
46. *A*, "Seventh Dialogue," §14, vol. 3, p. 307.
47. *Alciphron*, "Fifth Dialogue," §5, p. 178.

Bibliography

Aaron, R. I. *John Locke*, 2d ed. (Oxford: Clarendon, 1955).

Atherton, Margaret. "The Coherence of Berkeley's Theory of Mind," *Philosophy and Philosophical Research* 43, no. 3 (1983): 389–401.

Augustine, Bishop of Hippo. *Confessions and Enchiridion*, translated and edited by Albert C. Outler (London: Westminster, 1955).

———. *The City of God against the Pagans* (Cambridge: Cambridge University Press, 1998).

Austin, J. L. *Philosophical Papers* (Oxford: Oxford University Press, 1961).

———. "A Plea for Excuses." In Austin, *Philosophical Papers* (Oxford: Oxford University Press, 1961).

Ayer, A. J. *Language, Truth, and Logic* (New York: Dover, 1952).

Ayers, M. R. *Locke: Epistemology & Ontology* (New York: Routledge, 1991).

Barber, Kenneth F., and Jorge J. E. Gracia, eds. *Individuation and Identity in Early Modern Philosophy: Descartes to Kant*, edited by Kenneth F. Barber and Jorge J. E. Gracia (Albany: SUNY Press, 1994).

Beardsley, William. "Berkeley on Spirit and Its Unity," *History of Philosophy Quarterly* 18, no. 3 (July 2001): 258–77.

Benchley, Robert. "Mind's Eye Trouble." In *The Benchley Roundup* (New York: Harper, 1928).

Bennett, Jonathan. *Rationality: An Essay towards an Analysis* (New York: Humanities, 1964).

———. *Locke, Berkeley, Hume: Central Themes* (Oxford: Oxford University Press, 1971).

———. "Substratum," *History of Philosophy Quarterly* 4 (1987): 197–215.

———. *Learning from Six Philosophers*, vol. 2 (Oxford: Oxford University Press, 2001).

Berman, David. "Berkeley's Semantic Revolution," *History of European Ideas* 7 (1986): 603–7.

———. *George Berkeley: Idealism and the Man* (Oxford: Clarendon, 1994).

Berman, David, ed. *Alciphron in Focus* (New York: Routledge, 1999).

Blackburn, Simon. *Essays in Quasi Realism* (New York: Oxford University Press, 1993).

———. "Hume on Thick Connexions." In Blackburn, *Essays in Quasi Realism* (New York: Oxford University Press, 1993).

———. *Oxford Dictionary of Philosophy* (New York: Oxford University Press, 1996).

———. *Think: A Compelling Introduction to Philosophy* (New York: Oxford University Press, 1999).

Brandom, Robert. *Making It Explicit* (Cambridge, Mass.: Harvard University Press, 1994).

Burnyeat, M. F. "Idealism and Greek Philosophy: What Descartes Saw and Berkeley Missed," *Philosophical Review* 90 (January 1982): 3–40.

Butler, Joseph. *The Works of Joseph Butler*, edited by W. E. Gladstone, 3 vols. (Oxford: Clarendon, 1896).

Craig, E. J. "Berkeley's Attack on Abstract Ideas," *Philosophical Review* 77 (1968): 425–37.

Daniel, Stephen. "Berkeley's Christian Neoplatonism, Archetypes, and Divine Ideas," *Journal of the History of Philosophy* 39, no. 2 (April 2001): 239–58.

Davidson, Donald. *Essays on Actions and Events* (Oxford: Clarendon, 1980).

———. "Psychology as Philosophy." In Davidson, *Essays on Actions and Events* (Oxford: Clarendon, 1980), 229–39.

Dennett, Daniel. "Conditions of Personhood." In *Brainstorms: Philosophical Essays on Mind and Psychology* (Cambridge, Mass.: MIT Press, 1978), 267–85.

———. "Intentional Systems." In *Brainstorms* (Cambridge, Mass.: MIT Press, 1978), 3–22.

———. *The Philosophical Writings of Descartes*, translated by John Cottingham, Robert Stoothoff, and Dugald Murdoch (Cambridge: Cambridge University Press, 1985).

———. *The Intentional Stance* (Cambridge, Mass.: MIT Press, 1987).

———. "Three Kinds of Intentional Psychology." In Dennett, *The Intentional Stance* (Cambridge, Mass.: MIT Press, 1987), 43–68.

Flage, Daniel. "Berkeley, Individuation, and Physical Objects." In *Individuation and Identity in Early Modern Philosophy: Descartes to Kant*, edited by Kenneth F. Barber and Jorge J. E. Gracia (Albany: SUNY Press, 1994), 133–54.

Flew, Anthony. "Was Berkeley a Precursor of Wittgenstein?" In *Alciphron in Focus*, edited by David Berman (New York: Routledge, 1999).

Foster, John, and H. Robinson, eds. *Essays on Berkeley: A Tercentennial Celebration* (Oxford: Clarendon, 1985).

Frege, Gottlob. *The Foundations of Arithmetic*, translated by J. L. Austin (New York: Philosophical Library, 1950).

Garrett, Don. *Cognition and Commitment in Hume's Philosophy* (New York: Oxford University Press, 1997).

Hight, Marc, and Walter Ott. "The New Berkeley," *Canadian Journal of Philosophy* 34, no. 1 (March 2004): 1–24.

Hume, David. *An Enquiry concerning Human Understanding in Enquiries Concerning Human Understanding and the Principles of Morals*, edited by L. A. Selby-Bigge, revised by P. H. Nidditch (Oxford: Clarendon, 1975).

———. *A Treatise of Human Nature*, edited by L. A. Selby-Bigge, revised by P. H. Nidditch (Oxford: Clarendon, 1978).

Johnson, Samuel, *Elementa Philosohica*, (B. Franklin and D. Hall, 1752).

———. *Samuel Johnson, President of King's College: His Career and Writings*, edited by Herbert and Carol Schneider (Columbia University Press, 1929).

Kripke, Saul. *Naming and Necessity* (Cambridge, Mass.: Harvard University Press 1972).

Lennon, Thomas M. "Descartes' Idealism." In *Philosophy and Culture: Proceedings of the XVII World Congress of Philosophy* (Montreal: Montmorency, 1988), 4:53–56.

———. "The Problem of Individuation among the Cartesians." In *Individuation and Identity in Early Modern Philosophy: Descartes to Kant*, edited by Kenneth F. Barber and Jorge J. E. Gracia (Albany: SUNY Press, 1994), 13–40.

Lloyd, A. C. "The Self in Berkeley's Philosophy." In *Essays on Berkeley: A Tercentennial Celebration*, edited by John Foster and H. Robinson (Oxford: Clarendon, 1985), 187–209.

Loux, Michael J., and Dean W. Zimmerman, eds. *Oxford Handbook of Metaphysics* (New York: Oxford University Press, 2003).

Lowe, E. J. "Identity, Individuality, and Unity," *Philosophy* 78 (2003): 321–36.

Luce, A. A. *Berkeley and Malebranche* (Oxford: Clarendon, 1934).

Mackie, John. *Problems from Locke* (New York: Oxford University Press, 1975).

Malebranche, Nicolas. *Dialogues on Metaphysics*, translated by Willis Doney (New York: Abaris, 1980).

————. *The Search after Truth*, edited by Thomas Lennon and Paul Olscamp (Cambridge: Cambridge University Press, 1997).

McCracken, Charles J. "Berkeley's Notion of Spirit," *History of European Ideas* 7, no. 6 (1982): 597–602.

————. *Malebranche and British Philosophy* (Oxford: Clarendon, 1983).

————. "Berkeley's Concept of Mind," *Monist* 71, no. 4 (October 1988): 597–602.

Muehlmann, Robert. "The Substance of Berkeley's Philosophy." In *Berkeley's Metaphysics: Structural, Interpretive and Critical Essays*, edited by Robert Muehlmann (University Park: Penn State University Press, 1995), 89–105.

————. *Berkeley's Ontology* (Indianapolis, Ind.: Hackett, 1992).

Muehlmann, Robert, ed. *Berkeley's Metaphysics: Structural, Interpretive and Critical Essays* (University Park: Penn State University Press 1995).

Pappas, George. *Berkeley's Thought* (Ithaca, N.Y.: Cornell University Press, 2000).

————. "Abstraction and Existence," *History of Philosophy Quarterly* 19, no. 1 (January 2002): 43–63.

Pitcher, George. *Berkeley* (New York: Routledge, 1977).

Pittion, J. P., David Berman, and A. A. Luce. "A New Letter by Berkeley to Browne on Divine Analogy," *Mind* 7, no. 8 (1969): 375–92.

Pope, Alexander. *The Works of Alexander Pope*, edited by W. Warburton (1757).

Reid, Thomas. *The Works of Thomas Reid*, edited by Sir William Hamilton (Edinburgh: James Thin, 1850).

Rosenberg, J. F. *The Thinking Self* (Philadelphia: Temple University Press, 1986).

Sellars, Wilfrid. "A Semantic Solution of the Mind-Body Problem," *Methodos* 5 (1953): 45–82.

————. "Philosophy and the Scientific Image of Man." In Sellars, *Science, Perception, and Reality* (Atascadero, Calif.: Ridgeview, 1963), 4–40.

————. *Science, Perception, and Reality* (Atascadero, Calif.: Ridgeview, 1963).

————. "Some Reflections on Language Games." In Sellars, *Science, Perception, and Reality* (Atascadero, Calif.: Ridgeview, 1963), 321–58.

————. "Empiricism and the Philosophy of Mind." In Sellars (1963), 127–96.

————. "Science, Sense Impressions, and Sensa: A Reply to Cornman," *Review of Metaphysics* 2, no. 4 (1971): 391–447.

Taylor, C. C. W. "Action and Inaction in Berkeley." In *Essays on Berkeley: A Tercentennial Celebration*, edited by John Foster and H. Robinson (Oxford: Clarendon, 1985), 211–25.

Thomas, Dylan. *The Poems of Dylan Thomas* (New York: New Directions, 1952).

Tipton, I. C. "Berkeley's View of Spirit." In *New Studies in Berkeley's Philosophy*, edited by Warren E. Steinkrauss (New York: Holt, Rinehart, and Winston, 1966), 59–71.

————. *Berkeley: The Philosophy of Immaterialism* (London: Methuen, 1974).

Winkler, Kenneth P. *Berkeley: An Interpretation* (New York: Oxford University Press, 1989).

Wilson, Margaret Dauler. *Descartes* (London and Boston: Routledge & Kegan Paul, 1978).

Wittgenstein, Ludwig. *Philosophical Investigations*, 3d ed., translated by G. E. M. Anscombe, edited by G. E. M. Anscombe and R. Rhees (New York: Macmillan, 1968).

————. *Culture and Value* (Chicago: University of Chicago Press, 1984).

Index